Toward a Sociology of Irreligion

Colin Campbell

First published in Great Britain 1971 by Macmillan Press ltd
SBN 333 10672 5

Revised edition published 2013 by Alcuin Academics

ISBN 978-1-78018-003-8 (Printed edition)

Ebook versions 978-1-78018-004-5

Kindle version 978-1-78018-005-2

Toward a Sociology of Irreligion

Colin Campbell

Introduction by Lois Lee,

and new bibliography by Lois Lee

with Stephen Bullivant and Christopher R. Cotter

Contents

Preface

The curious reader who chances on this volume may well wonder why a book that has been out of print for nearly forty years is being republished; and what is more, re-published in its original form, without any attempt at revision. Part of the answer is to be found, as Lois suggests in her introductory commentary (see 'Resuming The Sociology of Irreligion' below), in its potential interest as an "historical artifact", although after such a long period of time there would also have been considerable obstacles to overcome if this work really were to be brought up-to-date. It is for both these reasons that it was decided, in lieu of any revision, that the original text would be accompanied by a contemporary commentary, one that would strive to bridge the intervening years by relating the current state of work in the field to some of the original themes, and in that respect try to pick up where the book left off all those years ago. Of course, from my own perspective, this book is less of an historical artifact than a biographical one, and like most people who in later life are confronted with evidence of their youthful behaviour, as much a source of embarrassment as pride. For now I can see all too clearly the unconscious omissions, logical difficulties and weaknesses of argument that evaded me at the time (but not, I note, some of the book's reviewers), and which Lois, in true generosity of spirit, has seen fit to play down.

As she notes in her introduction, the opening sentence of *Toward A Sociology of Irreligion* reads "No tradition for the sociological study of irreligion as yet exists and this book as been written in the hope that it will stimulate the development of just such a tradition". Looking back, I am not sure that I did actually have that much hope, when those lines were written in 1970, that this would come to pass. After all I was a junior academic, only having completed my PhD three years earlier, and hence had no particularly good reason to believe that anyone would take much notice of my work, although I did imagine – perhaps naively – that such an important topic would not continue to be ignored by academics for much longer; even though I was not so vain as to imagine that my own contribution to the field would, in itself, kick-start such a development. How wrong could one be? For, in the event, not only did my book have a negligible impact, but the study of irreligion continued to be neglected for a further three decades. It should perhaps be noted, in all fairness, that my optimism was not entirely without foundation, for there had been some stirrings of interest in this topic both in the USA and Europe in the late nineteen-sixties. Nor indeed was I the only academic interested in this area of study in the 1970s, as I discovered when I embarked on my research.

In the event these signs of interest proved to be indicators of a false dawn. Quite how long the wait would be before my hopes would be realised is rather starkly revealed by the citation data for the book. For, according to the Harzinger Publish or Perish data-base *Toward A Sociology of Irreligion* was cited a mere five times between its publication in 1972 and 2006; in other words about once every seven years. However, by 2011 it had been cited some 86 times, meaning that between 2005 and 2011 it was accumulating some 14 citations per year; evidence that my hope that the work might spark an interest in the study of irreligion was perhaps being realised after all. But then, as Lois notes in her discussion, this marked change of fortune raises an intriguing, if challenging, question. Why did it take so long for academics to become interested in this particular topic? This is not an easy question to answer, and I am not sure I am best qualified to attempt to do so, but I can at least answer a not entirely unrelated question, which is how it was that I became interested in the topic of irreligion in the first place.

In part the story is purely biographical, and relates to my involvement, at a relatively young age, in the Rationalist Press Association (the publishers of the magazine *The Humanist*), and subsequently the emerging British Humanist Movement. This meant that by the time I started my academic career in the early 1960s, I had direct personal experience of irreligious people and their organizations. It was therefore understandable, when contemplating what topic I might select for a PhD, to consider the British Rationalist and Humanist Movement, given that I knew it had not been the subject of academic study. What made this an even more tempting choice for me was that I had also taken the decision to specialise in the sociology of religion; the relevant point here being my growing belief – which is expressed in the book – that the study of the rejection of religion might well provide a new and fruitful perspective from which to interrogate some of the long-standing, and apparently intractable, problems in the sociology of religion itself. Consequently, almost as soon as I started my teaching career in November 1962, I registered for a PhD (as an external student of The University of London), the title of which eventually became "Humanism and the Culture of the Professions: A Study of the rise of the British Humanist Movement 1954-63". At first I had little idea where the thesis would take me, contenting myself with the modest aim of charting the nature and history of this movement whilst collecting as much demographic information about its membership as possible. The latter required a postal survey and hence a questionnaire was sent to all registered members of the British Humanist Association, The Ethical Union and The Rationalist Press Association, the results of which revealed that humanists tended to be male, young to middle-aged, married, with some experience of further education, and characteristically employed in the professions. It was this latter observation that became the basis for the central argument developed in the thesis.

Like many a graduating PhD student before me I naively hoped that it might be possible to publish the thesis more or less as it was. However, when the opportunity came along John Wakeford, who was the editor of the series in which the book would appear, as well as the publishers, Macmillan, felt that humanism was too narrow a topic for their "Perspectives" series, and hence pressed for a somewhat wider remit. Thus it was that although the thesis mainly concerned humanism and the humanist movement, the book had irreligion as its central focus. This change of emphasis did not bother me greatly at the time, given that my main concern was to ensure that some at least of the thesis material appeared in print. However in retrospect I do rather regret that the main theme of the thesis – to the effect that the socio-cultural basis of modern humanism was to be found in the culture of the professions – never actually saw the light of day. However, I can now see that tackling the broader topic of irreligion was actually a more interesting, and indeed challenging, enterprise; one that held a greater promise of advancing the discipline. What we can see from this brief biographical account is that I turned to the topic of irreligion principally as a consequence of a marriage of convenience between what was a personal interest on the one hand and a developing professional concern on the other, to which was added the special twist provided by publishing and editorial considerations.

Looking back, I think I assumed, given that the Humanist movement itself was growing fast in Britain in the 1960s, then so too would academic interest in both the existing alternatives to organized religion and the rejection of religion itself. What I don't think I had anticipated was that, while the one would certainly continue to flourish, at least for a while, the other would simply not take off. But then I was not the only sociologist who, in the late 1950s and early 1960s, made erroneous assumptions about future trends. For, viewed from the perspective of the twenty-first century, it is easy to forget that no-one at the time would have forecast the coming of the youth movement or counter-cultural revolt of the late sixties and early seventies, with its unique mix of bohemianism, radical politics, magic and mysticism.

I should perhaps stress that the reason I did not continue to pursue an interest in the study of irreligion after 1972 was not because my colleagues in the profession failed to share my enthusiasm for this field of study, let alone because of the lack of a strong positive response to the book. Rather it was due to a growing belief on my part – one I still hold – that phenomena such as religion and irreligion cannot be properly understood except in their larger socio-cultural context, a context that is necessarily both diachronic and synchronic in nature. In other words, that such phenomena need to be examined in terms of both their historical context (something I had already attempted) and their current socio-cultural systemic context (something I had not). So it was that, in the years after the publication of this work, I turned more and more to the study of the larger Western cultural system of which these phenomena were components.

This change of focus did not mean that I lost all interest in the sociology of irreligion, for my youthful enthusiasm for the topic meant that the subject still held a fascination for me. It was merely that it had ceased to be the focus of my research. Consequently, whatever the reason is for the current and long-overdue upsurge of academic interest in atheism, secularity and nonreligion, I am naturally delighted that it has happened, and especially grateful to Lois Lee and Stephen Bullivant for their part in enabling this process through their far-sighted initiative in launching the Non-Religion and Secularity Research Network (NSRN). But then I am, in addition, especially grateful to Lois, both for her part in persuading me that this work ought to be re-published, and in contributing what is for me an especially fascinating, as well as a thought-provoking, introduction. But then I should also thank Stephen and Christopher for their contribution in compiling a bibliography that, hopefully, students of irreligion will find invaluable.

Colin Campbell

York, March 2013

Introduction: Resuming a Sociology of Irreligion

Colin Campbell's book, *Toward a Sociology of Irreligion* (*TSI* hereafter), was originally published in 1971, some forty years ago. In it, Campbell presented a compelling argument for reconceiving of, and establishing the sociological study of, a significant counterpart to religion: 'irreligion'. Understanding secularisation, he said, requires not only the study of religion and the course of its marginalisation, but also the study of *irreligion*, that is, the acts and processes of rejecting religion. The difference between processes of marginalisation and processes of rejection is, at first glance, a subtle one, but there is a fundamental ontological distinction between the two things: in the former, the object of study is the *change* experienced by a widely discussed substantive phenomenon, religion; in the latter, a new substantive object is introduced into the picture. Irreligion is concrete and distinct, relational to religion but not reducible to its negative imprint (Lee, 2006). It is therefore etymologically relative but ontologically autonomous. It exists in and impacts upon the world, and it can in turn be shaped by forces acting upon it, including but not limited to religion.

The inclusion of the study of a new substantive concept (irreligion) alongside the established study of an analytical one (the marginalisation of religion) involves a profound change in the sociological study of secularisation and of religion itself. Introducing this new approach in comprehensive terms and showing how it might be taken up in practice, that is, in empirical research, are the most far-reaching of *TSI*'s achievements. On this basis, Campbell (2013: LVII; also discussed in Bullivant and Lee, 2013: 22) had good reason to hope that *TSI* would foreground a major new avenue for sociological research: 'No tradition for the sociological study of irreligion as yet exists,' he says, 'and this book has been written in the hope that it will help to stimulate the development of just such a tradition'.

Yet, for all that its recommendations were profound and penetrating, *TSI* failed to incite the broader sociological project that it looked towards. Subsequent contributions to the sociology of irreligion were not unknown, but they were few and far between and certainly never achieved the critical mass that might be called a 'tradition' (Bullivant and Lee, 2013: 22). A sociology of irreligion has implications for a number of fields of research – for the study of social movements, morality, patterns of association in modern societies, its forms of belief, and so on – yet it failed to impact on any of these literatures. Indeed, even on its home turf – the studies of religion and secularisation – it was, for several years, unclear whether the idea of a sociology of irreligion had even taken root. Almost as remarkable as this halting beginning, however, is the dramatic change in fortunes that has recently occurred. From a handful of (mainly) articles being published per decade in the later twentieth century, the first years of the twenty-first saw a few publications emerging per *year* and, by the end of the 00s, the annual rate of publication – of articles, book chapters and monographs – has increased to several scores. Thus, it now appears that a social scientific 'tradition' of studying irreligion and (complicatedly) related topics such as atheism and secularity has finally been established.

This change in fortunes has naturally reawakened interest in *TSI*. More than a curio for those involved in the revived sociology of irreligion, the book has been canonised as a foundational text for the new-wave social science of irreligion. There are several reasons for this, and the first task of this introduction is to review and underline these. Some of the contributions *TSI* makes to today's scholarship are widely recognised: *TSI* is, for example, commonly used as a resource for those seeking to provide a historical account of irreligious and secularist movements in modern Britain and America; and it has also been called upon to foreground and legitimise the new-wave sociology of irreligion (e.g. Lee, 2006; Zuckerman, 2010c; Bullivant and Lee, 2012).

Many of its other contributions have not been recognised or emphasised sufficiently, however. This is inevitable for a wide-ranging and exploratory text, which moves toward a sociology of irreligion by considering the potential sub-field from a variety of theoretical and practical angles: the resulting discussion is a rich one and it is to the book's credit that it is impossible to anticipate the variety of ways in which *TSI* will be taken up in future research. There are, however, three particular contributions that warrant attention sooner rather than later, because they stand to influence the rapidly developing social science of irreligion at its core. These relate to some epistemological and ontological assumptions that frequently have been taken up in the new field uncritically and I want, therefore, to argue that the understanding of *TSI* as a foundational text for this field of study should be extended to include these fundamental contributions. Campbell's discussion should be recognised as a tool to prompt and structure reflection on these important issues.

TSI is being re-published because of its important theoretical and empirical contributions, and because, impressively, these contributions remain salient to contemporary scholarship. On the other hand, at 40 years of age, Campbell's book is a historical artefact as well; and the fact that a vigorous sociology of irreligion did not immediately follow it makes it a singular resource for understanding its historical moment and the theoretical and other academic changes that have occurred since then. Some aspects of *TSI* now seem dated, but the contrasts between a sociology of irreligion situated in the late 60s/early 70s and the work being done today illuminate some of the social and cultural shifts that have occurred in that period. Many of these are heavily contested and, consequently, this historical and historiographical (or 'sociographical') analysis of *TSI* consequently stands to contribute to these debates. The final section of this introduction reflects on the halting development of the sociology of irreligion in light of this analysis, and, looking to the future, argues that conditions have fundamentally changed from those which met the original publication of *TSI* in 1971 and dampened its impact – and that this new wave of research activity is therefore likely to have the longevity that really justifies its being viewed as a 'tradition' in the making.

The Use of TSI in the Contemporary Sociology of Irreligion

As the number of scholars working with irreligion and related phenomena expands, a republication of *Toward a Sociology of Irreligion* is called for not only because the book provides a *seminal* account of irreligion but because it also provides a *singular* one. *TSI* is a small book but a wide-ranging one. Several of its contributions have not been revised, whilst others have not been recognised. It will therefore be useful to summarise even the more obvious uses to which *TSI* can be put.

First and foremost, *TSI* provides an intelligent and – as its reviewers unanimously said at the time – well-written precedent for a new generation of scholars attempting to (re)pioneer the study of irreligion and/or related phenomena. As well as more specific forms of guidance (more on this below), the existence of a high-quality *precedent* both legitimises and motivates further work; *TSI* has been important in this simple but fundamental regard. Nothing expresses this so clearly as the fact that *TSI* can claim the distinction of having provided the revived social scientific study of irreligion with its first cliché. This is to highlight the striking and almost irresistible contrast between Campbell's exuberant and extensive argument and title, the long years of dormancy in the sub-field and the suddenness and vibrancy of contemporary activity. 'In 1971', the rhetorical device runs, 'Colin Campbell published *Toward a Sociology of Irreligion*; it is only 35 years later that call has been heeded'.

This should not be dismissed as faint praise. In fact, it demonstrates the importance of *TSI* as a symbolic resource, one which means that today's scholars do not have to take that most daunting of steps; the first one. At the time, Campbell acknowledged how daunting the empirical project he proposed would be – taking on, as he suggested, an almost wholly uncharted field – and this statement is echoed In contemporary scholarship (e.g. O'Brian Baker and Smith, 2009: 730). Thus, his general discussion of the sub-field and his enthusiasm for its research should be viewed as a significant contribution – and one that has penetrated, and continues to penetrate, through an otherwise dauntingly vast project. Moreover, this symbolic resource has, in recent years, become a bridge between the

XVII

lonely, entrepreneurial irreligion researcher and precisely the tradition he hoped for: it has become a shared point of reference, mediating between scholars and helping, finally, to structure and consolidate the research community that it envisaged forty years ago. Without such a respectable precedent, twenty-first century irreligion research – both individual and communal – would have been much less articulate but also much less assured, much less resilient to the many critiques and miscomprehensions that a new field of study inevitably faces. As a symbolic resource, then, Campbell's book has achieved exactly what he hoped for it.

Frequent reference to *TSI* also reflects, however, the fact that many of Campbell's recommendations for this sociology are still leaders in the field. Extraordinarily, the book remains the sole sustained (and book-length) discussion of a social scientific approach to irreligion. Some important case studies are available (Budd, 1977; Hunsberger and Altemeyer, 2006; Zuckerman 2008) but unlike *TSI*, these works do not scrutinise the field of enquiry in more general terms. Campbell's exploration of the field of study still provides the most important single resource for anyone seeking to develop a research methodology in this area. Significant amongst its methodological contributions, the book makes a sustained attempt to theorise its core concept and to explore the sociological and methodological implications of that conceptualisation. This exploration is not only wide-ranging and intelligent, but it remains one of very few attempts to grapple with the concept of irreligion (or nonreligion) at all. Much discussion of irreligion and nonreligion is confused by an over-reliance on other concepts – 'atheism', 'secularism' and 'secularity' – which are used without scrutiny or, sometimes, much logic (see Lee, 2012 for a full discussion). The result has been a move against 'rigid terminologies' and, in the case of 'secular/ity/ism', a suggestion that the term be discarded altogether (e.g. Bader, 2011; Fitzgerald, 2007). Against this, Campbell's focus on irreligion, and his conceptual discussion of that term, is unusually constructive. 'Irreligion' presents a more tangible object than 'the secular': it is substantial where the secular is insubstantial, defined entirely by otherness, and focusing on it allows Campbell to begin to explore the methodological tools and challenges involved in its sociological investigation in much more concrete terms.

XVIII

This theoretical exploration of the field is combined with an example of this study in practice: a history of modern British and American irreligious and secularist movements. Whilst I agree with one of Campbell's reviewers that this focus is disappointingly conventional in some regards (Budd, 1972) and that relying so much on historical data means that more detailed methodological discussion and innovation is not something that *TSI* pushes forward, the empirical aspect of his book does allow Campbell to demonstrate his sociology of irreligion in practice. What is more, quite apart from its theoretical significance, the empirical section is still used today for its concise history of modern British and American irreligious and secularist movements. It is not the only study of these movements (e.g. Royle, 1974; Budd, 1977), but it is one of very few and its history has not been revised. Thus, *TSI* remains an important historical resource.

Getting more from reading TSI

If *Toward a Sociology of Irreligion* is recognised for its setting a precedent in exploring a new field of study as well as for the historical account it provides, the occasion of the book's republication is also an opportunity to return to it and consider anew what the text offers the area of research it outlines. It is not possible or desirable to anticipate every thread that might arise from the close reading of the book that I hope many new readers will undertake. I want, however, to highlight three contributions that have not received the attention they deserve. These are of particular significance to the field and also stand in opposition to some problems that are already emerging in the new wave sociology of irreligion.

Rich beginnings

The first thing to notice is the immense richness of Campbell's book. Some scholars referencing the text go little further than noticing the precedent and maybe the ambition of the project – and they are much the poorer for it. With a foregrounding methodological section, an empirical section and a theoretical exploration, the text as a whole has a broad scope that begins to hint at this richness. Given how pioneering the book was, Campbell's decision to make his discussion a wide-ranging one rather than focusing on one or other aspect of what a sociology of irreligion is a sage one. This means that the range of issues he considers is diverse. It includes the nature and forms of irreligion; its relationship to morality, politics, associational practice and, of course, religion; its causes and significance; and its role in earlier sociological accounts. What is more, even brief remarks are full of ambition and potential. Open any page and the reader is likely to find a passage that might push forward one's comprehension of the field and what is at stake in its study. This trait can be seen in almost any passage one turns to, but to take one example as means if illustration, let us consider Campbell's comments concerning irreligion and immorality, in which he relates specific empirical trends to a much deeper intellectual history. Referring to one of sociology's most central ideas – the relationship between religion and social cohesion – Campbell says, lightly, 'it is interesting to note how [a] popular argument about [the affinity between] irreligion and immorality has, as an academic counterpart, the thesis [...] that religion promotes integration' (2013: 100). He explains,

> The popular argument is that irreligion leads to immorality which, if unchecked, leads to societal disintegration. The academic argument emphasises the corollary of this, which is the role which religion plays in upholding the common system of integration in society. It would seem that the two arguments are to some degree mutually supporting, and the persistence of the latter despite the paucity of corroborative material for industrial societies might well be due in part to the continued existence of the former argument at a more popular level in society.

In *TSI*, asides of this sort provide rich resources for contemporary explorations of irreligion. In these few lines, Campbell is able to allude to the assumptions and normativities that underlie academic theories of religion and morality; to demonstrate how conceptions of religion and irreligion might be mutually constitutive, even across discursive spaces; to link this discussion to the question of social cohesion, one of sociology's most profound concerns; and, ultimately, to propose the affinity between irreligion and immorality as an empirical question. In *TSI,* Campbell offers no solution, but demonstrates how much is at stake in the project he outlines – and moves the discussion far beyond cruder one-up-manship discussions of (ir)religion and (im)morality that are still common, even in academic research.

Like so many other of the avenues *TSI* proposes, this one remains pertinent to contemporary social scientists. The concern with social cohesion that the 'founding fathers' of social science exhibited continues in contemporary social science and in the way the recent revival of fortunes for the sociologies of religion and the secular have been conceived. Once associated with the marginalisation of religion, the secular project has been reimagined as an attempt to harness the socially cohesive aspects of religion whilst maintaining the true purpose of secular settlements, namely the maintenance of order in face of religious wars of the sixteenth and seventeenth centuries (see various contributions to Levey and Modood, 2009, and especially Hunter, 2009; Taylor 2007). This more pro-religious notion of secularism, sometimes called 'post secularism', is accompanied by an emphasis on religious diversity, pluralism, multiculturalism and multifaithism. In all cases, the absence of irreligion in such discussions continues to be a problem, an issue that Gutkowski has raised (2010). In this way, contemporary scholars can be seen to be part of the paradigm which Campbell identifies and makes visible – and even his small asides have the potential to jolt the social sciences in quite profound terms.

These general reflections are intended to show how Campbell's analysis bridges many issues of profound importance to contemporary scholars of irreligion and secularism – and to encourage those who need it to the close reading of an (previously) out of print but not out of date text.

The Anti-essentialist Argument

Secondly, Campbell's careful anti-essentialist epistemology has not been given enough attention in discussions of *TSI*, partly because more naive approaches to definition and categorisation are commonplace in the new wave of irreligion sociology. For Campbell, irreligion is a response to religion and is therefore as amorphous and shifting an object as religion is. There is no fixed nature of irreligion; rather, irreligion responds to the religion of the day. As a result, specific phenomena like atheism are not, in Campbell's view, necessarily features of irreligion: atheism is only irreligious when theism is a significant aspect of the religious culture to which the irreligious respond, or, presumably, of another culture which is shaping the irreligious response. Alternatively, atheism can be invoked in an irreligious culture *regardless* of the local religious one. For example, atheism is important in 'New Atheism' (a particular brand of contemporary radical secularism and scientism) and its disputations, even in discussion of religions for which theism is not the most important aspect of the belief or practice. This historicising of irreligion is often absent in contemporary accounts – even those working with *TSI*. For example, Zuckerman's (2010a, 2010b) edited two-volume collection, *Atheism and Secularity*, uses Campbell's book to set the scene but does not follow Campbell's lead in scrutinising the title concepts and the issue of how 'atheism' and 'secularity' actually relate to one another (Zuckerman, 2010c). Elsewhere, and in general, the more constructivist approach that Campbell's text ends up advocating has been under-represented in the burgeoning 'nonreligion studies' (Lee, 2012). Whether his particular epistemological orientation is taken up or not, a close reading of Campbell's book should provide a rejoinder to some of the conceptual assumptions shaping the field today as well the chance to reflect upon this aspect of the sociological study of irreligion.

From Absence to Presence: The Substantive Account of Unreligion

A final important contribution of *TSI* that I want to highlight is its encouragement of the study of irreligion as distinct from the secular. Campbell persists with the notion that there are two main forms of unreligion. One of these is 'the secular' – a description of the marginalisation of religion or, rather, the space that is left after religion has withdrawn. It is a subtractive or absentive condition. The other is 'irreligion', a concrete phenomenon, identifiable by its presence in the empirical world. In this distinction, Campbell offers nothing contradictory to the orthodox view of secularisation as having the negative, subtractive 'secular' as its endpoint: in engaging with the secular, he suggests that irreligion can be seen as a temporary phenomenon and one which motors the process of secularisation. This makes his work perfectly consistent with contemporary secularisationists like Bruce (2002, 2011), Zuckerman (2008; 2010c) and Bagg and Voas (2010). Bruce (2002: 42), for example, says:

> In so far as I can imagine an endpoint [of secularisation], it would not be self-conscious irreligion; you have to care too much about religion to be irreligious. It would be widespread indifference (what Weber called being religiously unmusical); no socially significant shared religion; and religious ideas being no more common than would be the case if all minds were wiped blank and people began from scratch to think about the world and their place in it. This is an important point, because the critics often assume that the secularization paradigm supposes the human default position to be instrumental, materialism atheism.

Significantly, this view has emerged in the work of leading instigators of the new nonreligion and secularity research. Zuckerman, for example, cites high levels of 'indifference to religion' as proof that 'certain segments of Scandinavian society are about as secular as is sociologically possible' (2008: 97) and that 'when millions of people are just benignly indifferent to religion, we can thus truly characterize religion as being somewhat insignificant in that society' (ibid.: 106).

The focus on empty secularity rather than substantive irreligion impacts also on methodologies and analysis. Several scholars in the field of nonreligion studies conceive of their project as precisely the qualitative study of the *absence* of religion (e.g. O'Brian Baker and Smith, 2009). And Zuckerman explains that 'a constant theoretical and methodological question for me during my time in Scandinavia' was precisely 'how to study the relative *absence* of something' (Zuckerman, 2008: 76). He claims that the 'fascinating sociological and theoretical implications' of his work are 'not only for our understanding of religion, but for our understanding of its absence' (ibid: 57). In practical terms, therefore, Zuckerman is concerned to 'describe and understand men and women as they go about living their religion-less lives' (ibid: 96). This is not all he was doing, however: in fact, Zuckerman interviewed Scandinavians about their relationship to religious organisations and practice and, whilst he finds many Scandinavians to be indifferent to theology, he also shows a range of ways in which people engage with but reject religion, and how these rejections of religion are entwined with their experience of their local and national communities, social relations and irreligious beliefs. One woman, for example, mentions discussing religion with her family, memories of her confirmation, participating in Church life, and engagements with people of less familiar religious traditions – experiences that seem meaningful in her life and autobiography – yet Zuckerman (ibid: 87-91) says, paradoxically, that 'religious concerns, concepts, ideologies, participation, and beliefs are quite marginal in [Gitte's] sense of self'. In fact, he associates people like Gitte with 'indifference to religion'. In this way, a focus on the secular – meaning the absence of religion – does not do justice to the complexity and range of substantive forms of irreligion that Zuckerman in fact presents us with.

Whilst Campbell (2013) sees irreligion as an agent of secularisation rather than a description of its endpoint, the emphasis of his work consistently pushes towards an appreciation of the socio-cultural significance of irreligion. His empirical work describes not flash-in-the-pan movements but movements working toward longer-term and concrete goals. The impression is not merely incidental to his goal of stating the importance of the sociology of irreligion; in fact, as he says, even a *minimal* study of irreligion would improve upon what has gone before, in which, '[c]ompared with the alacrity with which sociologists of a functional persuasion point to the fact that religion exists in all societies, there exists a remarkable reluctance to mention the fact that irreligion exists in *any* society' (2013 : 9, emphasis added). But elsewhere he points out that irreligious acts and emotions are likely to number into the many millions in any society in contact with religious culture. Contrary to repeating the secularisationist's view that irreligion is essentially a transitional phenomenon, the weight of *TSI* is precisely towards putting this meta-narrative to one side and researching, in sociological detail, the myriad ways in which irreligion exists within and shapes contemporary societies.

From today's vantage point, we are in a position to consider the secularisationist view empirically, to ask whether irreligion has in fact become less significant in societies which have secularised further. The example from Zuckerman's important work is used in order to illustrate the extent to which the argument for a focus on substantive irreligion rather than subtractive a-religion (or, in Zuckerman's terminology, 'secularity') has yet to penetrate, but it also anticipates a possible counter-argument: that irreligion would be far more significant in the more religious societies of the 1960s and 70s, and that these rejections of religion, grand and small alike, are likely to be less frequent and less meaningful in the far more secularised societies of the twenty-first century West. By contrast, Zuckerman's discussion with Gitte gives a brief illustration of ongoing interaction between 'secularised' or irreligious individuals and religious organisations. It indicates, therefore, the ongoing relevance of a sociology of – not 'atheism' and 'secularity' as Zuckerman later proposed (2010a, 2010b, 2010c) – but of *irreligion* explicitly, of 'outsider' relationships with religion. Thus, Campbell's sociology of irreligion does not force a researcher to take a view on the secularisation question: the sociological study of irreligion might be part of a critique of secularisation theory, undermining the notion of the secular as post-religious, for example; but equally, it might contribute to a secularisationist narrative, as Campbell intended in 1971. In fact, this ambivalence helps to open up one of the most important theoretical questions against which the sociology of irreligion will provide insight: what *is* the relationship between irreligious activity and secularisation?

Moreover, Campbell's discussion of substantive irreligion should provide yet another opportunity for contemporary scholars to reflect – and to reflect sensitively – on the continuing ambivalence concerning the relationship between substantial irreligion and insubstantial secularity. In fact, in this way *TSI* foreshadows – and sheds new light on – a conceptual discussion that has recently become prominent in the study of secularism in particular. In this, a similar distinction has been made between secularism as a skeletal framework for arranging cultural phenomena (religions) in the public sphere and secularism as an ideological and therefore much more weighty phenomenon (see, for example, Asad (2003)). This has contributed to what is now identified as a 'post-secular turn' in sociology (McLennan, 2007; 2010). Campbell's more modest intervention foreshadows this much-lauded discussion by some decades. Moreover, *TSI* is also ahead of its time in dealing with secularism and irreligion concurrently: in his empirical analysis and theoretical discussion, Campbell discusses both secularist political arrangements and various forms of personal and public irreligion, as well as considering the relationship between the two – the way, for example, secularist politics might benefit certain groups and how this benefit might give rise to irreligious belief on the personal level. Today's work on secularism typically ignores the irreligious perspective altogether (see Gutkowski, 2010) or conflates it with secularism (whilst letting secularism be the dominating concept) in a confused and unproductive way (Lee, 2011; Lee, 2012). Treating irreligion, as well as secularism, as substantive aspects of secularity provides a broader and more sociologically compelling approach.

In short, whether it is practical and methodological or more extensively upsets deep-seated theories of secular modernity, the shift in attention which Campbell proposes, from the study of religion's absence to the study of irreligion's presence, is a profound one. Indeed, his argument is forceful enough that it might be extended beyond itself. Campbell's focus was irreligion, a concept which conjoins hostility and indifference towards religion into a general notion of the rejection of religion. Yet, his sociological and theoretical discussion of irreligious action and movements details empirical examples for which rejection, 'irreligion's principal defining characteristic' (2013: 36), arguably provides too narrow and too negative a summary. Instead, the richness and range of practice he demonstrates persistently shows that the object of study can be conceived of in more positive terms. Thus, the logic of this argument can be used to extend Campbell's sociology beyond an exclusive focus on irreligion, that is, the rejection of religion, and towards a field more broadly conceived: the study of all of those phenomena which are defined by how they differ from religion, that is (in my terminology at least), nonreligion (Lee, 2012). This notion of nonreligion is inclusive of more stable and less antagonistic modes, positions and practices. Thus, *TSI* foregrounds a sociological project more expansive in scope than even it, at times, conceives of – just one way in which this slim volume provides a beginning for a project much vaster than could be accounted for in *several*.

Historicising the Sociology of Irreligion

As well as being of intrinsic interest to scholars in this field, *TSI* is also of extrinsic interest as a historical artefact. Being one of a very few contributions to the study of irreligion of its day, the book itself becomes an important data point for an intellectual history of changing academic views of irreligion and the contexts that gave rise to them. The implications of when and why a sociology of irreligion has become more or less popular – and what this tells us about popular and academic cultural environments – was, in fact, something that Campbell considered in his own discussion of the literature (2013: 8-13), but *TSI* has now become an object of this mode of enquiry as much as an example of it. Indeed, due to the halting development of the field subsequent to *TSI*'s publication, it has become a particularly interesting one.

Given the richness of this text, and the elegance and enthusiasm with which it is presented, the slow beginnings of the sociology of irreligion that Campbell envisaged are somewhat surprising – and all the more intriguing when one compares it to the speed at which the second wave of irreligion sociology has grown. *TSI* may have taken a step along the path toward the sociology of irreligion (and nonreligion), but there were to be very few advances beyond this in the decades that followed, with infrequent contributions, typically in article form. Campbell himself moved onto other subject matter or, rather, turned to questions he considered to be prior to the study of irreligion: he came to feel that neither religion nor irreligion could be understood in isolation from the larger cultural system of which they both were a part (Campbell, *personal communication*). Although he became known as an authority on consumerism, in fact this work also arose from his interest in understanding broader cultural systems – as the title of his first major product of this approach, *The Romantic Ethic and the Spirit of Modern Consumerism* (Campbell, 1987), reveals. Theoretically connected as the projects might have been, still this shift of approach meant that Campbell moved away from the task of providing detailed and dedicated accounts of ir- and non-religious movements. Ultimately, the following decades saw these subjects either ignored or left as the preserve of theological, philosophical and historical scholarship and, more recently, of lively journalistic commentary – against which Campbell's book offered a singular alternative.

Then, in the mid-00s, a change occurred. The Non-religion and Secularity Research Network (NSRN), an interdisciplinary body founded in 2008, provides a bibliography of work in this area and this gives some indication of the steady increase of activity, with 10 and 12 publications in 2003 and 2004 respectively, rising to 33 and then 68 in 2009 and 2010. (available at www.nsrm.net, accessed January 2012). This body of work is the sum of different sub-projects, often isolated from one another by terminology and/or theoretical frameworks despite a common empirical interest (a problem that Campbell foresaw in 1971 (2013: 18) and which is noticed by contemporary scholars (e.g. Pasquale, 2007: 760; see also Lee, 2012)). In 2003, Talal Asad called for what he termed an 'anthropology of the secular', a call since taken up by other scholars (see especially Cannell, 2010); irreligion plays a role in these notions of secularism, though it is an under-theorised one. Two years later, Barry Kosmin and Ariela Keysar established the Institute for the Study of Secularism in Society and Culture (ISSSC) at Trinity College, Hartford, CT. Despite its self-association with 'secularism' (a term now mainly applied to ideologies which seek to constrain religion), in fact the ISSSC focuses especially on micro-level irreligion of all forms, attested to by the contents of their first publication, *Secularism and Secularity: Contemporary International Perspectives* (2007). In addition to this text, a spate of book-length publications also marked the changing fortunes of the study of irreligion and nonreligion: noteworthy contributions include Hunsberger and Altemeyer's study of organised nonreligion (2006), Zuckerman's study of Scandinavian 'societies without God' (2008), his two edited volumes on global 'atheism and secularity' (2010a, 2010b) and Amarasingham's edited collection on New Atheism (2010). As well as the ISSSC, the social scientific study of nonreligion has achieved other institutional footholds: the Non-religion and Secularity Research Network (NSRN) held its inaugural conference in 2009; the first taught course on 'atheism and non-religion' was established in 2010 (Bullivant, 2011), with other modules emerging since then (see www.nsrn.net for further information); and, as of Autumn 2011, Pitzer College in California has offered the possibility of majoring in 'Secular

Studies' – placing these Secular Studies alongside Religious Studies, Sociology, Science, and Philosophy in the college's prospectus. It is notable that these projects were being conducted in parallel, appearing on the scene at a similar time, with several celebrating *TSI* and presenting it as a reference which legitimised their (so they thought) isolated enterprises.

This almost overnight change in fortune are remarkable, and beg the question of why it occurred at the time and with the vigour that it did. In a recent survey of the emerging field, Bullivant and Lee (2013: 2) have argued that it is too early to understand precisely why the study of irreligion, nonreligion and secularity have experienced such an upsurge and why at this moment. The renewed visibility of religion and of irreligious movements like the New Atheism obviously play a role – although the nature of this role and the extent to which these phenomena operate dependently and independently from each other is a question for empirical research and remains to be seen. As in the 1970s, the membership of organised irreligious and secularist bodies like the National Secular Society (NSS) and British Humanist Association (BHA) are witnessing a rise in their membership. Certainly, this general popular interest will have had an impact on the academy.

A more subtle line of reasoning can be taken up from Campbell's own explanation of the non-existence of the sociology of religion before the late 1960s. He partially explains the absence of social scientific treatments of irreligion by the irreligiosity of social scientists themselves, a perception which can be evidenced by some significant cases – Marx, Weber and Durkheim's various forms of irreligiosity – and, today, by some more systematic studies of the academy (Gross and Simmons, 2009; in Bullivant and Lee, 2012). Campbell's argument is that these nonreligious social scientists treat religion as some kind of oddity, requiring of explanation, whereas their own nonreligion, whilst not necessarily normative in society at large, is at least subjectively normative and therefore does not attract their attention (2013: 8). Concrete evidence for this theorem comes from the fact that the few incidences in which irreligion received social scientific attention come out of *religious* contexts and typically (but atypically for classical social science) treat irreligion as anomalous and requiring of explanation. Campbell's main example is the interest in irreligion coming out of universities from countries in which the Catholic Church had a great influence (ibid: 9). Drawing on Stephen Bullivant's historical studies (2009a; 2009b: 41-7), Bullivant and Lee (2012) provide further examples. They note that Vetter and Green's 'Personality and Group Factors in the Making of Atheists', published in 1932 and probably the first the Anglophone study of the psychology of atheism, appeared in the *Journal of Abnormal and Social Psychology* and described atheists – like 'Single Taxers, Fundamentalists [and] Communists' – as having '[e]xtremes of social, political and religious outlook' (Vetter and Green, 1932, in Lee and Bullivant 2012). They also provide specific examples of the Catholic Church's interest in explaining nonreligion. In interwar and post-WW2 France, for example, it was the Catholic Church which, concerned about marked declines in levels of traditional religiosity, commissioned a number of large-scale quantitative and qualitative studies into the 'social character not only of present unbelief, but of its causes and its origins' (Congar, 1938, in Bullivant and Lee, 2012). Such studies continued into the 50s and 60s, in France and elsewhere (e.g. Lepp, 1963 and Steeman, 1965, in Bullivant and Lee 2012) and, in 1960, an Institute for Higher Studies on Atheism was opened at the Pontifical Urban University in Rome. Most overtly, in the years between Campbell's completing his doctoral thesis (1968) and publishing a developed version of that thesis as *TSI* (2013; originally published 1971), the first social scientific conference on the topic of nonreligion was held by the Vatican. This responded to the Second Vatican Council's request for a 'more thorough treatment' of the causes and nature of contemporary atheism, and the resulting conference on 'the culture of unbelief' was held in March 1969 (Caporale and Grumelli, 1971). The fact that the majority of studies which remained engaged with this subject matter in the later decades of the twentieth century came out of America would also be consistent with this model: American populations have become irreligious at a much slower pace than its European counterparts.

The limits of this argument include the fact that the first wave of irreligion research did not always come out of religious settings, and Campbell's own *TSI* is a chief example of this. What is more, this model would not explain the current boom in irreligion studies, emanating out of Europe as well as America despite their different (ir)religious profiles and

xxx

normativities (Voas and Ling, 2010). The increase in discussion about religion might provide an additional explanation, but there are serious limitations here too. The fact that the most high-profile irreligious movement in the West today, New Atheism, is particularly associated with America and Britain (and, to a lesser extent, Germany) and thus correlates with the most prolific areas of irreligion research, seems to suggest that this cultural explanation is significant. Yet, we then need to explain the incidence of New Atheism in turn and this raises new problems: if, for example, this irreligious movement is explained as a reaction to religion, why is it that it appeals in such similar ways to these two differently (ir)religious populations, the Americans and the British? Certainly, the view that Europe and especially northern Europe is profoundly secular attracts a consensus that cuts across these theoretical contestations – and this means that some substantial parts of the revived irreligion studies are taking place in contexts of unchallenged secularity; this in turn means the idea that religious normativity gives rise to irreligious research provides a partial explanation only.

A necessary addition to this explanation might, however, be extrapolated from Campbell's theory: perhaps emerging irreligious movements alert those with an investment in religion to the importance of irreligion as a socio-cultural reality that *might* be worthy of study but that *what is then important is how worthy of study it proves to be*. Bullivant and Lee (2012) notice that the late 60s/early 70s is the moment at which nonreligion moved from being a primarily deviant phenomenon to a much more respectable and widespread one. Campbell (after Becker (1950), in Campbell, 2013: 6; 17; see also Lee, 2012) conceives of 'irreligious' as related to concepts such as 'heretic' and 'infidel'– concepts which are expressive of religious rather than non-religious normativity. According to various histories of the secularisation of Britain and Europe, the real thrust of secularisation was just taking place. Thus, Campbell's view of irreligious movements as agents of secularisation makes sense at this moment. It might be, however, that a **sustained** sociological interest simply rests upon more embedded and widespread irreligion in society – an empirical reality which provides much more material for research and makes the socio-cultural significance of irreligion much clearer. In keeping with the spirit of *TSI*, if not with all of its explicit statements, the project of this sociology would then become less interested in the transitional forms of irreligion, but more so in far more stable forms. Indeed, my interest in 'nonreligion' as a broader concept than 'irreligion' might be seen to reflect this change. As we have discussed, the 'founding fathers' of sociology as well as others working within the secularisation paradigm did not anticipate that secularity would have any content; therefore it is only once secularity is established that the many and nuanced ways in which this secular population engages with religion and 'religious' themes becomes widely visible. As part of this process, irreligion – or, less narrowly, nonreligion – will come loose of its original theoretical moorings: if nonreligion is normal and normative, the focus on irreligion as an agent of secularisation is recast as merely one form or impetus for incidents of it. This, in my view, adds a new momentum to the sociology of irreligion and non-religion, and this is what may be finally giving rise to an established and widely-recognised tradition of research.

Advancing the Sociology of Irreligion

The shift from a narrower sociology of irreligion to a more broadly conceived sociology of irreligion, or – to make the distinction – a sociology of nonreligion, only expands the scope of the project Campbell began 40 years ago. His text remains the most important methodological resource for scholars in this area, whether they also take up the study of counter-religious movements arising in religious-normative settings, or whether they take up the study of places in which nonreligion occupies a dominant position rather than a deviant one, as seen both in certain parts of the West but also in Socialist and post-Socialist localities, where irreligion has been associated with elite groups and 'top-down' power dynamics.

In fact, the resuming of a sociology of irreligion would be far *less* auspicious if it could be described in such simple terms – as an easy picking up where Campbell left off 40 years ago. In fact, the field is changed and changing, and it is precisely this dynamism which makes the resumed project so promising. If revision is a sign of this activity, part of fulfilling this promise will be the revising of some of Campbell's empirical arguments – as more studies concerning irreligious and other nonreligious social movements and organisations are amassed – as well as his theoretical ones. We can already see that the parameters of the field as he envisioned them are shaped by the relative marginality of nonreligion at that time, and the focus on anti-religion and secularism is one expression of that marginality. I think, however, that *TSI*'s place as the foundational text for nonreligion studies will be permanent. It is the starting point of debates, elaborations, amendments, counter-arguments and counter-theory. And if the vitality of the broader field of nonreligion means that *TSI* can no longer be seen as the final word in this project – or 'stillborn', as Demerath III put it (1969, in Pasquale 2012) – this makes the book's contribution more rather than less significant for contemporary sociology.

Lois Lee

January 2013

Cited work

Amarasingam, Amarnath (ed). 2010. *Religion and the New Atheism: A Critical Appraisal*. Leiden and Boston: Brill.

Asad, Talal. 2003. *Formations of the Secular: Christianity, Islam, Modernity*. Stanford, CA: Stanford University Press.

Bader, Veit. 2011. Beyond Secularisms of All Sorts. *Immanent Frame* (online). SSSR, 11 October 2011. Available at http://blogs.ssrc.org/tif/2011/10/11/beyond-secularisms-of-all-sorts/ [accessed 9 December 2011].

Bagg, Samuel, and David Voas. 2010. The Triumph of Indifference: Irreligion in British Society. In *Atheism and Secularity: Volume 2: Global Expressions*, edited by Phil Zuckerman. Santa Barbara: Praeger: 91-111.

Bruce, Steve. 2002. *God is Dead: Secularisation in the West*. Oxford: Blackwell.

Bruce, Steve. 2011. *Secularization: In Defence of an Unfashionable Theory*. Oxford: Oxford University Press.

Budd, Susan. 1972. Review: Toward a Sociology of Irreligion. *British Journal of Sociology*, 23 (2): 255-256.

Budd, Susan. 1977. *Varieties of Unbelief: Atheists and Agnostics in English Society 1850-1960*. London: Heinemann.

Bullivant, Stephen. 2009a. From *"Main Tendue"* to Vatican II: the Catholic Engagement with Atheism, 1936-65. *New Blackfriars*, 90 (1026): 178-87.

Bullivant, Stephen. 2009b.'The Salvation of Atheists: A Critical Exploration of a Theme in Catholic Dogmatic Theology', Unpublished PhD thesis, Oxford University, 2009.

Bullivant, Stephen. 2011. Teaching Atheism and Non-religion: Challenges and Opportunities. *Discourse*, 10 (2): 93-110.

Bullivant, Stephen and Lois Lee. 2012. Introduction: Interdisciplinary Studies of Non-religion and Secularity: The State of the Union. *Journal of Contemporary Religion*, 27 (1): 19-27.

Campbell, Colin. 1968. Humanism and the Culture of the Professions: A Study of the Rise of the British Humanist Movement, 1967-1963. Unpublished PhD thesis, University of London.

Campbell, Colin. 2013 [1971]. *Toward a Sociology of Irreligion*. Alcuin Academics.

Campbell, Colin. 1987. *The Romantic Ethic and the Spirit of Modern Consumerism.* Oxford: Basil Blackwell.

Cannell, Fenella. 2010. The Anthropology of Secularism. *Annual Review of Anthropology*, 39: 85-100.

Corporale, Rocco and Antonio Grumelli. 1971. *The Culture of Unbelief: Studies and Proceedings from the First International Symposium on Belief Held at Rome, March 22-27, 1969*. Berkeley, CA: University of California Press.

Fitzgerald, Timothy. 2007. *Discourse on Civility and Barbarity: A Critical History of Religion and Related Categories*. Oxford: Oxford University Press.

Gross, Neil, and Solon Simmons. 2009. 'The Religiosity of American College and University Professors. *Sociology of Religion,* 70: 101–29.

Gutkowski, Stacey. 2010. From Multiculturalism to Multifaithism? The Panel Debate. *Studies in Ethnicity and Nationalism*, 10 (2): 319-322.

Hunsberger, Bruce and Bob Altemeyer. 2006. *Atheists: A Groundbreaking Study of America's Nonbelievers*. Amherst, NY: Prometheus Press.

Hunter, Ian. 2009. The Shallow Legitimacy of Secular Liberal Orders: The Case of Early Modern Brandenburg-Prussia. In *Secularism, Religion and Multicultural Citizenship*, edited by Geoffrey Brahm Levey and Tariq Modood. Cambridge: Cambridge University Press: 27-55.

Kosmin, Barry A. and Ariela Keysar (ed.s). 2007. *Secularism and Secularity: Contemporary International Perspectives.* Hartford, CA: ISSSC.

Lee, Lois. 2006. The 'Secular' Individual in Britain: Toward a Sociology of (Ir)religion. Unpublished MPhil dissertation, University of Cambridge.

Lee, Lois. 2011. From Neutrality to Dialogue: Constructing the Religious Other in British Non-religious Discourses. In *Modernities Revisited*, edited by Maren Behrensen, Lois Lee and Ahmet S. Tekelioglu. Vienna: IWM Junior Visiting Fellows' Conferences 2011., 29. Available at www.iwm.at. [accessed 23 Jun. 2011].

Lee, Lois. 2012. Research Note: Talking About a Revolution: Terminology for the New Field of Non-religion Studies. *Journal of Contemporary Religion*. 27(1): 129-139.

Levey, Geoffrey Brahm and Tariq Modood (ed.s). 2009. *Secularism, Religion and Multicultural Citizenship*. Cambridge: Cambridge University Press.

McLennan, Gregor. 2007. Towards Postsecular Sociology? *Sociology*, 41: 857-870.

McLennan, Gregor. 2010. The Postsecular Turn. *Theory Culture Society*, 27 (3): 3-20.

O'Brian Baker, Joseph and Buster Smith. 2009a. None Too Simple: Examining Issues of Religious Nonbelief and Nonbelonging in the United States. *Journal for the Scientific Study of Religion*, 48 (4): 719-733.

Pasquale, Frank L. 2012. The Social Science of Secularity. *Free Inquiry*, 33(2): 17-23.

Pitzer College, 2011. *Pitzer College, 2011-2012 Course Catalog*. Pitzer College, CA. Available at http://www.pitzer.edu/academics/curriculum/pdf/Course_Catalog.pdf [accessed 22 Feb 2012].

Royle, Edward. 1974. *Victorian infidels: the origins of the British secularist movement, 1791-1866.* Manchester: Manchester University Press.

Taylor, Charles. 2007. *A Secular Age*. Cambridge, MA: Belknap Press of Harvard University Press.

Voas, David and Rodney Ling, 2010. Religion in Britain and the United States. *British Social Attitudes: The 26th Report.* London: Sage/National Centre for Social Research.

Zuckerman, Phil. 2008. *Society without God: What the Least Religious Nations Can Tell Us about Contentment*. New York: New York University Press.

Zuckerman, Phil (ed). 2010a. *Atheism and Secularity: Issues, Concepts and Definitions*. Vol. 1. Santa Barbara, CA: Praeger.

Zuckerman, Phil (ed). 2010b. *Atheism and Secularity: Global Expressions*. Vol. 2. Santa Barbara, CA: Praeger.

Zuckerman, Phil. 2010c. Introduction. In *Atheism and Secularity - Volume 1: Issues, Concepts and Definitions*, edited by Phil Zuckerman. Santa Barbara: Praeger, vii-xii.

Irreligion: A Contemporary Bibliography

Lois Lee

With Stephen Bullivant and Christopher R. Cotter

Developed from an empirical account of the British Humanist movement (Campbell, 1968), Campbell has recently reflected that, at the time of writing it, he had not 'fully appreciated the extent to which *Toward a Sociology of Irreligion* (2013 [1971]; *TSI* hereafter) was not so much a contribution *to* the field of study as an exploration *of* the field of study' (personal communication, 2012). It is, of course, both things. It may be true to say, however, that the latter is the book's more profound and far-reaching contribution. Campbell's lack of awareness of how far he had achieved a general exploration of the field is possibly explained precisely by his dedication to the case study he had before him, with the 'exploration *of* the field' incidental to that study, emerging as a condition of the pioneering research he wanted to do. If this is true, Campbell's awareness of the range of conceptual, methodological and theoretical foundations of his project shows that he was already looking like the rigorous researcher that he was to become known as. But it would also show the benefits of attending to conceptual, methodological and theoretical issues with a concrete research project in mind, something that, intentionally or not, may have enabled him to probe these issues as deeply as he does. Whatever the reason, the resulting book has provided a wide-ranging and astute discussion that is still of active use to researchers and students entering the field.

In recent years, however, there have been contributions to this field that take some of Campbell's exploration and empirical contribution further. In the Introduction to this volume, I give several reasons why these contributions should not be seen as usurping the value of *TSI*, which remains a rich and singular resource. Although by no means exhaustive, and focused on English language contributions, this contemporary bibliography is intended to locate this resource in broader contemporary context as well as indicate other material of note. The bibliography follows the structure of *TSI* itself, and each section can be used as further reading to the individual chapters of Campbell's book.

1 The Sociology of Irreligion

Campbell's book opens with general introduction to the sociology of irreligion and a discussion of what is at stake in such a sociology. He considers the overall nature of this sociological project as well as its potential contribution to the sociology of religion and to its theoretical cornerstone, secularisation theory. As I have discussed (Introduction), Campbell's account remains superlative in the latter regard, that is, in terms of considering the ontology of irreligion and nonreligion in relationship to theories of the secular and secularisation. Most authors assume a certain relationship between irreligion and secularisation and do not discuss it explicitly (ibid.); therefore my own work (see especially Lee, 2012a and Lee, 2012b) is notable if only by virtue of being a still fairly isolated attempt to take up the question.

In terms of general treatments of the field, all interventions make some statement concerning their own empirical and theoretical contribution, but Campbell's short but general discussion of the value of the field as a whole has not often been repeated. Bullivant and Lee's (2012) introduction to a recent, guest-edited special issue of the *Journal for Contemporary Religion* on 'Interdisciplinary Studies of Non-religion and Secularity' provides one survey of the field, as does Pasquale's (2012) article for *Free Inquiry*. Bullivant's (2008) research note on the sociology of, in this case, atheism provides a useful indication of how far the field has developed in a few short years, and Pasquale's earlier discussion of the field (2007) gives another erudite statement of why this area of research is useful. These authors all touch on the contribution a sociology of irreligion stands to make to the study of religion, but a deeper theoretical discussion of this relationship will rely on more extensive and empirically grounded conceptualisations of irreligion. This work will beneficially engage with 'genealogical' discussions of the concepts of irreligion, nonreligion and/or the secular, and the argument that these categories and various categories relating to 'religion' are mutually constitutive; Talal Asad (1993), Timothy

Fitzgerald (2007) and Kim Knott (2010) provide different but equally important contributions here.

Anthropologists have also begun to discuss a new field of study. Lacking the precedent that Campbell has provided sociologists, this anthropological work has repeated some of the work Campbell has done, but is of note in other regards. Talal Asad's discussion of the secular and secularism (2003) and his suggestions of what such an anthropology might look like (2003: ch. 1) mirror Campbell's discussion, and Fenella Cannell (2010) has recently provided a general account of the sub-discipline of an anthropology of secularism. Also notable is Ruy Llera's (2006) exploration of what the researchers' own irreligiosity might mean for their research, an important piece of reflection that it would be useful for sociologists to consider and replicate. In turn, this anthropological work stands to benefit from considering their approach alongside Campbell's (and other sociologists') – in terms of scrutinising their current practice of using the term 'secularism' in a way that conflates the political-ideological with the personal-philosophical and makes it difficult, for example, to conceptualise people who are religious and politically secularist at the same time; or those who personally identify as atheist but who are more ambivalent secularists; on this topic, see Lee (2012a) and also Gutkowski (2010).

NSRN Online and its (open access and peer-reviewed) journal, *Secularism and Nonreligion*, provide further general resources to researchers. In addition, Bullivant's (2011) reflections on teaching the study of nonreligion and atheism as part of an undergraduate curriculum looks towards a wider discussion of teaching and other academic practice in this new academic sub-discipline.

Asad, Talal. 2003. Formations of the Secular: Christianity, Islam, Modernity. Stanford, CA: Stanford University Press.

Asad, Talal. 1993. Genealogies of Religion: Discipline and Reasons of Power in Christianity and Islam. London: John Hopkins University Press.

Bullivant, Stephen. 2011. Teaching Atheism and Nonreligion: Challenges and Opportunities. Discourse, 10 (2): 93-110.

Bullivant, Stephen. 2008a. Research Note: Sociology and the Study of Atheism. Journal of Contemporary Religion, 23 (3): 16-31.

Cannell, Fenella. 2010. The Anthropology of Secularism. Annual Review of Anthropology, 39: 85-100.

Fitzgerald, Timothy. 2007. *Discourse on Civility and Barbarity: A Critical History of Religion and Related Categories*. Oxford: Oxford University Press.

Gutkowski, Stacey. 2010. From Multiculturalism to Multifaithism? The Panel Debate. *Studies in Ethnicity and Nationalism*, 10 (2): 319-322.

Knott, Kim. 2010. Theoretical and Methodological Resources for Breaking Open the Secular and Exploring the Boundary Between Religion and Non-religion. *Historia Religionum*, 2: 115-133.

Lee, Lois. 2012a. Research Note: Talking About a Revolution: Terminology for the New Field of Non-religion Studies. *Journal of Contemporary Religion*. 27(1): 129-139.

Lee, Lois. 2012b. Being Secular: Towards Separate Sociologies of Secularity, Nonreligion and Epistemological Culture. Unpublished PhD thesis, University of Cambridge, 2012.

Llera Blanes, Ruy. 2006. The Atheist Anthropologist: Believers and Non-Believers in Anthropological Fieldwork. *Social Anthropology* 14 (2): 223-234.

NSRN Online. Published by the Nonreligion and Secularity Research Network (NSRN). Available at http://nsrn.net .

Pasquale, Frank L. 2012. The Social Science of Secularity. *Free Inquiry*, 33(2): 17-23.

Pasquale, Frank L. 2007. Empirical Study and Neglect of Unbelief and Irreligion. In *The New Encyclopaedia of Unbelief*, edited by Tom Flynn. Amherst, NY: Prometheus Books, 760-766. Available at http://www.trincoll.edu/Academics/centers/isssc/Documents/Unbelief%20and%20Irreligion,%20Empirical%20Study%20and%20Neglect%20of.pdf [Accessed 20 December 2011.]

Secularism and Nonreligion. Published by the Institute for the Study of Secularism in Society and Culture (ISSSC) and the Non-religion and Secularity Research Network (NSRN). Available at http://secularismandnonreligion.org .

2 The Nature and Forms of Irreligion

The first substantive section of Campbell's book considers the concept of irreligion in some depth. Firstly, it provides guidance in terms of definition, a topic on which there has been little subsequent scrutiny. Lee (2012a) provides a survey of the terminological literature, discusses the problems that arise from a lack of conceptual reflexivity in the field and suggests some conceptual proposals for use and further scrutiny. Cragun and Hammer (2011) have also provided an interesting discussion on how terminology in this field is shaped and constrained by religious agendas in the American academy. McCutcheon (2007) and Fitzgerald (2007) discuss irreligion and/or related categories in relation to religion, arguing that the concepts are co-dependent and ideological. Knott (2005, 2010) considers religion, the secular/non-religious and the postsecular in spatial terms, making these 'spaces' autonomous enough that one can study how people and objects move around them and interact between and against them. Religion-focused conceptual works have also started to make the irreligious and/or the secular more central to their work, as in Griel and Bromley's edited collection (2003), *Defining Religion: Investigating the Boundaries Between the Sacred and Secular.* In addition, edited collections which touch on the topic of irreligion give some attention to conceptual work, in dedicated chapters and introductory remarks to the collections and to the individual studies. Such collections include those by Corporale and Grumelli (1971), Kosmin and Keysar (2007) and Zuckerman (2010a, 2010b).

In considering its nature, Campbell is emphatic about irreligion being expressed in action and emotion and, following from this, argues that irreligiosity is a common experience and one by no means confined to groups we might label as irreligious. Since 1971, the study of practice and culture has advanced extensively in sociology and Lee's (2012c) discussion of the locations of nonreligion in mind, body and space reflect this shift. Knott and Franks' (2007) study of how secular values are enacted in the context of an English medical centre shows how such an approach to irreligion might be conducted in practice, and is an important precedent in that respect. Campbell's (1996) own exploration of superstition in secularised contexts provides another resource for considering 'religious' action in irreligious context. In addition, irreligious action and experience that is situated in religious space or is, at least, not part of a clearly bounded irreligious culture has been explored by Bullivant (2008b), who extends William James' (2008) concept of 'religious experience' to this domain, resulting in the notion of 'irreligious experience'. With Campbell, Bullivant begins to develop a framework that might help theorise studies of religious 'doubt' (e.g. Hunsberger et al., 2002) in more sophisticated ways.

Work on the range and types of irreligiousness is likewise only in its formative stages, with the majority of contributions so far questioning – as Campbell does – the notion that unreligious populations are homogenous, as well as the validity of research methods built on this basis. O'Brian Baker and Smith (2009a, 2009b), Hadaway and Clark Roof (1979) and Lim et al. (2010) provide empirical support for this view, and Bullivant (2008a) demonstrates why categories relating to irreligion and atheism are unreliable tools for survey research. Several projects developing typologies of irreligion are in progress, but some typological work has already been completed concerning what Campbell (2013 [1971]: 31) calls the 'twilight zone' between religion and irreligion: Storm (2009), Voas and Day (2007), Voas (2009) and Day (2011).

An interesting possibility that might be developed from the sociology of irreligion is the study of *rejections* of irreligion. This approach would make the growing 'postsecular' literature relevant to the study of irreligion, to the extent that that literature surveys critics of irreligious-secular thought. See Gregor McLennan (2007, 2010) for a good overview of the 'postsecular turn' in sociology. Of course, most of this literature is theoretical, but it points to a possibly fascinating branch of the sociology of irreligion and is therefore worth indicating.

Bullivant, Stephen. 2008a. Research Note: Sociology and the Study of Atheism. *Journal of Contemporary Religion*, 23 (3): 16-31.
Bullivant, Stephen. 2008b. Introducing Irreligious Experiences. *Implicit Religion*, 11 (1): 7-24.

Campbell, Colin. 1996. Half-belief and the Paradox of Ritual Instrumental Activism: A Theory of Modern Superstition. *The British Journal of Sociology,* 47 (1): 151-165.

Corporale, Rocco and Antonio Grumelli. 1971. *The Culture of Unbelief: Studies and Proceedings from the First International Symposium on Belief Held at Rome, March 22-27, 1969.* Berkeley, CA: University of California Press.

Cragun, Ryan T. and Joseph H. Hammer. 2011. 'One Person's Apostate is Another Person's Convert': What Terminology Tells Us About Pro-Religious Hegemony in the Sociology of Religion. *Humanity and Society,* 35: 149-175.

Day, Abby. 2011. *Believing in Belonging: Belief and Social Identity in the Modern World.* Oxford: Oxford University Press.

Fitzgerald, Timothy. 2007. *Discourse on Civility and Barbarity: A Critical History of Religion and Related Categories.* Oxford: Oxford University Press.

Griel, Arthur L., and David G. Bromley (eds). 2003. *Defining Religion: Investigating the Boundaries between the Sacred and Secular.* Oxford: JAI.

Hadaway, C. Kirk, and Wade Clark Roof. 1979. Those Who Stay Religious 'Nones' and Those Who Don't: A Research Note. *Journal for the Scientific Study of Religion* 18 (2): 194-200.

Hunsberger, Bruce, M. Pratt, and S.M. Pancer. 2002. A Longitudinal Study of Religious Doubts in High School and Beyond: Relationships, Stability, and Searching for Answers. *Journal for the Scientific Study of Religion* 41 (2): 255-266.

James, William. 2008. *The Varieties of Religious Experience: A Study in Iluman Nature.* London: Routledge.

Kosmin, Barry A. and Ariela Keysar (ed.s). 2007. *Secularism and Secularity: Contemporary International Perspectives.* Hartford, CA: ISSSC.

Knott, Kim. 2010. Theoretical and Methodological Resources for Breaking Open the Secular and Exploring the Boundary Between Religion and Non-religion. *Historia Religionum,* 2: 115-133.

Knott, Kim. 2005. *The Location of Religion: A Spatial Analysis.* London: Equinox.

Knott, Kim and Myfanwy Franks. 2007. Secular values and the Location of Religion: A Spatial Analysis of an English Medical Centre. *Health and Place*, 13 (1): 224–237.

Lee, Lois. 2012a. Research Note: Talking About a Revolution: Terminology for the New Field of Non-religion Studies. *Journal of Contemporary Religion*. 27(1): 129-139.

Lee, Lois. 2012b. Being Secular: Towards Separate Sociologies of Secularity, Nonreligion and Epistemological Culture. Unpublished PhD thesis, University of Cambridge, 2012.

Lee, Lois. *2012c.* Locating Nonreligion, in Mind, Body and Space: New Research Methods for a New Field. *Annual Review of the Sociology of Religion: Volume 3: New Methods in Sociology of Religion*, edited by Luigi Berzano and Ole Preben Riis. Leiden: BRILL.

Lim, Chaeyoon, Carol Ann MacGregor and Robert D. Putnam. 2010. Secular and Liminal: Discovering Heterogeneity Among Religious Nones. *Journal for the Scientific Study of Religion*, 49 (4): 596-618.

McCutcheon, Russell T. 2007. 'They Licked the Platter Clean': On the Co-Dependency of the Religious and the Secular. *Method and Theory in the Study of Religion* 19: 173-199.

McLennan, Gregor. 2010. The Postsecular Turn. *Theory Culture Society*, 27 (3): 3-20.

McLennan, Gregor. 2007. Towards Postsecular Sociology? *Sociology*, 41: 857-870.

O'Brian Baker, Joseph and Buster Smith. 2009a. None Too Simple: Examining Issues of Religious Nonbelief and Nonbelonging in the United States. *Journal for the Scientific Study of Religion*, 48 (4): 719-733.

O'Brian Baker, Joseph and Buster Smith. 2009b. The Nones: Social Characteristics of the Religiously Unaffiliated. *Social Forces* 87 (3): 1251-1263.

Storm, Ingrid. 2009. Halfway to Heaven: Four Types of Fuzzy Fidelity in Europe. *Journal for the Scientific Study of Religion*. 48 (4): 702-718.

Voas, David. 2009a. The Rise and Fall of Fuzzy Fidelity in Europe. *European Sociological Review*, 25 (2): 155-168.

Voas, David and Abby Day. 2007. Secularity in Great Britain. In *Secularism and Secularity: Contemporary International Perspectives*, edited by Barry A. Kosmin and Ariela Keysar. Hartford, CA: ISSSC: 95-110.

Zuckerman, Phil (ed). 2010a. *Atheism and Secularity: Issues, Concepts and Definitions*. Vol. 1. Santa Barbara, CA: Praeger.

Zuckerman, Phil (ed). 2010b. *Atheism and Secularity: Global Expressions*. Vol. 2. Santa Barbara, CA: Praeger.

3 Modern Irreligious Movements in Britain and America – and Elsewhere

The study of irreligion has always been more visible in historical than social scientific research and some treatments of past irreligious movements in Britain and America are available in addition to Campbell's. Focusing first on the UK, subsequent to *TSI*, Campbell's contemporaries, Edward Royle and Susan Budd, published books on, respectively, the origins of the British secularist movement (1974) and Atheists and Agnostics in English society between 1850 and 1960 (1977). In the following decade, Ian MacKillop (2012[1986]) published a book-length study of the British Ethical Societies of the nineteenth and twentieth centuries and, like *TSI*, this book has recently been republished. Contemporary researchers, however, are turning to new methodologies to understand irreligious movements. Especially important is the range of qualitative methods being taken up, with promising moves towards the use of situated ethnography and material cultural approaches now visible. Much of this work is in progress, but Cotter (2011a) provides a useful summary of some important contemporary projects that are currently underway and Lee (2012) discusses some of the potential of these approaches.

It is interesting to note that even historical treatments of irreligious movements have only begun to emerge more recently in the US. Seaman's (2005) study of 'America's Most Hated Woman', Madelyn Murray O'Hair, the prominent American Atheist activist, points at one reason why this interest has been delayed in the US case: in the past, irreligious movements have not been associated with literary and normally male elites, as in the UK, but with more marginal individuals, who were associated with eccentricity rather than respectability.[1] Indeed, the gendered aspect of irreligion is taken up by Kirkley in her book, *Rational Mothers and Infidel Gentlemen: Gender and American Atheism, 1865-1915*. In addition, Susan Jacoby (2004) has provided a popular but significant history of American secularist movements and public irreligion, albeit one used to make a normative (pro-secularist) argument.

Given the marginal status of irreligious views in American culture, this kind of normative framing is common in contemporary US contributions to the field, but another result of this situation is that interest in irreligious movements reawakened slightly earlier in the US than in the UK. Thus, there are already some important sociological studies of contemporary irreligious movements available: Hunsberger and Altemeyer (2006), Pasquale (2010) and Smith (2011) are strong examples. Interesting longitudinal perspectives are also emerging, as in Cimino and Smith's work (2007) on how contemporary American movements respond to their historic failure to get a foothold in society and culture, and Schmidt's (2011) attempt to understand contemporary forms of public irreligion (and especially the New Atheism) in comparison with past forms – specifically, the American Association for the Advancement of Atheism.

Indeed, the study of the New Atheism – an irreligious movement associated with Richard Dawkins, Sam Harris, Christopher Hitchens and Daniel Dennett, and which combines a contemporary scientism with a radical and often anti-religious agenda – is a significant subject matter in contemporary irreligion studies and the likely cause of much popular and academic interest in the subject. Social scientific accounts are still relatively rare, although some contributions to Amarasingam (2010) move beyond the more common theoretical and critical engagements. In addition to Amarsingam (ibid.), several contributions (Beattie, 2007; Stenger, 2009; Bradley and Tate, 2010, Cotter, 2011b) provide a scholarly framework for those interested in taking up the much-needed sociological study of New

---

[1] This observation is indebted to Stephen Bullivant.

Atheism: And, as in so many of the areas discussed in this bibliography, a number of sociological studies are in progress and will become available in coming years. It is worth noting, however, that, though it of course makes no mention of New Atheism, *TSI* is an important resource for its study, enabling scholars to take the long view in understanding this recent, flashy phenomenon: *TSI* is full of analyses that could be applied to the New Atheism – something which helps check the idea that New Atheism is wholly new in nature as well as in name.

One important development in the contemporary sociology of irreligion is a movement towards the study of irreligious movements outside of Anglophone and Western settings – work that both enriches our understanding of irreligious movements and provides opportunities for comparative work. Johannes Quack's (2011, 2012) work on organised irreligious movements in India is a significant example, as is the literature beginning to deal with state Atheism in Socialist and post-Socialist societies (Husband, 2000; Lewis, 2000; Froese, 2004a, 2004b; Zrinšak, 2004; and Luehrmann, 2011) – examples which provide an important point of comparison to the typically 'grass-roots' type of irreligious organisation seen in Western societies. Regional variation has also been noticed and theorised, in Block's (2010) study of the highly irreligious States of Columbia and Washington and in Voas and McAndrew's (2012) discussion of variation in the UK.

Writing in a religious-normative setting, Campbell's 1971 study focuses on organised irreligious movements in much the same way as contemporary US scholars do. In Europe, however, many settings are irreligious-normative and those working with political secularism have shifted attention from irreligious movements to how irreligious and secularist assumptions are interwoven into political and administrative institutions. There is not space here to point to the increasingly numerous general and critical accounts of secularism, but some more particular discussions include Shakman Hurd's (2008) work on secularism in International Relations, Gutkowski's (2012) work on the 'British secular habitus' and its enactments in British involvements in Iraq and Afghanistan in the 'War on Terror', and a growing literature devoted to the role of religion in (secularist) legal frameworks; Doe and Sandberg (2010) and Doe (2011) provide impressive compendiums of this work.

Amarasingam, Amarnath (ed). 2010. *Religion and the New Atheism: A Critical Appraisal*. Leiden and Boston: Brill.

Beattie, Tina. 2007. *The New Atheists: The Twilight of Reason and the War on Religion*. London: Darton, Longman and Todd.

Block, Tina. (2010). Religion, Irreligion, and the Difference Place Makes: The Case of the Postwar Pacific Northwest. *Social History,* 43(85): 1-30.

Bradley, Arthur and Andrew Tate. 2010. *The New Atheist Novel: Fiction, Philosophy and   Polemic After 9/11*. London: Continuum.

Budd, Susan. 1977. *Varieties of Unbelief: Atheists and Agnostics in English Society 1850-1960*. London: Heinemann.

Cimino, Richard, and Christopher Smith. 2007. Secular Humanism and Atheism beyond Progressive Secularism. *Sociology of Religion*, 68 (4): 407-424.

Cotter, Christopher R. 2011a. Qualitative Methods Workshop: NSRN Methods for Nonreligion and Secularity Series). *NSRN Events Reports* (online). NSRN, June 2011. Available at: http://nsrn.net/events/events-reports/. [Accessed 19 December 2011.]

Cotter, Christopher R. 2011b. Consciousness Raising: The Critique, Agenda, and Inherent Precariousness of Contemporary Anglophone Atheism. *International Journal for the Study of New Religions* 2 (1): 77-103.

Doe, Norman. 2011. *Law and Religion in Europe: A Comparative Introduction*. Oxford: OUP.

Doe, Norman and Sandberg, Russell. 2010. *Law and Religion: New Horizons*. Leuven: Peeters.

Froese, Paul. 2004a. After Atheism: An Analysis of Religious Monopolies in the Post-Communist World. Sociology of Religion 65 (1): 57-75.

Froese, Paul. 2004b. Forced Secularisation in Soviet Russia: Why an Atheistic Monopoly Failed. *Journal for the Scientific Study of Religion* 40 (1): 35-50.

Gutkowski, Stacey. 2012. The British Secular Habitus and the War on Terror. *Journal of Contemporary Religion*, 27 (1): 87-103.

Hunsberger, Bruce and Bob Altemeyer. 2006. *Atheists: A Groundbreaking Study of America's Nonbelievers*. Amherst, NY: Prometheus Press.

Husband, William B. 2000. *Godless Communists: Atheism and Society in Soviet Russia 1917-1932.* DeKalb, Illinois: Northern Illinois University Press.

Jacoby, Susan. 2004. *Freethinkers: A History of American Secularism*. New York: Metropolitan Books.

Kirkley, Evelyn A. 2000. *Rational Mothers and Infidel Gentlemen: Gender and American Atheism, 1865-1915*. Syracruse, NY: Syracruse University Press.

Lee, Lois. 2012. Locating Nonreligion, in Mind, Body and Space: New Research Methods for a New Field. *Annual Review of the Sociology of Religion: Volume 3: New Methods in Sociology of Religion*, edited by Luigi Berzano and Ole Preben Riis. Leiden: BRILL.

Lewis, David C. 2000. *After Atheism: Religion and Ethnicity in Russia and Central Asia*. New York: St Martin's Press.

Luehrmann, S. 2011. *Secularism Soviet Style: Teaching Atheism and Religion in a Volga Republic*. Indiana: Indiana University Press.

MacKillop, I.D. 2012 [1986]. *The British Ethical Societies*. Cambridge: Cambridge University Press.

Pasquale, Frank L. 2010. A Portrait of Secular Group Affiliates. In *Atheism and Secularity: Volume 1: Issues, Concepts and Definitions*, edited by Phil Zuckerman. Santa Barbara, CA: Praeger: 43-88.

Quack, Johannes. 2012. Organised Atheism in India: An Overview. *Journal of Contemporary Religion* 27 (1): 67-85.

Quack, Johannes. 2011. *Disenchanting India: Organized Rationalism and Criticism of Religion in India*. New York, Oxford University Press.

Royle, Edward. 1974. *Victorian infidels: the origins of the British secularist movement, 1791-1866.* Manchester: Manchester University Press.

Seaman, Ann Rowe. 2005. *America's Most Hated Woman: The Life and Gruesome Death of Madelyn Murray O'Hair*. New York: Continuum.

Schmidt, Leigh Eric 2011. A Society of damned Souls: Atheism and Irreligion in the 1920s. *Perspectives in Religious Studies* 38 (2): 215-226.

Shakman Hurd, Elizabeth. 2008. *The Politics of Secularism in International Relations.* Princeton, NJ: Princeton University Press.

Smith, Jesse M. 2011. Becoming an Atheist in America: Constructing Identity and Meaning from the Rejection of Theism. *Sociology of Religion* 72 (2): 215-237.

Stenger, Victor. 2009. *The New Atheism: Taking a Stand for Science and Reason*. New York: Prometheus.

Voas, David and Siobhan McAndrew. 2012 [Jan]. Three Puzzles of Non-religion in Britain. *Journal of Contemporary Religion*. 27 (1).

Zrinšak, Siniša. 2004. Generations and Atheism: Patterns of Response to Communist Rule among Different Generations and Countries. *Social Compass* 51 (2): 221-234.

4 Irreligion and Society

Many of the ideas and analyses presented in this section of *TSI* have not been extensively pursued since. This is probably by virtue of a focus on the secular (the absence of religion) as opposed to irreligion (a concrete socio-cultural phenomenon) in the social scientific work (discussed in the Introduction in this volume, and in Lee, 2013). Many of these issues (causes of irreligion, social, moral and political aspects of irreligious activity, etc.) are, however, raised in the treatments of organised irreligion discussed above. They are also sometimes dealt with in quantitative studies, but these often present basic correlations only, and correlations which are hindered by an issue which Campbell (2013 [1971]) and subsequent sociologists have raised concerning the treatment of the irreligious as an undifferentiated group in survey methodologies. In addition, Campbell shows irregularities in these correlations and insufficiencies in the data that have not been responded to; this is one of several cases in which there is no 'further to' *TSI*.

One sociological question concerning irreligion that has advanced further to *TSI* has been the discussion of the relationship between irreligious and religious groups. More subtle studies of anti-religious viewpoints (e.g. Kane, 2010; Lee, 2011) have been supplemented by work on anti-*irreligious* viewpoints: Edgell et al., 2006; Harper, 2007; Goodman and Muellar, 2009; Gervais et al., 2010; Cragun et al., 2012. Bullivant (2009) has considered how the Catholic Church has engaged with atheism,

L

demonstrating another way in which scholarship of religion and irreligion might be conducted in combination.

Campbell's discussion of irreligion and class identity and action has not yet been sufficiently addressed in the new sociology of irreligion. Some intersections between irreligion and other social categories are beginning to emerge: Cavalcanti and Schleef (2005) discuss the role of nonreligion in immigrant processes of cultural integration; work in progress is analysing the intersections between race and irreligion taking up issues developed in an early an isolated contribution by Welch (1978)dealing with blackness and non-affiliation.

Campbell's discussion of 'the springs of irreligion' emphasises variety – that there are as many causes of irreligiosity as for religion itself. Against this, treatments of disaffiliation processes present a limited view, and are focussed on the 'abandoning of religion', to use Altemeyer and Hunsberger's phrase (1997) rather than the taking up of irreligion, as Campbell focuses on. Examples of this literature include articles by Sandomirsky and Wilson (1990); Sherkat and Wilson (1995); Shariff et al. (2008); Schwadel (2010); Merino (2012); and book-length works by Altemeyer and Hunsberger (1997) and Zuckerman (2011). In addition, studies of organised irreligion mentioned above often include some discussion of how and why individuals chose to participate in such associations, groups and movements. Campbell's argument that changes in morality give rise to irreligion (2013 [1971]: 106) is something taken up in Callum Brown's approach to secularisation (2009) and will presumably be explored in his ongoing research, with David Nash, into contemporary irreligion.

Altemeyer, Bob, and Bruce Hunsberger. 1997. Amazing Conversions: Why Some Turn to Faith and Others Abandon Religion. New York: Prometheus.
Bullivant, Stephen. 2009. From "Main Tendue" to Vatican II: the Catholic Engagement with Atheism, 1936-65. New Blackfriars, 90 (1026): 178-87.
Brown, Callum. 2009. The Death of Christian Britain: Understanding Secularisation 1800-2000, 2nd edition. London: Routledge.

Cavalcanti, H.B., and D. Schleef. 2005. The Case for Secular Assimilation? The Latino Experience in Richmond, Virginia. Journal for the Scientific Study of Religion 44 (4): 473-483.

Cragun, Ryan, Barry Kosmin, Ariela Keysar, Joseph H. Hammer and Michael Nielsen. 2012. On the Receiving End: Discrimination Toward the Non-religious. Journal of Contemporary Religion, 27 (1): 105-127.

Edgell, Penny, Joseph Gerteis and Douglas Hartmann. 2006. Atheists as Other: Moral Boundaries and Cultural Membership in American Society. American Sociological Review 71 (2): 211-234.

Gervais, W.M., Azim F. Shariff, and Ara Norenzayan. 2011. Do You Believe in Atheists? Distrust Is Central to Anti-Atheist Prejudice. Journal of Personality and Social. Journal of Personality and Social Psychology 101 (6): 1189-1206.

Goodman, Kathleen M., and John A. Mueller. 2009. Invisible, Marginalized, and Stigmatized: Understanding and Addressing the Needs of Atheist Students. New Directions for Student Services 125: 55-63.

Harper, Marcel. 2007. The Stereotyping of Nonreligious People by Religious Students: Contents and Subtypes. Journal for the Scientific Study of Religion 46 (4): 539-552.

Kane, Michael N. 2010. Research Note: Perceptions about the Ridicule of Religious and Spiritual Beliefs. Journal of Contemporary Religion 25 (3): 453-462.

Lee, Lois. 2012. Being Secular: Towards Separate Sociologies of Secularity, Nonreligion and Epistemological Culture. Unpublished PhD thesis, University of Cambridge, 2012.

Lee, Lois. 2011. From Neutrality to Dialogue: Constructing the Religious Other in British Non-religious Discourses. In Modernities Revisited, edited by Maren Behrensen, Lois Lee and Ahmet S. Tekelioglu. Vienna: IWM Junior Visiting Fellows' Conferences 2011., 29. Available at www.iwm.at. [Accessed 23 Jun. 2011]

Merino, Stephen M. 2012. Irreligious Socialization? The Adult Religious Preferences of Individuals Raised with No Religion. Secularism and Non-religion 1: 1-16.

Sandomirsky, S., and J. Wilson. 1990. Processes of Disaffiliation: Religious Mobility among Men and Women. Social Forces 68: 1211-1229.

Schwadel, P. 2010. Period and Cohort Effects on Religious Nonaffiliation and Religious Disaffiliation: A Research Note. Journal for the Scientific Study of Religion 49 (2): 311-319.

Shariff, Azim F.A., Adam B. Cohen, and Ara Anorenzayan. 2008. The Devil's Advocate: Secular Arguments Diminish both Implicit and Explicit Religious Belief. Journal of Cognition and Culture 8 (3-4): 417-423.

Sherkat, Darren E., and J. Wilson. 1995. Preferences, Constraints, and Choices in Religious Markets: An Examination of Religious Switching and Apostasy. Social Forces 73 (3): 993-1026.

Welch, Michael R. 1978b. The Unchurched: Black Religious Non-Affiliates. Journal for the Scientific Study of Religion, 17 (3): 289-293.

Zuckerman, Phil. 2011. Faith No More: Why People Reject Religion. New York: Oxford University Press.

5 Functionalist Explanations and the Longevity of Irreligion

TSI concludes with a discussion of irreligion *vis-a-vis* functionalist accounts of religion. Functionalism has since fallen by the wayside in the sociology of religion, and in sociology in general, but Campbell's treatment of potential functions of irreligion is more generally useful as an almost anthropological study of its role in human life. Thus, Campbell's concluding discussion pre-empts two branches in the contemporary social science of irreligion: that dealing with (i) irreligion, health and wellbeing and (ii) cognitive anthropological approaches to irreligion. As mentioned, the marginal status of irreligion in the US means that this nation has produced the most work dealing with irreligiosity as a healthy (and/or not necessarily unhealthy) condition; see, e.g., Hwang, 2008a, 2008b; Zuckerman, 2008, 2009; and Hwang et al., 2011.

In many ways, cognitive approaches to religion, both psychological and anthropological, are the heir to past functionalism: they look for traits that are universal to the human population and understand those traits in terms of their utility or their relationship to some functional process like evolution. As Campbell observes of contemporaneous functionalists, so today's cognitivists have been emphatic about the prevalence of religion across societies and cultures, whilst few have been willing to admit that irreligion exists in *any* (2013 [1971]: 9). What is more, explanations of religion are sometimes so impressive that irreligion and ignorance of religion come to seem like pathological cases. This situation is beginning to be redressed, however, and Saler and Ziegler (2007) have made an important contribution, developing arguments from William Sims Bainbridge (2005) (who has also provided a function-focused account of nonreligion (2007)) and Justin Barratt (2004); see also Caldwell (2009), Geertz and Markússon (2010), Hunter (2010) and Lanman (2012).

Bainbridge, William Sims. 2007. *Across the Secular Abyss: From Faith to Wisdom*. Lanham, MD: Lexington Books.

Bainbridge, William S. 2005. Atheism. *Interdisciplinary Journal of Research on Religion*, 1 (1): 1-24.

Barratt, Justin L. 2004. *Why Would Anyone Believe in God?* Walnut Creek, CA: Altamira Press.

Caldwell, C.L. 2009. The Puzzle of Nonbelief. In How Differently We Work! *Case Studies at the Overlap of Religion and Psychology*, ed. Nathaniel F. Barrett and Robert Cummings Neville.

Geertz, Armin W. and Guðmundur Ingi. 2010. Religion is Natural, Atheism is Not: On Why Everybody is Both Right and Wrong. *Religion* 40: 152-165.

Hunter, Laura A. 2010. Explaining Atheism: Testing the Secondary Compensator Model and Proposing an Alternative. *Interdisciplinary Journal of Research on Religion* 6.

Hwang, Karen. 2008a. Atheists with Disabilities: A Neglected Minority in Religion and Rehabilitation Research. *Journal of Religion, Disability & Health* 12 (2): 7-24.

Hwang, Karen. 2008b. Experiences of Atheists with Spinal Cord Injury: Results of an Internet-Based Exploratory Survey. *SCI Psychosocial Process* 20: 4-17.

Hwang, K., J.H. Hammer, and R. Cragun. 2011. Extending the Religion-Health Research to Secular Minorities: Issues and Concerns. Journal *of Religion and Health* 50 (3): 608-22.

Lanman, Jonathan A. 2012. The Importance of Religious Displays for Belief Acquisition and Secularization. *Journal of Contemporary Religion*, (27)1: 49-65.

Saler, Benson, and Charles A. Ziegler. 2007. Atheism and the Apotheosis of Agency. *Temenos* 42 (2): 7-41.

Zuckerman, Phil. 2009. Atheism, Secularity, and Well-Being: How the Findings of Social Science Counter Negative Stereotypes and Assumptions. *Sociology Compass* (3): 949-971.

Zuckerman, Phil. 2008. *Society without God: What the Least Religious Nations Can Tell Us about Contentment*. New York: New York University Press.

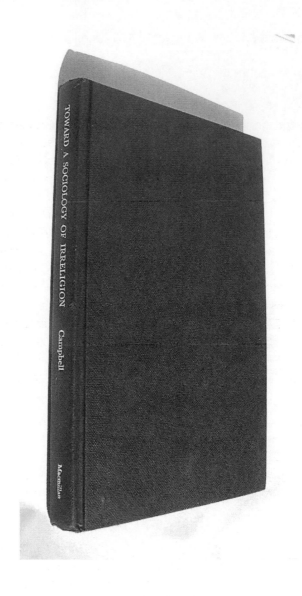

Cover of 1971 edition

Introduction

No tradition for the sociological study of irreligion as yet exists and this book has been written in the hope that it will help to stimulate the development of just such a tradition. Lacking a foundation on which to build, however, meant that writing such a book presented a very real problem. How was the subject-matter to be approached? Which of the many respected perspectives and intellectual currents within contemporary sociology would be appropriate to an examination of irreligion? As it transpired, these questions were academic in both senses of that word, for the mode of treatment has been largely dictated by the nature of the information available. Some of the topics which it was originally intended to include have had to be omitted for lack of adequate data, whilst others have been discussed in a restricted fashion for the same reason. In the event, the ensuing discussion relies upon historical material much more than was originally anticipated, although in no sense has it been the intention to substitute a historical for a sociological treatment of the phenomenon of irreligion.

The book is divided by chapters into five main parts, each of which attempts to make a different contribution to the development of a sociology of irreligion. In Chapter 1 there is a brief outline of the setting against which the emergent study of irreligion exists, both with respect to the historical background of the rise of irreligion in contemporary Western society and the intellectual background of the neglect of this phenomenon by sociology. Then, in Chapter 2, there follows an analytic exploration of the nature and varieties of irreligion. The emphasis here is on morphology, with special attention given to the difficulties surrounding the delineation of the boundaries of irreligion. Chapter 3 constitutes a marked change of perspective in order to introduce the concrete phenomenon of irreligion through a brief account of the major irreligious social movements of the nineteenth and twentieth centuries. This is followed in Chapter 4 by an attempt to explore some of the major points of articulation between irreligion and other spheres of social life. This is approached directly in the case of morality and politics and then indirectly in the consequent discussion of the sources and functions of irreligion. Finally, Chapter 5 investigates some of the implications which the sociological study of irreligion has for the functionalist tradition within the sociology of religion.

The aim of this book is to explore the possibilities for the development of the sociological study of irreligion. This, it was felt, could be best achieved by allowing the discussion of the material to generate its own perspectives, rather than by employing particular developed sociological viewpoints. It seems, in retrospect, that this has enabled the subsequent exploration to make critical observations on the sociology of religion and that, in general, the spirit which animates the following discussion is, in keeping with the subject-matter itself, that of the sociological sceptic and iconoclast.

1 Prologue: Toward a Sociology of Irreligion

It would be wrong to suppose that irreligion is a creation of the twentieth century. Although we are accustomed to hearing the age we live in described as the 'secular age' or the 'age of doubt', previous periods of history could justifiably be similarly labelled. To the Christians of the time, the last years of the Roman Empire must have seemed a time in which scepticism and heresy flourished, just as to the orthodox Christian of the eighteenth century the rise of Deism and the French Revolution indicated that he was living in an 'age of infidelity'. Even the Middle Ages, frequently treated as the epitome or an era of faith, was seen by medieval writers as a time of spiritual crisis, in which witchcraft, heresy and paganism were constant threats to the faith. The principal reason why our perspective of history is such that we view our own time as characteristically irreligious and contrast it with what we believe to be the prevailing faith of all previous epochs is because we live in the shade of the late nineteenth century. And it is the religious activity of that period which we tend to use as the yardstick by which to measure our own lack of faith. But as Mayor has observed of England, the mid-Victorian era was a time of religious boom:

> . . . never in the memory of anyone living had so large a proportion of the population been in church and the religious leaders exercised so large an influence in the national life. If active participation in church life, and a sincere and earnest attempt to live by the teachings of the Church day by day, are marks of religious vitality, there has rarely in the modern world been a country so religious as late nineteenth-century England. The flourishing Protestantism of that age has so impressed its mark on English history, and even on the obscure but perfectly real corporate memory of the people, that the crowded churches and silent Sabbaths of three generations ago still seem to a great number of English men and women the normal, and the present social code either a temporary aberration or a welcome revolution, according to taste.[1]

Bearing this in mind, we ought to be more cautious before we finally declare our own age to be typified by a lack of religious faith, and we might focus instead on the question of whether the later part of the nineteenth century should be described as a period of an excess of faith. Viewed in this way, it could be that our own age is closer to the norm, assuming that any norm for the level of religious faith in society can ever be established, than was that of our grandfathers.[2]

However, even if irreligion is not itself a creation of the twentieth century and the widespread feeling that it is, is largely to be attributed to a form of historical visual illusion, it is the case that irreligion does occupy a somewhat unique position in contemporary society. For it is only in recent history that irreligion has appeared as a phenomenon among the masses as opposed to the elite. Also appearing for the first time in the last century have been specifically irreligious social movements. As a direct result of these changes irreligion now occupies an established position in society of comparative respectability. It is this, and not the emergence of irreligion itself, which is characteristic of the twentieth century. Traditionally, the holding of heretical, including irreligious, views has been a prerogative of the societal elites. A form of upper-class intellectual delinquency, it was usually tolerated because it constituted no real challenge to the established belief system or threat to the power structure of society. The one clear condition on which toleration was extended, however, was that the irreligious did not engage in active proselytising, especially of the lower classes. Typical of this outlook is the remark attributed to Frederick the Great that religion was necessary 'as a discipline for the masses' but that scepticism should be reserved for 'the elite only'.

Today this state of affairs no longer holds and irreligious views can be encountered at any level of society. Indeed for a period in the middle and late nineteenth century irreligion was as widespread among the working classes in Britain as any other section of society. That this change represented a fundamental dividing line between contemporary and traditional societies was recognised by those who lived through it. Thus J. M. Robertson wrote at the turn of the century:

If any one circumstance more than another differentiates the life of today from that of older civilizations, or from that of previous centuries of the modern era, it is the diffusion of rationalistic views among the 'common people'. In no other era is to be found the phenomenon of widespread critical scepticism among the labouring masses : in all previous ages, though chronic complaint is made of some unbelief among the uneducated, the constant and abject ignorance of the mass of the people has been the sure foothold of superstitious systems.[3]

Many factors were associated with this change, which can roughly be taken as dating from the French Revolution. The story of how this change came about in Britain and America will be considered in Chapter 3. The fact remains that contemporary Western society, as illustrated by the experience of Britain and America, is to be distinguished from traditional pre-industrial Western societies not so much by the extent of irreligion but by the general distribution of expressions of irreligion throughout all social strata. This is not, of course, to say that all social classes are equally irreligious or that they express their irreligion in the same form, but only to comment on the democratisation of the irreligious outlook.

Parallel with this move away from the elitist basis of irreligious expression has been a development of specifically irreligious social movements. In pre-industrial Western society, radical movements of protest, whether primarily racial, political, economic, social or ideological, traditionally found expression in some variety of Christian sectarianism. However, by the end of the eighteenth century it was no longer the case that movements of dissent would automatically take this form. Whilst retaining the organisation and outlook of the sect, movements of protest increasingly came to include non-Christian and irreligious elements in their ideology.[4] Almost all the full range of irreligious attitudes appear as adjuncts to the main ideological stance of the political and religious philosophies which originated at this time, but of primary concern in this context is the emergence of social movements in which the associated ideology is essentially irreligious. Just as it is possible to distinguish before the period of industrialisation between radical movements which, although religious in form, were basically movements of economic or political protest, and radical movements, which were essentially religious

3

movements, so it is possible to distinguish in the modern era between social movements which, although irreligious in tone, are essentially protests against the economic or political *status quo,* and social movements which are fundamentally protesting against religion *per se.* The 'political religions' of Communism, Fascism and Nationalism are clearly examples of the former phenomenon which, although irreligious in character (at least in the traditional sense), are not primarily irreligious movements. On the other hand, the free-thought and secular movements of the nineteenth century and the ethical and humanist movements of the twentieth are primarily defined by their attitudes of antagonism or criticism toward established religion. The emergence of specifically anti-religious social movements thus marked a significant change in the religious life and climate of Western societies and was, of course, the means by which the democratisation of irreligion was accomplished.

The direct consequence of the formation of movements such as these was that irreligion, long a cultural force, was for the first time a social and political force as well. These movements were much more than mere propaganda agencies for irreligious outlooks. They represented the interests of the irreligious and generally fought for full democratic rights to be extended to them, both as individuals and as social organisations. And although these organisations generally were very active in a wide range of social and political reforms, and in doing so collaborated with other radical bodies, this was a struggle necessarily very much their own, and one in which they could not rely on outside support. Fundamentally the irreligious in the nineteenth century (and to some extent in the twentieth) were fighting the same battle for social acceptance and equality before the law which the Dissenters had fought and won before them. To date, the irreligious have not been as successful as the Dissenters, but they have significantly altered the status of irreligion in modern society and they are still altering it. To be irreligious in the mid-nineteenth century was to risk not only social ostracism, petty persecution and accusations of immorality but criminal proceedings as well. Blasphemy was a crime in England which brought forth sentences of up to a year's imprisonment on secularists found guilty of the offence. In courts of law and in standing for public office, secularists were refused the rights extended to everyone else. The situation was little better in America during the same period. However, the

4

irreligious reacted to persecution and imprisonment much as did their religious predecessors, and with the same result. There was no shortage of volunteers for martyrdom in the cause of irreligion, and continued persecution only stiffened the will to resist and helped rally support. As a result, the irreligious were eventually successful and the legal disadvantages under which they long suffered have now almost disappeared. Successfully campaigning for changes in the law is of course a very different matter from effecting a change in traditional and social attitudes, and it remains true that the irreligious may still find themselves indicted before the bar of public opinion. Nevertheless, the existence of irreligious social movements has effectively changed the legal and constitutional basis of British and American society in such a way that irreligion can now be said to 'exist' as an element in the pluralist structure of these societies - something that was not true a century ago.

All this suggests that the role which irreligion occupies in contemporary societies is a distinctive feature of those societies. As far as the evidence allows one to judge, irreligion (if it existed at all) performed no such role in pre-literate societies, the early civilisations or feudal society. This is not to say that modern societies are basically irreligious; rather the reverse, they are still in general more religious than irreligious, and in this way they exhibit continuity with traditional societies. But in the existence of irreligion, both organised and unorganised, manifesting itself to some extent in all social strata and having a degree of social and legal recognition, modern societies appear to be unique.

Irreligion and Secularisation

A consideration of the place of irreligion in contemporary society necessarily involves some discussion of the secularisation debate. The irreligious and the secular are frequently associated, and are even sometimes used as if they were rough synonyms for one another. It is therefore worth quoting Becker's statement about the relationship between the two concepts: 'The secular is not synonymous with the profane, infidel, godless, irreligious, heretical, unhallowed, faithless, or any similar term. It subsumes them, but... includes a great deal more.'[5]

Thus, although a discussion of the rise of irreligion as a social phenomenon is relevant to a consideration of the secularisation debate, it is far from being directly equatable with such issues. In fact the relationship between the irreligious and the secular is less clear-cut than Becker's quote would lead us to believe. For, although in general the secular is a broader term than the irreligious, considerable ambiguity exists over the correct meaning to be attached to the terms 'secular' and 'secularisation'. Shiner remarks on the 'dominant' connotations of 'indifference, anti-clericalism and irreligion' which still cling to these words and which therefore tend to mitigate against their use in the context of religious neutralism.

Secularisation itself is a peculiarly ambiguous concept, and this makes the task of relating irreligion to the various hypotheses particularly formidable. Shiner has distinguished five main usages of secularisation in sociological and theological thought.[6] The first usage is where it is conceived as the decline of religion, the second is where it is conceived as conformity with the world, the third is where it is conceived as the desacralisation of the world, the fourth is where it is conceived as the disengagement of society from religion and the fifth where secularisation is conceived as the transposition of beliefs and patterns of behaviour from the religious to the secular sphere. None of these five ideal types employs assumptions about the changing status of irreligion, and although the rise of irreligion would not, on the face of it, be inconsistent with any one of them, it is not necessarily the case that secularisation and irreligion should go together. The 'decline of religion' hypothesis, for example, may or may not be associated with a rise of irreligion. On the other hand there are good grounds for assuming that the rise of irreligion will be associated with secularisation, at least in some of the forms outlined by Shiner. This is because the political aim of most irreligious movements has been the realisation of a secular society. Free thought, secular, ethical, rationalist and humanist organisations have all worked in different ways and different contexts to achieve the complete separation of Church and State, the abolition of privileges granted to religious bodies, the repeal of religiously-based legislation, and a completely secular system of education, as components in a complete programme for secularisation. Even today, the 'secularisation of society in fullest measure' remains the political aim of the humanist movement.[7]

The fact that irreligious movements act as agents of secularisation has strangely enough been overlooked by sociologists in their contribution to the continuing secularisation debate. Yet they play a significant role in this respect, especially in bringing about formal and legal modifications of the basis of society. In the cultural context as well they act as propagators of a rational-scientific world-view and thus contribute to the decline of the traditional supernatural perspectives. Alternatively, irreligion in its organised or unorganised form can be taken as evidence of secularisation and the growth of irreligious movements treated as data indicating the decline of religion in much the same way that statistics for religious membership and attendance at worship have been used. However, one has to search hard to find examples of sociologists referring to material about irreligion in this context.

Fundamentally sociologists have been principally concerned with debating the verdict that is to be returned on the positivist prophecies about the 'end of religion'. The majority of nineteenth-century intellectuals were greatly influenced by Positivism and were prone to argue that as religion is based on ignorance and superstition it will eventually die away. The founding fathers of sociology reflected this view in their own writings. Naturally enough a good deal of sociological discourse has examined the evidence for pronouncing this prophecy true or false. Parsons and Lenski are two sociologists among many (mainly American) who have unequivocally judged it to be false.[8] Sorokin is a representative of those who have expressed the view that the prophecy has been realised.[9] It seems very likely that the debate will continue for a good while yet. However, one consequence of the predominance of this debate within the sub-discipline of the sociology of religion is that the focus of attention on the future of religion tends to obscure the question of the future of irreligion. It may be true that the participants in this debate believe that the one issue contains the other within it and that a clear determination of the 'fate' of religion would also imply knowledge of the fate of irreligion. This view, however, is not entirely tenable, for religion may well continue to exist as a cultural and social phenomenon despite a rise in organised and unorganised irreligion, or indeed because of such a rise. In any event irreligion as a social and cultural phenomenon is worthy of serious investigation, independent of any light which such investigations may shed on the future of religion or the secularisation thesis.

7

Sociology and Irreligion

The blunt fact is that until very recently sociologists have entirely ignored irreligion. This in itself requires some explanation, since as we have seen irreligion is not merely an obvious feature of contemporary industrial societies, but in some ways a distinctive feature of such societies. How is it that sociologists have failed even to consider irreligion as a subject for investigation? This can hardly be because they have failed to recognise its existence, for even in an overtly religious society like contemporary America, sociologists as members of the intellectual elite occupy that 'one structural situation . . . where irreligiousness is common'.[10] Indeed one suspects that irreligiousness is far from uncommon among sociologists themselves. It may be, of course, that this very fact makes the phenomenon too close to home to be noticed or alternatively to be studied in comfort. If this interpretation were true, it might explain the marked preference which some sociologists show for studying religious beliefs and practices which are a very long cry from their own. However, this seems an unconvincing explanation and one looks instead at the basic premises which have long guided research in the sociology of religion.

Sociology was founded as an intellectual discipline at a time when Positivism was a major influence in intellectual life, and although not all sociologists could be said to have been equally under its spell, it did to some extent dictate the nature of the problems which sociology was to consider. Foremost among these was 'the problem of religion'. From the standpoint of Positivism, religion was a problem in the sense that its beliefs and practices were not rational and scientific and thus their very existence required some explanation. The nature of the explanations offered by these early sociologists constituted the beginning of the sociology of religion. In almost every case, however, the positivistic ethos of the age caused them to present religion and not irreligion as the problematical phenomenon. The central problems were : why is religion apparently a universal feature of human life? what functions does it fulfil for the individual and society and what is its origin or cause ? By contrast, it appears that irreligion was assumed to be self-explanatory; as the natural state of mature civilised men (and of not a few early sociologists) it hardly required any discussion, let alone explanation. Paradoxically, therefore, it may be because sociology has its origins in an irreligious epoch that irreligion itself has not become a subject for study in sociology.

Support for this view can be found in the odd fact that irreligion is just as neglected as an object of sociological inquiry in the formally irreligious societies of the Communist bloc as it is in the religious societies of Europe and North America. Marxist sociology no less than the various forms of non-Marxist sociology prevalent in the West takes its starting-point from the same positivist assumption that religion (not irreligion) is the problematical phenomenon. Indeed it is only by going outside of the discipline of sociology altogether, to an intellectual tradition which long preceded it, that one can find irreligion presented as a problem requiring explanation. This cultural tradition is the one associated with the Roman Catholic faith, and it is in those countries where Catholicism has imposed its demands on sociology that the signs of sociological interest in irreligion have begun to emerge.

There is another reason why irreligion has been overlooked, at least in the West. This is the pre-eminent role which functionalism has occupied in the study of religion. The perspective which functionalism brings to the investigation of religion is one which focuses the eye of the sociologist on the positive consequences which religious belief and ritual have for the maintenance of society. In so doing, a form of theoretical induced blindness is prone to afflict the sociologist, so that not only does he not see the negative consequences but neither does he see any 'negative religion'. So fundamental to this perspective is the assumption that religion is a universal feature of societies and is in the main beneficial in its effects, that one looks in vain for any consideration of the functions of irreligion. Compared with the alacrity with which sociologists of a functional persuasion point to the fact that religion exists in all societies, there exists a remarkable reluctance to mention the fact that irreligion exists in any society. As for the question of whether irreligion might exist in all societies, this remains unasked to this day.

Although the total neglect of irreligion must be accounted for primarily in terms of the prevailing assumptions guiding research in the sociology of religion, there are other contributing factors. One of these is the tendency to view irreligion as a phenomenon that is confined to the nineteenth

9

century, and to view whatever manifestations occur in the twentieth as 'survivals'. Such an attitude clearly leads to irreligion being defined as a subject more suitable to historical than sociological investigation. Unfortunately, historians have also tended to neglect irreligion, although not to the same extent. The comparative paucity of historical material must, however, be included as another factor which has inhibited the development of a sociology of irreligion. Another factor of major importance in preventing sociologists from studying contemporary irreligion is the lack of sufficient data. The sociology of religion has grown up on a diet of social surveys, opinion polls and local and community studies. Many of these sources provide some material on irreligion, usually through the use of residual categories such as 'no religion' or 'atheist or agnostic', but in the vast majority of cases the information is of little use. In the first case, the population chosen is either that of a geographical area or one which possesses some distinguishing religious characteristic (such as membership of a religious body). In few instances is an attempt made to ensure that a representative number of irreligious people are included. The results presented for the irreligious are thus usually based on insufficient sample size. In addition, since it is the religious and not the irreligious who are the focus of study, little care is taken in the construction of the irreligious categories. It is therefore hard to escape the conclusion that even the small amount of information on irreligion which studies of this sort have produced is really of little value. This deficiency is clearly a severe handicap when it comes to the formulation of hypotheses about the irreligious.

The lack of material from surveys and community studies need not have been disastrous for an incipient sociology of irreligion, because material on the irreligious could easily have been obtained by studying the various irreligious social movements with their accompanying social organisations. However, this has not been done and is only now getting under way, and thus the lack of material on irreligion has been an almost total one. There seems to be little doubt that one of the main reasons why irreligious organisations have not been the objects of study before now is the widespread belief that the irreligious are typically social isolates and are not to be found in organisations.[11] In as much as this erroneous assumption is itself associated with the functionalist view of the integrative role of religion, it represents another example of how the functionalist perspective on religion has inhibited the study of irreligion. It could be argued that irreligious organisations have not been studied because in general their membership is very small, especially in comparison with the main religious denominations, but as there has long been a tradition of studying small religious sects and cults, it is clear that size alone can hardly have been a deterrent. Indeed, it is much more likely that irreligious organisations have been neglected for the very reason that the study of religious sects has flourished. This is that a distinct and coherent theoretical framework for the study of sects has existed in sociology since the early work of Troelsch and Weber. By contrast the potential student of irreligious organisations is in the position of having no obvious theoretical tradition present itself and is in addition faced with the difficult decision of whether or not to treat the object of study as if it were a religious sect or denomination.

There are now signs that this period of total neglect is coming to an end. An awakening of interest in irreligion is discernible among sociologists on both sides of the Atlantic, and for the first time the subject has received explicit recognition as a relevant topic to be discussed at conferences of the sociology of religion.[12] As yet, research on the subject is negligible and a body of literature hardly exists, but the portents are there. Why, after such a long period of neglect, should this change be occurring now? Although it may well be too early to be certain of the causes of this emerging interest, it is possible to point to two sets of factors which appear to be jointly responsible. One of these is internal to the sociology of religion, the other external and concerns reorientation on the part of religious organisations themselves. This latter, external factor has been the most obvious precipitator of the recent activity to stimulate sociological inquiry into irreligion.

Catholic pastoral sociology, especially in France, has long exhibited a concern with the 'lapsed' Catholic, and to a lesser extent with the phenomenon of anti-Catholic irreligion. This tradition within continental sociology has recently received a marked stimulus from the establishment of the Vatican Secretariat for Non-Believers in the spring of 1965. The background to that decision within the Catholic Church was a growing concern with atheism and the development of the view that 'there is no more important or topical problem for the Church today than [the] intellectual and pastoral encounter with atheism'.[13] It is, of course, not the first time that the Roman Catholic Church has shown a marked concern over atheism, but this time there is a difference. Instead of responding to atheism directly through propaganda and with missionary and proselytising zeal, the concern expressed now is a concern to understand. One of the main functions of the Secretariat is to 'investigate the grounds and causes of modern atheism'. Cardinal König quotes Pope Paul: 'Our pastoral solicitude prompts us to probe into the mind of the modern atheist, in an effort to understand the reasons for his mental turmoil and his denial of God.'[14] This necessitates on the one hand the establishment of dialogues with non-believers and on the other enlisting the help of sociologists and psychologists in order to map the phenomenon of irreligion. This development has thus led to a direct stimulus to the sociological investigation of at least the 'atheistic' variety of irreligion.

This, however, has occurred at a time when there are signs that sociology itself is beginning to find an interest in irreligious phenomena. This is most obvious within the sociology of religion, where there have been signs of a growing realisation that the boundaries of the discipline need to be redrawn. At the same time that increasing doubt is being thrown on traditional methods of distinguishing religious and non-religious phenomena, so the traditional restrictions on what constitutes a 'religion' are becoming blurred. In addition, distinctions within 'the non-religious' are being commented on for the first time. All this is suggestive of a major state of flux and it seems clear that when the boundary lines emerge again, a clear place will be allotted to irreligion. Outside of the sociology of religion as such, interest has also been shown in irreligious organisations and movements for the light which they can shed on hypotheses in the sociology of social movements.[15]

One of the more interesting developments discernible in this state of flux is the growing tendency to see the study of irreligion as part and parcel of the study of religion. Increasingly one comes across the argument that the study of religion implies the study of irreligion, and that the nature of religious activities and beliefs cannot be understood except in terms of the social context of nonreligion.[16] There is no doubt considerable force to this argument and it may well be that the development of a combined sociology of religion and irreligion could prove very beneficial. It could also be, however, that as most of the investigators who give this argument are already working within the field of religion, this is the rationalisation they require in order to investigate this phenomenon at all. In any case, there seems no *a priori* reason why the study of irreligion should not benefit other areas of sociological inquiry in much the way that the study of religion has. Unless this latter possibility receives greater emphasis, there does seem to be real danger that the new-born sociology of irreligion will be treated as if it were merely the sociology of religion 'stood on its head'. The need to treat irreligion as 'an independently valid scholarly focus' must not be lost sight of.[17]

Sociology of Irreligion as a Devil's Advocate

This last point draws our attention to the fundamental question of why irreligion should be regarded as an important subject for sociological inquiry. Why should it be cause for concern that a sociology of irreligion does not exist? What justification is there for suggesting that sociologists should pay more attention to this phenomenon than to some other which has suffered from partial or total neglect? It must be said at once that basically no justification need be offered for the serious study of anything; the academic impulse 'blows where it listeth', and irreligion is no exception. However, if no justification is required for one's own interest in a subject, some explanation is certainly required if one hopes to convince one's colleagues that they should show some interest in it. Since this has been implied in the argument so far, some reasons must be advanced to show that the continued neglect of irreligion would be unwise. Two of these have already been given: these are that the study of irreligion will greatly benefit the study of religion, and that the special social and cultural characteristics of irreligious organisations means that they constitute particularly suitable objects of study for the sociology of social movements. Of these two, the former is clearly the more important.

The study of irreligious phenomena appears to offer a unique and untried vantage-point from which to gain a fresh grip on the slippery tangle of assumptions, hypotheses and predictions which constitute the sociology of religion. Tenets which are traditional in the discipline and which date

13

back to the work of Durkheim, Weber and Marx have proved to be notably unyielding in the face of efforts to operationalise and verify them. Functionalist assumptions remain vague, ambiguous and disputed, whilst Marxist prophecies remain unfulfilled; even definitions of religion are no more satisfactory now than they were at the turn of the century. Although the total picture is by no means as bleak as this, the frustrated sociologist of religion can be excused if he turns to irreligion primarily with the hope of gaining new insights into old problems. The temptation is obvious enough, although it is not quite so obvious that the eventual rewards will make the effort worthwhile. The immediate attraction must be that of testing the inverse of traditional hypotheses in the sociology of religion. For example, as religion is traditionally linked to societal integration and attachment to society's goals, is it also the case that irreligion is associated with disintegrative tendencies and experiences of anomie? Does irreligion weaken social control in the way that religion is identified as strengthening it? Does the irreligious individual suffer additional unresolved frustrations and uncertainties, a weakened morale and sense of identity, compared with his religious counterparts? Clearly the list of hypotheses here is as long as the hypotheses current in the sociology of religion. Few of them have ever been examined and it seems likely that a consideration of some of them would prove profitable in terms of the light thrown on corollary hypotheses. There are, however, serious problems with this procedure. One is the difficulty raised by the question of functional alternatives. The task of identifying functional alternatives and specifying their scope makes the job of studying religion through the examination of irreligion much more difficult than it might appear at first sight. Associated with this is the question of how far it is reasonable to assume that the social forces which govern the appearance and form of irreligion are in fact the obverse of those which control religion. Whilst it may be true in some instances, it may also be the case that religious and irreligious responses are the products of the same social forces. Thus, although it is tempting to establish a sociology of irreligion by stating, as initial hypotheses, the obverse of well-tried theories about religious phenomena, it is a procedure which should be approached with caution. Nevertheless, despite this proviso, it is the case that any information provided about the social role of irreligion is likely to be relevant to the study of religion. As has already been suggested, such information is relevant to the secularisation debate.

It could also cast fresh light on discussions of religion and socio-economic deprivation, religion and social change, and the various hypotheses involved in the assertion of religion's role in providing answers to the 'problem of meaning'. All this suggests that it would be well worthwhile for the sociologists of religion to invest some time and effort in a consideration of irreligion.

A nascent sociology of irreligion is clearly eminently suited to play the devil's advocate to a saintly sociology of religion, and it would definitely be wrong to imagine that a consideration of irreligious phenomena would lead to a confirmation of theoretical presuppositions in the sociology of religion. Indeed on the face of it the reverse is much more likely to be true. In the absence of any serious investigations, what has been believed about irreligion is whatever constitutes the 'popular view', and on a subject such as this the opinions of the general public are notoriously unreliable. In general, opinions about irreligion were forged in the white-hot furnace of emotion surrounding the great religious debates of the late nineteenth century. At the time both sides were capable of believing almost anything to the disadvantage of the other, and although now the furnace has burnt very low, underlying attitudes linger on. Thus, although most people no longer tend to view the irreligious as friendless, tortured souls, prone to suicide and deathbed repentance, as did the Victorians, the remains of this attitude linger on in the tendency to assume that the irreligious are social isolates, existing in anomic situations and likely to be aggressive or psychologically disturbed. Similarly, the Victorian belief that religion was the very basis of civilisation and an ordered society, and the principal support for morality, continues in the common assertion of the necessary link between religion and morality. One suspects that this is no less true of sociologists than of the general public. It might even be more true of sociologists because in many ways the sociology of religion in its own writings has embodied the popularly held opinions about religion and irreligion current at the turn of the century. The Durkheimian emphasis on the association of religion and social order is eminently Victorian, as is the linkage of social isolation with irreligion. Perhaps - and here the devil's advocate is guilty of heresy-the neglect of irreligion has prevented the realisation that most of what is held dear in the sociology of religion is merely an elaboration of what was the popular wisdom of half a century ago. If this should prove to be the case, even in a small measure, then the

15

study of irreligion would have certainly justified itself, and not merely for the light shed on the sociology of religion but also because of the light thrown on sociology itself.

2 The Nature and Forms of Irreligion

The claim of the sociology of irreligion to be accepted as an important and viable sphere of study clearly cannot be admitted until its specific subject of investigation has been outlined. Irreligion itself must be identified, delineated and defined and its various forms described. This itself is a difficult task and may even prove to be a thoroughly daunting one, if the experience of the sociology of religion is anything to go by. Since irreligion is defined primarily by reference to religion, the notable lack of success in defining the latter term is hardly a good omen for success in defining the former. On the other hand, it is possible that the attempt to define irreligion may itself help in some way to provide a solution to this perennial and thorny problem. Whatever the accompanying expectations, the attempt must be made, for without even a provisional delineation a sociology of irreligion cannot exist. At a popular level the specification of irreligion seems straightforward enough; one thinks immediately of such phenomena as atheism, agnosticism, total indifference to religion, anti-clericalism and the like. By contrast, the sociological specification of irreligion is formidable indeed, because in addition to the familiar problems associated with defining religion one has additional ones arising out of the quality of rejection which the prefix 'ir-' implies.

One of the major hindrances to a successful definition of irreligion is the existence of a condition of terminological confusion. This does not so much surround the word 'irreligion' itself -which is in practice a comparatively little-used word - but rather surrounds the family of words with which it is linked. Words like 'atheist', 'agnostic', 'free-thinker', 'humanist', 'infidel', 'pagan', 'rationalist' and 'secularist' are all dangerous ones for the social scientist who is not aware of their ambiguity or sensitive to their etymology. Confusion can arise in the first place because several of the terms have two or more distinct meanings. 'Humanism', for example, can refer either to the culture associated with classical learning and the Renaissance or to an 'atheistic or agnostic insistence on the self-sufficiency of the human race'.[1] 'Agnosticism' can refer either to the belief that mankind is incapable of finding out whether God exists or to the position of those who say that they do not know whether God exists. 'The secular' can be used to refer either to neutrality or to hostility in religious matters. This

17

ambiguity is made worse by the fact that the meaning of these words can vary according to the contexts in which they are used. Of particular significance here is the fact that several are used in both a religious and an irreligious context, and although the general sense may be the same the definitive content is different. Hence, 'rationalism' is used in both religious and irreligious contexts to refer to the treatment of reason as the ultimate authority, but in the irreligious context it has the additional connotation of implying the use of reason for the destruction of religious belief.[2] Similarly, 'free thought' is a term used in both contexts to imply a reaction against constraint on thinking and a questioning of conventional doctrine. But again it has atheistic and agnostic overtones when used in an irreligious context.[3] In part, these differences are the result of the secularisation of language, in the sense that these terms were used in a religious context prior to their adoption for irreligious purposes. This process itself, however, did not render them redundant in their former context and so they have continued to function in both sacred and secular language.

This problem is itself only part of a wider problem of the development of specialised vocabularies for distinct disciplines. This need not be a problem for sociology, which has certainly excelled in producing such a vocabulary for its own use, except that when confronted with a virgin area of territory to survey it is highly confusing to find the land covered with the signposts of explorers from other disciplines. In this case, the land of irreligion has been crossed and re-crossed by parties of explorers representing theology and philosophy, a fact which is likely to make the sociologist's task that much more difficult. Nevertheless, these terminological problems need not represent insurmountable obstacles. As long as care is taken to state in what context a word is being used and with which of its various meanings, confusion can be avoided.

A more serious difficulty is the lack of common agreement in the labelling of social phenomena as religious or irreligious. The field of irreligion has to be delineated before it can be defined, and initially, at least, the sociologist has to use common-sense categories in order to identify the boundaries of this field. Any lack of common agreement about these boundaries is then a grave handicap. In part this is just the 'other side of the coin' of the problem of defining religion. On the other hand the problem is not precisely the same, if only because of the difference in the standpoint adopted. It is true that the conventional solutions to the problem of defining religion, such as drawing the line between theism and non-theism, or between the supernatural and the natural, are open to objections from the point of view of defining irreligion. Just as some traditional religions have contained non-theistic elements, so have some irreligious movements allowed for the possibility of theism.[4] Similarly, belief in a non-natural power or force may occur in ostensibly irreligious movements such as the political religions of Nazism and Communism.

However, the problem of defining irreligion is in some ways more intractable than the problem of defining religion because there is no corresponding conventional consensus. All agree that Roman Catholicism is a religion, even if they argue the merits of extending the term to such phenomena as baseball.[5]

In other words, there does exist a core phenomenon which goes unquestioningly by the name of 'religion'; but it is more difficult to find a similar core of irreligious phenomena. Convention would suggest that atheism and agnosticism (and perhaps anti-clericalism) might constitute such a core, but to some extent each of these positions has been claimed as a legitimate element in the general religious tradition. It almost seems as if there is no area which irreligion might claim for its own which has not also been claimed by religion. This does not mean that there is no such phenomenon as irreligion or that the claims of religion are irrefutable, but it does indicate the elasticity of use of the term 'religion' contrasted with the comparative rigidity of the term 'irreligion'. Indeed it is not long after irreligion has laid a claim to a territory of its own, as with Huxley's coining of the term 'agnosticism' in 1869, than the Church discovers that it also possesses co-ownership of the deeds.[6] This form of territorial aggrandisement on the part of religion is one of the reasons why a core content of irreligion is hard to come by.

There is also the problem of the confused state of irreligionists themselves about whether their own position is or is not a functional alternative to religion, and if it is, whether this justifies their describing themselves as religious. This confusion certainly existed in the Anglo-American ethical movement as some people clearly regarded the movement as religious, largely on the grounds that it was doing the work of religion, whilst others saw it as a-religious on the grounds that it was

19

entirely neutral on questions of theism and metaphysics.[7] A similar debate on the applicability of the term 'religion' has occurred in the more recent past in the humanist movements in Britain and America.[8]

It almost seems as if to venture to define and delineate irreligion (or religion) is to enter an Alice-in-Wonderland world where words can be used to mean whatever one wishes them to mean and reality divided into the religious and the irreligious in any way one chooses, according to whim or fancy. In fact, this impression is largely the result of trying to discuss irreligion in an a-historical and non-structural situation, as if some absolutely valid substantive definition of irreligion was obtainable. One only needs to be reminded that in the ancient world the Christians were called atheists because they refused to acknowledge the Roman gods and that, as Robertson claims, the Old Testament prophets were among the earliest free-thinkers, to realise the necessity of a historical and cultural perspective for the study of irreligion.[9] To seek to define irreligion in terms of the rejection of a specific belief or practice is necessarily to limit the term to the cultural tradition concerned and by so doing to risk being caught out by the twists and turns of history :

> From the earliest times to the present day belief has changed, and will go on changing. ... In the opinion of men who lived not very long ago he who did not believe that the world was made in six days was an infidel; he who did not believe that the sun moved round the earth was an infidel; he who did not believe that a man lived three days in the belly of a fish was an infidel. To go further back, he who did not believe that the moaning of the wind in the trees was the voice of the god of the wind was an infidel.[10]

Clearly the infidel of one age may well be the orthodox believer of the next, or, in Matthew Arnold's phrase, 'The Freethinking of one age is the common sense of the next'. A similar relativity may also apply geographically and culturally at one point in time. We are therefore bound to conclude that irreligion cannot be defined substantively in terms of identifiable beliefs and practices but only as a general form of response to religion, the content of the irreligious response itself varying as the content of religion varies. The nature of this response is well indicated by the meanings given to the word 'irreligion', which, according to the 'Oxford

English Dictionary', implies such attitudes as hostility, disregard and indifference toward religion.

Thus, although the attempt to specify the content of irreligion has in a way only returned us to the problem of identifying the content of religion, it is still possible to identify irreligion as a characteristic set of responses to religion. And these responses exist as ever-present options in societies, in a way that specific responses like atheism may not. If, as we are led to believe, some form of religion has existed in all societies, then the possibility of reacting with hostility or indifference toward it must also have been a feature of all societies. Potentially at least, the sociology of irreligion has as wide a field of application as the sociology of religion.

We have now arrived at the point at which we can formulate a minimum definition of irreligion as a reaction or alienative response to established religion. More specifically, irreligion is those beliefs and actions which are expressive of attitudes of hostility or indifference toward the prevailing religion, together with indications of the rejection of its demands. This definition, however, will only serve as a preliminary statement as there are many problems yet to be tackled before the area of irreligion is fully mapped. Hostility and indifference may themselves take many forms or appear in various guises and contexts; they may spring from different sources and be directed at any one of the many elements which comprise religion. The irreligious response may be latent, manifest or covert, organised or unorganised, a minority or majority tradition in relation to the structure of religious orthodoxy. All these features and forms of irreligion need to be examined prior to any definitive statement of the nature of irreligion, and in particular before the boundaries between irreligion and religious heresy and reform on the one hand, and between irreligion and the secular on the other, have been plotted.

Irreligious Belief and Action

It is conventional to equate irreligion with a lack of religious belief. In contemporary Anglo-American society it is the non-theists who are considered as the main illustration of irreligion, just as on the Continent Catholic sociologists are prone to substitute atheism for irreligion. Clearly this usage is to some extent historically justifiable; the rejection of religious belief and the teachings of the Church have been associated with anti-religious feeling. On the other hand the failure to believe is not necessarily any indication of hostility or indifference toward religion. The phenomenon of the religiously sympathising unbeliever is not unknown; there are probably many within and without the churches who, whilst thoroughly in sympathy with religion, find that although they would like to believe they cannot. Many of these people may indeed define themselves as religious, in line with the tradition which equates religion with ethical behaviour or ritual practice. There is therefore a danger that, by equating irreligion with unbelief, individuals who are not really evidence of an irreligious response will be classified as such. There is in addition an even greater danger that the reverse process will occur.

Jay Demerath has provided one of the very few sociological definitions of irreligion which, despite its merits, refers to irreligion as 'unbelief . . . in . . . religious doctrine'. Although he recognises that there might be other 'dimensions of irreligiosity', he considers unbelief to be sufficiently salient to warrant its use as the defining variable.[11] This seems unnecessarily restrictive as it focuses attention solely on the cognitive manifestations of hostility and indifference toward religion; irreligious feeling and action, if indeed they are recognised as existing at all, are relegated, *a priori,* to a secondary position, as if, by implication, they are derivatives of irreligious belief. This rationalistic bias is inherently suspect, reminiscent as it is of a similar bias which prevailed in the sociology of religion at the beginning of this century. In any case irreligious emotion and action cannot be relegated to the epiphenomenological periphery. Much evidence suggests that anti-clerical and anti-ecclesiastical feeling are as likely to be the precursors of the loss of religious faith as their consequences.[12] Certainly irreligious emotion and action are very real dimensions and clearly must be treated as independent of each other, and of the belief dimension, in exactly the same way that the dimensions of religion are treated, until such time as the nature of their relationships can be established. Once this precaution is adopted it can be seen that the equating of irreligion with unbelief is liable to exclude an important area of irreligious phenomena. Irreligion, however it is defined, must refer to all aspects of behaviour (belief, action, attitudes and experience) in just the way that religion does. The concept of irreligious action can cover a very wide range of discrete acts, from the large-scale desecration of churches or persecution of clergy such as occurred during the French Revolution down to the simple act of abstinence from church services or even profane swearing. Of course, it may well prove very difficult to establish whether given acts are truly expressive of criticism or indifference toward religion or stem merely from unconsidered custom, ignorance or laziness. By convention we are reluctant to identify acts as in fact irreligious if any other possible interpretation is open. It is likely therefore that we are overlooking a considerable amount of irreligiosity. One suspects that isolated and personal acts of rebellion by both schoolchildren and adults are far from rare, and the refusal to kneel during prayers, or perhaps to close one's eyes, or even merely a refusal to say the Lord's Prayer, are far from uncommon events in contemporary society. One may of course try to take the sting out of such actions by suggesting that their real motivation is not irreligious, but is to be understood in terms of social or personal dissatisfaction. But such an argument can naturally also be applied to those who conform to religious convention. Thus if one chooses to disregard the fact that most soldiers engage in 'foul, immoral, and blasphemous language' as not signifying irreligiosity but merely a customary mode of language use, then the fact that the same soldiers utter a hasty prayer to God in the heat of battle should similarly be treated as signifying little more than a similar 'usage'.[13]

Varieties of Irreligion

The central point of reference for defining irreligion is the nature of the response to religion, and so far we have referred to this in the language of the 'Oxford English Dictionary' as 'hostility' or 'indifference'. We must now consider the form of this response more carefully and in so doing distinguish the varieties of irreligion. The first point to make is that attitudes presuppose awareness. To hold an attitude of hostility or sympathy toward a religion is necessarily to have a minimal awareness of it. Conversely, to be unaware of it precludes the holding of attitudes. Thus if any part of the population of a society is genuinely unaware of the established or dominant religion, then with reference to that religion they cannot be either religious or irreligious. They are what our forebears would have called 'pagans' and are perhaps best described as the unreligious. It seems difficult to imagine that such people could exist in contemporary society, where almost universal literacy and all-penetrating mass media make some acquaintance with the predominant religion unavoidable. And yet the unreligious were a feature of the society of the recent past and may well be a feature of the society of the future. Among the 'great ecclesiastical unwashed' of the nineteenth century there were those who did not know that St Paul's was a church as well as those who had barely heard the name Jesus Christ.[14] Whilst perhaps few were totally ignorant of anything to do with religion, 'Darkest England' was only a shade lighter than 'Darkest Africa'. Strictly speaking, the unreligious position as described here falls outside what has been outlined as the irreligious phenomenon. It does, however, shade over into the irreligious, in so far as what awareness exists is associated with indifference or hostility toward religion.

Throughout the discussion so far the irreligious position has been characterised by the use of the two words 'indifference' and 'hostility'. Clearly they are not synonyms but refer to very different attitudes and thus relate to contrasting forms of irreligion. Where an awareness of the established religion is associated with its rejection and the expression of hostility towards its beliefs, personnel or practices, one has the classic instance of an anti-religious response. Where, on the other hand, a similar awareness is associated with, at the most, a merely implicit rejection and behaviour expressive of indifference toward the religion, one has an instance of an a-religious response.[15] These constitute the two principal varieties of irreligion, and one of the main tasks of a sociology of irreligion is that of discovering the circumstances which lead to the emergence at a given point of time of one of these forms rather than the other. Both represent irreligious standpoints in that they are responses to the established religion other than that of commitment. The contrasts between them are important, being significantly related to variations in the socio-cultural structure in general.

Observers have long commented on the fact that the irreligious can be subdivided into the anti-religious and the a-religious. Those who refrained from attending church in East London at the turn of the century were described as falling into two classes, 'the estranged and antagonistic and the apathetic and careless'.[16] In addition there has been considerable discussion of the tendency for the a-religious response to have gradually supplanted the anti-religious response as the primary form of irreligion in British society. The first half of the nineteenth century had been marked by virulent anti-religious campaigns, but by mid-Victorian times these had died down and instead of attacking religion 'many people were simply uninterested in religion or else regarded it as a curious historical phenomenon destined like others to pass away'.[17]

It is clear that religion-irreligion is closer to a continuum than a dichotomy, and consequently difficulty is experienced when one comes to the phenomena near the centre of the continuum. This difficulty will be encountered more than once in the attempt to present a sociology of irreligion and arises here because of the need to distinguish the primary forms of irreligion. The two principal forms of irreligion we have identified as anti-irreligion and a-religion, and we have already suggested that at the boundary, marked ignorance of religion, these shade into the non-irreligious category of unreligion. There is, however, the problem of the other boundary, the boundary between irreligion and religious commitment. In the no-man's-land in this direction we can distinguish another category - briefly mentioned earlier - which might be claimed as a variety of irreligion. This is the religiously sympathising unbeliever, a person who neither possesses commitment to a religious position nor regards religion with hostility or indifference, but on the contrary is favourably disposed toward it. Such a person is not easily fitted in to the sphere of irreligion as we have outlined it above, but is equally unamenable to inclusion in the category of the religious.

The status of such a person is similar to the concept of 'seeker-ship' proposed by Glock and Stark and developed by Lofland and Stark.[18] As originally proposed, this concept referred to those people who 'have the concern [to discover the purpose and meaning of life] but who have not resolved it'.[19] Lofland and Stark, however, define it more precisely as a 'floundering among religious alternatives, an openness to a variety of religious views, frequently esoteric, combined with failure to embrace the specific ideology and fellowship of some set of believers'.[20] This latter definition, however, necessarily restricts the term to use only with people who are unable to make up their minds about rival religious ideologies, whereas the original implication was that seekership could also refer to those unable to decide between religious and non-religious world-views. In this broader sense the term could relate to the religiously sympathising unbeliever, who may indeed be a 'seeker' in the sense implied. The similarity is only partial, however, since seekership is not necessarily implied by a sympathetic but unbelieving attitude toward religion. Such a person may indeed have 'found' the answers he was seeking. The distinguishing characteristic of the category envisaged here is the combination of a lack of religious commitment with a pro-religious attitude; clearly the question of seekership is only tangentially related to such a position. Some people fall into both categories, notably those whose loss of belief was reluctantly conceded and who, like Malcolm Quinn, became 'unbelievers' although nevertheless wanting a 'religion'.[21] Others perhaps, being in Weber's graphic term 'religiously unmusical', are just fascinated by a phenomenon which they recognise as beyond their experience.

The above discussion of the varieties of irreligion clearly indicates that it is the specific attitude of rejection which is irreligion's principal defining characteristic. That attitude of rejection may be more implicit than explicit, as is suggested in the attitude of indifference, but it is by the nature of the response to religion that irreligion is defined. In this crucial respect the approach adopted here differs from those attempts to specify irreligion which have concentrated on the absence of religious commitment as the defining characteristic. This difference is important and requires some explanation.

The main reason for defining irreligion in terms of the rejection rather than the absence of religion is that it seems to avoid several difficulties involved in the 'irreligion equals unbelief equation. In the first place the 'definition through absence' approach requires a careful statement of what constitutes religious commitment in order that its absence can be established. This in turn immediately plunges the issue straight into the labyrinth of complex issues surrounding the definition of religion, in particular the problem of functional alternatives. In the second place irreligion becomes easily confused with the secular. Where religious commitment is absent, commitment to political, economic, educational, familial and other secular values is almost certain to be present. In view of the considerable difficulty in establishing that religious commitment is not present in any form or other, there is a standing temptation to resort to asserting that commitment to secular values is such as to preclude religious commitment. Thus what started as the sociology of irreligion becomes the sociology of the secular. If this danger is avoided it is likely to be by means of the no less satisfactory tactic of defining irreligion as the absence of a particular form of religious commitment. This is patently unsatisfactory, because, as discussed earlier, the dimensionality of religion (and irreligion) is lost, together with the possibility of examining the variable content of irreligious forms of protest in different cultural and historical contexts. The sociology of unbelief will then need to be counterbalanced by sociologies of 'un-'practice and of 'un-'experience. In any case there are more fundamental reasons for not defining a field of study in terms of the absence of a given phenomenon. The absence of religious belief should either be because on the one hand it was 'available' but was rejected, or on the other because it was never available. If the absence of religious commitment in a society or group in society is because it was never an available option, then this ceases to be a very interesting sociological fact. The study of the non-existence of the non-available is hardly the stuff from which intellectual disciplines are built.

On the other hand, the study of the rejection of social and cultural forms which are available is potentially sociologically very interesting. It is for this reason that irreligion is here defined as the rejection of available religious traditions rather than as the non-existence of certain religious beliefs. Charles Glock, for example, has suggested that it is possible to conceptualise non-belief in such a way that it is culture-free, sensitive to variations within and between cultures, and a-historical.[22] In order to realise this aim, however, he is forced to propose four very general types of belief (objectivist supernatural, objectivist natural, subjectivist supernatural and subjectivist natural) with, correspondingly, four main types of non-belief. However, any one of these four varieties of non-belief may appear in association with one of the remaining forms of belief. What people accept and what they deny are part and parcel of the same complex of beliefs, and one cannot invoke just any particular variety of beliefs as a standard from which to judge that they are 'believers' rather than 'non-believers'. Definitions in terms of cultural content such as these are very prone to seem arbitrary and based on cultural bias. In addition, however, they lack social relevance, being based exclusively on cultural nonconformity. As sociologists define religion as a social and not merely as a cultural phenomenon, so too must they define irreligion as a social phenomenon. It constitutes social nonconformity just as much as cultural nonconformity; the failure to express an attitude of seriousness during a church service but to express amusement instead might well be just as much an expression of irreligion as polite agnosticism about God. Clearly, however, it is hard to envisage a culture-free conceptualisation of irreligious acts! Irreligion, like crime, is a function of what society formulates as the norm, and there is no more possibility of constituting a universal concept of irreligion than there would be of gaining universal agreement on what constituted criminal acts. However, just as crime can be defined as a relationship to the norm (or law), so can irreligion be denned as a relationship to established religion.

Contextual Aspects of Defining Irreligion

The specification of the nature of irreligion as a relationship of hostility or indifference toward religion still leaves an important problem unresolved. As we have seen, irreligion can only be specified within a given social and cultural context, and this process of specification is crucial if we are ever to identify examples of irreligious belief and behaviour. Contextual specification, however, gives rise to fresh difficulties.

The essence of this problem is the identification of the religion or religious tradition which is to be the yardstick by which we measure the expressions of hostility or indifference. Clearly there is no difficulty in those situations where societies possess one single dominant and coherent religion, for in such situations irreligion must necessarily take the form of resentment against that tradition. In societies marked by religious pluralism or even by denominational pluralism, however, the situation is necessarily more complex. The very disparate nature of religion makes the identification of attitudes of hostility and indifference more difficult and there is a greater danger of confusing irreligion with religious prejudice on the one hand and religious radicalism on the other. In order to escape these dangers one looks first to those elements which are common to the various religious traditions, and thus by identifying a 'lowest common denominator' of religious belief and practice one restores the possibility of defining irreligion with respect to this 'societal religious tradition'. Rejection of this tradition is then the equivalent of the rejection of the state Church in a religiously monistic society. However, whilst it is true that the rejection of the common factor constitutes an irreligious response, to conceive of irreligion as equitable with this factor is to restrict the concept considerably. For although, from the point of view of the total society, the rejection of elements not part of this common factor is not irreligion, from the perspective of individuals or sub-groups in society it may be. Religion, as the relevant point of reference for individuals within the society, will consist of more than the common factor, and their specific irreligiosity may manifest itself in the expression of hostility or indifference toward those features of religion which are most central to them. Thus the irreligion of the Roman Catholic apostate may focus as much on hostility toward the Pope and the priesthood as on the rejection of belief in God or the divinity of Christ. Thus there is a form of sub-cultural irreligiousness to be set alongside the central irreligiousness constituted by rejection of the religious common factor.

Nevertheless, it is the case that religious pluralism does not destroy the possibility of discriminating between religious traditions in terms of their socially defined orthodoxy. One can have an established orthodoxy within a diverse and pluralistic religious structure, as is the case with Anglicanism in Britain or, in a rather different way, with Protestantism, Catholicism and Judaism in America. The concept of religious orthodoxy provides yet another possible point of reference for the exercise of delineating irreligion. In this case the problem is that of distinguishing irreligion from what is merely an expression of religious radicalism. Frequently, those who attempt to present a radical conception of a religious tradition are accused by the more orthodox of being in fact converts to irreligion.[23] Conversely, those who come to believe that their own radical beliefs are so unacceptable as to constitute irreligion may in fact be mistaken, and a wider knowledge of their own religious tradition may later lead them to the realisation that they have been espousing an 'acceptable', if unorthodox, interpretation of the faith. Clearly the problem here surrounds the question of the nature of the structure of the religious tradition. The minimal assumptions one can make are that such traditions will contain some notion of comparative orthodoxy, in practice as well as belief, together with some conception of the permitted range of unorthodox variations. This in turn implies the existence of a boundary which lies between extreme unorthodoxy and tentative irreligion. Objectively, this boundary is defined by the religious organisations themselves in terms of some minimal commitment, whether it be to doctrine or to discipline. In practice, although this boundary may be ill-defined or in dispute, a belief that it exists seems indispensable to all religious bodies built on the assumption of a distinction between 'the faithful' and 'the rest'. Subjectively, the boundary can be said to lie in the difference between the person who still hopes to change the religious tradition into a form closer to his own ideal, and the person who considers that the tradition must be abandoned, either without replacement, or simply replaced by another 'religion'.

Some of the considerable difficulties which surround the identification of this boundary between the unorthodox and the irreligious are likely to arise out of a discrepancy between the objective and subjective mode of definition. Hence, to take the most obvious case, those who consider themselves to be merely reforming the religious tradition may well be considered to have rejected it by the authorities of the Church. Several of the 'irreligious' movements considered in this book originated in movements of this kind. Adler, for example, considered himself to be reforming Judaism, but was regarded by his Jewish congregation as going too far to be considered still within the framework of the Judaic faith.

Stanton Coit's Ethical Church had a somewhat similar relationship with Anglicanism. Whether reform movements are retained within the framework of the religion concerned, or forced outside it, will depend on the tolerance level of the organisations, which is thus a critical factor in determining whether the forces for religious reform will eventuate in an irreligious movement or not. In so far as the reformist impulse involves an element of hostility toward the established variant of the religious tradition, it clearly has direct kinship with the more generalised irreligious response. Only the difference in the breadth of objects for attack and the contextual difference of aim between modification on the one hand, and replacement or abolition on the other, distinguish the two responses.[24]

So far we have considered the problem of how to distinguish the boundary between religious radicalism and irreligion using the notion of religious orthodoxy as a point of reference. It is, however, also useful to consider the problem from the reverse perspective, that is, from the point of view of irreligious orthodoxy. Although irreligion rarely has a dominant or established status in society, in the same way that religious traditions frequently have, this does not preclude the possibility of employing the notion of irreligious orthodoxy.[25] Some organisation or body is likely to claim to represent the irreligious, and to the extent that it can be said to do so, its ideology can be treated as a notional orthodoxy. Even where there is no ideology which can be so treated, there will be a popular conception of irreligion which could be treated as a conventional norm. Thus, in very general terms irreligion would be Deism in the late eighteenth century but atheism in the nineteenth. The introduction of this reverse orthodoxy means that discrepancies can also arise between objective and subjective modes of definition from this perspective. Those who are unorthodox in their irreligion may find themselves condemned as 'religious' by the 'official' representatives of irreligion. The boundary between unorthodox irreligion and religion may be as difficult to distinguish as the related boundary between unorthodox religion and irreligion. It would seem necessary to specify a 'twilight zone' wherein lie these two boundaries, and where the application of our categories becomes, to a large measure, an arbitrary matter.

The Range of Irreligiousness

The foregoing discussion has indicated something of the difficulties which are to be expected in any attempt to identify and delineate the irreligious response in a modern pluralistic society. Some expressions of hostility are probably readily identifiable, especially in relation to the dominant or established religious orthodoxies. Problems arise, however, where cultural pluralism has given rise to multiple orthodoxies or where the religious tradition is itself so tolerant of variant forms that an orthodoxy barely exists. In these situations the irreligious response may merge and mingle with expressions of unorthodox, or merely just unusual, religious expressions, in such a way that it becomes barely possible to distinguish between the two.

Partly, this difficulty arises out of the desire to retain both a subjective and an objective point of reference for the definition of irreligion. As long as these two criteria overlap, there is no problem. Where a person defines his own behaviour, and it is defined by others, as constituting the rejection of religion, then he is clearly irreligious. Where these two criteria do not overlap, then the problems mentioned above become very real. However, the degree to which the criteria are likely to overlap is related, among others factors, to the range of the irreligious response.

The range of the irreligious response refers to the variation in the number of religious components against which hostility or indifference is directed. At the one end of the scale, hostility may only be directed against one element in a religious system of belief and practice. This element may be religious personnel, as with anti-clericalism, or a specific religious belief, as in the case of anti-theism, or a specific class of religious acts, as with anti-church-going, but it is clearly possible for such specific irreligiosities to exist unassociated with irreligiousness in any other form. At the other end of the scale, there is the response of total or absolute irreligiousness, where the rejection covers not just a complete class of religious components such as beliefs, experiences or practices, but the very fact of religion itself as a social and cultural phenomenon of any kind. It is this latter form of irreligiosity, rather than any more specific or partial irreligiosity which is commonly given the name 'irreligion'. And yet such a response is probably comparatively rare, since the arousal of hostility is usually the product of experience in connection with some particular religious tradition and usually too in relation to some particular component of that tradition. Thus even though the response may thereafter be generalised to include religious traditions with which the individual is not directly acquainted, the basic expression of hostility will most probably be directed against the native variety.

There are clearly two different contexts in which it is possible to discuss the range of irreligiousness. The one is with respect to the dimensions of religion itself — belief, experience, practice and organisation - whilst the other refers to the diversity of religious expression, the variation in content with respect to these dimensions. The irreligious response can be specific or general in varying degrees with respect to either or both of these contexts. The distinction in terms of content is more frequent than that in terms of religious component. Langmead Casserley, for example, distinguishes between 'relative irreligion' - which is the rejection of some particular religion — and 'absolute irreligion', which is 'neither professing nor practising any form of religion at all'.[26] Distinctions of this kind would suggest that much irreligion is relative rather than absolute, in so far as it constitutes a rejection of a particular religious tradition rather than of all religions. Most irreligion in contemporary Europe and America is probably relative in this sense, being Christian irreligion rather than absolute irreligion. In a narrower context still, one may distinguish between Protestant and Catholic irreligion and possibly even Anglican and Methodist irreligion. It is pertinent in this context to reproduce Mayor's remark that, in British society, 'many agnostics are at least Protestant Agnostics'.[27] This attitude of relative or specific irreligion may indeed be associated with attitudes of sympathy for other religions, and it is thus not uncommon to find secularists or humanists who speak favourably about Buddhism whilst condemning Christianity. At the same time it is necessary to recognise that a position of absolute or general irreligion can exist. Such cases most commonly appear as positions of thoroughgoing rationalism in which all forms of religious expression are dismissed as 'mere superstitions'. Distinctions may, of course, still be made even in a position of total irreligion, between religions which are more or less 'harmful', but none is in any way regarded with favour. Indeed, such a position frequently attacks on a wider front even than religion, denouncing perceived irrationalism or superstition in such fields as the visual arts, literature and politics.

The other context in which irreligion can be said to vary in its 'range' is in respect to the components of religion. The principal ones are those of belief, experience, practice and organisation.

But even these are capable of further subdivision, so that in its very minimal form irreligion may appear as a single isolated act of hostility, defiance or rejection. The general divisions are nevertheless comparatively clear. There are those irreligious acts which concentrate on belief, there are those acts which concentrate on religion as practice and there are those acts which concentrate on religion as a form of social organisation. As religion comprises all these components in differing degrees, it seems on the face of it to be unlikely that the irreligious response will remain for long *solely* one of hostility toward one component. A 'spill-over' of hostility to the other components seems more or less inevitable.

On the other hand, it is quite usual for differential importance to be attached to the various components, so that one or another is denned as a 'central' or 'crucial' characteristic of religious commitment. In such a situation, it is common to define religious and irreligious commitment alike by reference to that component alone, as is the case in contemporary Britain and America where theistic belief is the component of religion singled out in this way. Nevertheless, even where one factor is singled out as crucial, the possibility that the irreligious response may originate in relation to practice or organisation remains open. Perhaps the more realistic procedure would be to talk in terms of the 'focus' of the irreligious response in relation to these components. Thus, to take perhaps the best example of a specific irreligious response in relation to the components of religion, anti-clericalism constitutes a focus of hostility on the clergy but is clearly likely to have a degree of 'spill-over' into organisation, practice and possibly belief, at those points where these latter components are most obviously related to the clergy themselves.

Accepting that the irreligious response can be either specific or general in relation to either the components of religion, or to the range of religious forms, the question arises as to the relationship between these two dimensions of irreligion. Does a rejection of all the components of religion tend to be associated with a rejection of all religions more often than with the rejection of a single tradition? Or alternatively, does the process of generalisation from one religion to all religions proceed more easily where the response is limited to one aspect of religion, such as theology or clericalism ? Clearly, such questions cannot be decided *a priori* but must wait the outcome of careful investigation. However, certain clues do suggest that a relationship between the substance and the form of the target of the irreligious response may be readily identifiable. Where the response is overwhelmingly anti-Catholic, for example, it is also frequently anti-clerical; similarly, where it is overwhelmingly anti-Nonconformist it tends to be principally anti-scriptural. Such associations are obvious enough and illustrate the general point that the nature of the irreligious response is largely determined by the nature of the individual's perception or experience of religion.[28] What remains unclear, however, is what determines whether the generalisation of the irreligious outlook follows the substantive path or the component path-or indeed if generalisation proceeds equally along both paths.

The introduction of the notion of the range of irreligiousness allows us to speculate on the possibility of constructing a hypothesised 'ideal' or 'pure' type of irreligious response. Although the building of types is something of an occupational hazard for sociologists and one for which they are quite rightly frequently rebuked, they can nevertheless have a heuristic value. In this case, the presentation of irreligion in an ideal-type form might assist the process of distinguishing irreligion from its various associated phenomena of religious reform, religious prejudice, quasi-religions and secularity. This it can do because the construction of a type allows for the exaggeration of elements found in reality and for the omission of factors which, although present in reality, may not be 'intrinsically' involved in the phenomenon under discussion. In this context the exaggeration of aspects of reality can be achieved by treating the one end of the range of irreligious-ness, that of general or total response, as if it were typical of the irreligious reaction in general. Hence the pure type of irreligion would involve the rejection of all religions and of all components of religious phenomena.

The Setting of the Irreligious Response

So far, an attempt has been made to define what constitutes the essence of the irreligious response, what forms it can take, within what limits it can vary, and in what ways it can be distinguished from related phenomena such as that of religious reform. There remains the question of the setting and the source of the response, if not the more fundamental question of its origins. The factors which actually give rise to the irreligious response are likely to be as complex and as diverse as the causes of religious commitment and thus could only be adequately examined at considerable length. A step in this direction, however, is that of considering the differences in the social and cultural setting in which this response emerges. Principally, this question centres on whether the response stands alone, a social or cultural tradition defined by its irreligiousness, or appears in association with other traditions, movements, philosophies or ideologies which are defined other than by a rejection of religion. Up to this point irreligion has been discussed as if it were a discretely independent phenomenon, a clearly circumscribed response, which, although possessing kinship with other phenomena, was not to be seen as part of any more inclusive response. This is clearly not necessarily the case; irreligion can indeed be part of a larger cultural or social pattern. The most obvious example of this would be the incorporation of an irreligious outlook into Communism, where irreligion is a response which is derived from commitment to a more general world-view. Such a setting contrasts sharply with an autonomous or 'primary' response, which is not a derivative of a more general commitment, but stands alone, generated directly from the life-situation. This latter response is essentially irreligious in a way that the former cannot be and is thus taken as the more 'typical' response for purposes of constructing an 'ideal-type' of irreligion. The appearance of the irreligious response in association with secular ideologies or philosophies is not necessarily an indication that it is derived from them. On the contrary, they may be called upon to legitimise the response or to provide a supporting framework for it.

Alternatively, they may provide mutual support for each other. Whatever the relationship, it seems possible to distinguish between irreligion as a primary and derived response and as a 'pure' (and thus primary) response and as an 'associated' (though not necessarily derived) response. In fact it seems that the pure and primary irreligious response is something of a rarity, as irreligion is more often to be found in association with some developed philosophy of life which is not itself a mere elaboration of the rejection of religion. Among many examples of such philosophies which could be given would be Positivism, Utilitarianism, Idealism, Rationalism, Humanism, Communism, Nationalism, Nazism, and Existentialism. The relationship between these various 'isms' and irreligion is clearly a more complex problem than can be encompassed by the three crude categories set out above; it is thus a subject which warrants further examination.

There is another and associated sense in which it is possible to speak of a 'purely' irreligious response and which relates to the likelihood of the response appearing in association with a secular ideology. This refers to the perception of irreligious agitation as a sufficient end in itself and not merely as a means to some higher end. This is likely to be the case where religion is seen as an unmitigated evil, a hindrance or 'barrier' to the progress of mankind. The aim thus becomes the simple one of the elimination of religion altogether, both as a secular power and form of social organisation and as a system of cultural symbolism. The alternative to this is the view which sees religion as having fulfilled, albeit partially and inadequately, some necessary individual or social functions, functions which remain to be fulfilled, even though religion in its pre-existing form must be judged to be wanting, or to have fallen into decay, or to be riddled with hypocrisy, or whatever. Therefore, the elimination of religion is in itself inadequate. It must be replaced by some viable alternative or alternatives.

In this view the irreligious response is just a means to the real end of replacement, and thus irreligionists of this ilk are necessarily involved in the formulation of some ideology and/or system of social organisation which will be able to function as a replacement for religion. Such an outlook can be said to be less purely 'irreligious' than the abolitionists' one, since a commitment to the replacement ideology exists alongside the irreligious commitment *per se.* At the same time such a position is clearly likely to bring irreligion into association with a secular ideology, although not necessarily in the form of a derivative of it.

There is a long history of hostility between the abolitionist and the replacement schools of thought in the irreligious tradition, inasmuch as the former accuse the latter of being 'half-hearted' and of 'playing at religion' whilst the latter accuse the former of being 'merely negative'. Apart from this, however, they do recognise a common cause in their opposition to the prevailing religion and differ primarily in their perception of the appropriate strategy, the replacement school tending to the view that what is established cannot effectively be eliminated but only displaced, whilst the eliminationist school tends to the view that nothing new can be effectively introduced until what exists has been destroyed entirely.[29]

In considering irreligion as a cultural and social force, attention has been given to the form which the rejection of religion may take, the range of items rejected and the setting and source of the rejection. Throughout this discussion irreligion has been treated as a conscious process, a deliberate and intentional act or acts aimed at demonstrating that the claims of religion are denied. It is now necessary to consider the possibility that irreligion may exist as an unconscious or unrealised phenomenon, or possibly in some other way as a 'hidden' element in social life. The very posing of such a question suggests that people might be 'irreligious without knowing it' or alternatively that they might be consciously religious while being subconsciously irreligious. It has long been known that human behaviour can be understood in meaningful terms even when originating from a level other than that of consciousness. Such behaviour is not, however, the main concern of sociologists, although they cannot afford to ignore its existence. In order to cater for the possibility of a subconscious, or at least not fully conscious, rejection of religion, it is necessary to introduce the concept of latent irreligion. There are a variety of circumstances in which the irreligious response might take a latent form. It could be that the realisation that one possesses a tendency to reject religion is so painful that the realisation is repressed. Alternatively, it could be that the irreligious response is not brought into consciousness because it is not needed. A thoroughly secularised person finds religion to be so irrelevant to his daily life that he is not even conscious of the fact that he has rejected it. In such situations the latent response may well become manifest if the individual is forced to come face to face with religion in the form of a social or cultural reality. The experience of compulsory church parades in the Army appears to be the sort of experience which is capable of rendering manifest a latent irreligiosity.[80]

Finally, there is another form of irreligion which may have affinities with irreligion in its latent form. This is covert irreligion. In this case there is little doubt that the individual is fully conscious of his own irreligiousness but he refrains from proclaiming it, with the result that other people are unaware of his true position. There have clearly been many instances in the recent past when individuals have found it more prudent to hide their irreligion than to display it. Naturally enough, the extent of covert irreligion is very hard to estimate, but it is significant that Post mentions it as one of the main difficulties in the way of estimating the extent of infidelity in America at the beginning of the nineteenth century.[31]

Organised Irreligion

It is an odd but interesting fact that sociologists have tended to assume that irreligion is an individual phenomenon. References to atheists and agnostics in contemporary society clearly give the impression that such individuals are considered to be 'loners', lacking the mutual support for their beliefs which membership of an irreligious organisation could bestow. One can guess at some of the reasons why this should be. In the first place, the long tradition of associating religion with the integration of society has naturally created a predisposition to associate irreligion with a lack of integration and hence with individualism. In the second place, the Victorian caricature of the atheist as a depraved, friendless and tortured soul has left its mark on the collective consciousness of contemporary society (and equally upon contemporary sociology) in the form of a tendency to view his modern counterpart as an aggressively nonconforming and neurotic person who is alienated from his social milieu.[32] Lastly, the fact that irreligious organisations have only very infrequently organised themselves on the communal pattern associated with traditional religious bodies has caused sociologists either to overlook their existence altogether or to view them as only quasi-organisations. However, whatever importance should be attached to these factors as responsible for the persistence of this assumption, the assumption itself remains virtually unchallenged. Glock and Stark state that 'Atheists have no ethnic or organizational identity' and that 'typically . . . atheists and agnostics cannot be found in organized groups'.[33] Other studies clearly make the same assumption, if not so explicitly.

Whilst it may be the case in contemporary American society that atheists and agnostics lack 'visibility' as an organised group, it is not true, even there, that they lack any form of organisational identity.[34] Organisations catering for agnostics and atheists in America have existed in the recent past and still exist today; they include the American Association for the Advancement of Atheism, Freethinkers of America Inc., United Secularists of America, the Rationalist Association Inc., the American Rationalist Federation, the Freethought Society of America, the Secular Society of America, the American Ethical Union, the Humanists and the American Humanist Association at the national level and a multitude of other locally based groups and societies. Whilst it is true that some of these organisations have only a 'paper' identity, or act merely as a publishing house, this in itself hardly warrants their complete dismissal. If, in addition, attention is directed outside America to Britain and the Continent, then it becomes patently absurd to assume that the irreligious lack organisational identity.[35] It is therefore necessary to turn our attention to the phenomenon of organised irreligion and to consider its various forms and its relationship to its unorganised manifestations.

Irreligion appears in two major forms, either organised in social movements of protest, reform or propaganda, or unorganised, taking the form of an aggregate of unco-ordinated individual acts of hostility or indifference. While sociologists and psychologists are more likely to concentrate their attentions on the latter, historians have recognised the importance of the former. Both, however, are equally worthy of serious consideration by the sociologist, as is the general question of what determines which form predominates in any given social context. Also, the relationship between the two forms requires examination. Do they tend to appear side by side or are they alternative forms of the irreligious response? Do irreligious social movements recruit their members from an existing pool of irreligious isolates, or do they find their members among dissatisfied members of other religious organisations, the isolates preferring to remain outside any organisational framework? These and many other questions suggest themselves about the manner in which organised and unorganised irreligion are related.

A necessary first step before such questions can be examined is a discussion of the nature of irreligious organisations. Some of the prominent irreligious movements and organisations of the nineteenth and twentieth centuries will be considered in the next chapter, but first there is the problem of the character of irreligious organisations. It was noted above that whilst sociologists have tended to overlook the fact that irreligious organisations exist, what is also true is that when such organisations are noted they are invariably described as 'loose-knit', 'ineffective' or 'unsuccessful'. A substantial body of comment exists on the nature of irreligious organisation and it is all along these lines. Sperry deems humanists incapable of organising themselves into effective social groups, Budd feels that the nature of their ideology and the personality type they recruit render effective organisation impossible, and Demerath and Thiessen that irreligious groups are rendered precarious by their dissidence and illegitimacy.[36] Other observers have emphasised that the ineffectiveness of irreligious organisations stems from their fear of sectarianism and their consequent preference for loosely-knit and unformalised organisational structures.[37] Earlier irreligious movements no less than the contemporary ones have been characterised in the same way. Referring to free thought in America between 1820 and 1850, Post comments on the fact that 'freethinkers did not readily organize', whilst Warren, referring to a later period, observes that 'with the possible exception of the anarchists, freethinkers were among the most loosely-knit of any social group'.[38]

Clearly, there would appear to be something distinctive in the prevailing form of irreligious organisation, something which appears to observers as a 'loose-knit' structure and for which a variety of explanations have been offered. Understandably perhaps, there appears to be more agreement about what this distinctive characteristic is than about what causes it, or whether indeed it is an inevitable feature of irreligious movements. Over and above the description and explanation, however, it is possible to detect in most observers of this phenomenon an element of evaluation, an assessment of irreligious organisations as less than successful in relation to the criteria of the commentator himself. This fact is of interest because it clearly derives, at least in part, from an implicit comparison of irreligious organisations with religious organisations — a comparison which necessarily presents the irreligious organisations in an unfavourable light. Irreligious organisations are judged to be ineffectively organised because they lack certain characteristics of the traditional

41

religious denomination or sect, that is a definite and positive ideology, a centralised and formalised organisational structure, a clear system of authority, a formal procedure for resolving disputes, a *gemeinschaftlich* atmosphere and a permanent and loyal group of members.[39] Because these characteristics are lacking, such organisations are deemed (in comparison with churches) to fail in their efforts to influence effectively either society or the lives of their members. There are exceptions, but these are those organisations which most resemble the traditional model of a religious organisation, such as the positivist churches or the ethical societies. However, it is not clear how these bodies are judged to be any less effective than for example the Unitarian Church or the Bahai faith. It may be true that the majority of the more 'purely' irreligious organisations appear as pale shadows of effective social forces when compared with traditional religious bodies, but is this a reasonable comparison to make? Is it useful to judge rationalist and humanist groups in relation to Methodist chapels and Anglican churches and conclude that they are less 'closely-knit' than the latter? Not only is it possible that judgements by comparisons of this sort are mainly expressions of preference for the traditional religious model, but they may also serve to obscure the distinctive features of irreligious organisations. For, as we have seen, not all irreligious organisations are formed in an attempt to serve as substitutes for conventional churches, and because they have different aims from the churches it should not be surprising if they choose, or evolve, different organisational structures. One may indeed learn more from a comparison with political parties, pressure groups or general interest groups than from a comparison with church. After all, the irreligious response frequently includes a rejection of ecclesiasticism and sectarianism and so it should not be surprising if the irreligious choose to turn elsewhere than to the churches for their organisational models.

Once we escape from the constraint of considering the nature of irreligious organisations through the process of implicit comparisons with the churches, it is possible to understand their characteristics more fully. Most of these characteristics in fact stem from the break with tradition which these organisations represent. This break means that no one pattern of organisation is held sacred and no virtue is held to exist in standardisation. There exists therefore a variety of organisational forms.

At one extreme we find the substitutionists who are still attracted to the religious model. Comte's Religion of Humanity is the best example because it is modelled entirely on the traditional religious pattern, even including a full-blooded ecclesiastical system with pontiff and priesthood. The basic organisational unit is a local community church with its own minister, and its fundamental activities are religious in the traditional mould; Congreve's Church of Humanity fits this description. Moving one stage away from this model we find the ethical societies. These too are basically local community units and have an obvious kinship with the churches, but they have made more of a break with ecclesiasticism (at least in England), and have no official 'priesthood'. Nevertheless, the pattern of membership participation and activity is like that of a 'liberal' Christian denomination. There then comes a radical break between the substitutionists and the abolitionists, for the latter explicitly reject the traditional religious model as appropriate for their organisations. Irreligionists of this ilk are deeply suspicious of elaborate formal organisation which in any way resembles the church pattern. Partly theirs is a fear of authoritarianism arising out of their anti-clericalism, partly a fear that the individual's freedom of action and expression will be unnecessarily eroded and partly an intense dislike of the sanctimonious superiority and exclusiveness which are seen as the hallmarks of a sectarian outlook. This latter secto-phobia is an outstanding characteristic of many irreligious individuals and movements.[40] These individuals are more likely to turn to the political model than the religious for inspiration in building an organisational structure. The National Secular Society, for example, was a truly national organisation with local branches which were not autonomous and which held annual national conferences to formulate policy on the lines of the typical trade union structure. The branches were run on the usual democratic model of an elected committee with chairman, secretary and treasurer and periodic business meetings. In practice the N.S.S. was never composed entirely of abolitionists and the church model was never entirely lost sight of.

Other secular models have influenced the nature of irreligious organisations in addition to those of political parties and trade unions. In nineteenth-century England there was very real rivalry between the church and the pub.[41] Many secularists clearly saw the latter as a more appealing model for their organisations than the churches or chapels. Certainly some secular societies seem to have had more of the characteristics of working men's clubs than of the middle-class churches. In general, however, the leaders of the model were strongly opposed to activities which might make it harder to claim that secularists were thoroughly respectable, and the club model did not prevail. On the other hand mechanics' institutes had played an important part in educating the leaders of the nineteenth-century urban working class, and the atmosphere of earnest endeavour and self-improvement which surrounded them could be detected in some secularist meetings.

Of more significance than whether the organisational model is a religious or a secular one is whether it is a communal or an associational one. The church or chapel model, together with the club, all emphasise the functions which membership fulfils for the member; in this sense the organisations are orientated internally to their members. The trade union branch or the learned society on the other hand emphasise the functions they fulfil for society and are oriented externally toward some aspect of their 'environment'. Very different organisational consequences follow depending on whether primacy is attached to fulfilling the individual member's needs or those of society.

At the opposite end of the continuum from the *gemeinschaft-lich* nature of the church model of organisation there is the purely associational character of national organisations of individual members. The Rationalist Press Association is a good example of this kind of irreligious organisation, having a purely individual membership the majority of whom never meet another member of the association. There are annual conferences and annual general meetings, but only a very few of the members are able or willing to attend. They are thus bound together only through their subscription to a common journal and the general allegiance which membership implies. Many humanist movements have individual memberships of this kind in conjunction with a federation of local groups, and therefore they can be said to lie a little nearer the church end of the continuum. The associational style of organisation is often seen as appropriate for those bodies whose primary aim is propaganda or education. The point which requires to be emphasised, however, is that this latter form of organisation is not a 'less successful' form of organisation than the church model, or even necessarily a 'lower-order' form of organisation; it is principally a different form of organisation conceived to fulfil different ends or similar ends in a radically different environment. This point is glimpsed by Lenski, who describes the humanist organisation in America as having 'a very loose-knit form of organization geared to modern developments in the field of communication, with its members communicating as often through the mass media as through face-to-face contacts'.[42] Clearly the success of any irreligious or religious organisation can only be judged in terms of its stated goals.[43]

A consideration of the character of irreligious organisations is an appropriate point at which to turn away from the general analysis of irreligion and consider instead the individual and historical manifestations which have appeared in Britain and America during the last hundred years. This we turn to next, and in the following chapter we shall consider the secularist, positivist, ethical and humanist movements of the nineteenth and twentieth centuries. In discussing the origins, character, success and consequences of these movements it is hoped to provide illustrations of the analytic categories discussed above. At the same time it is hoped that some of the foregoing conceptualisation will contribute something new to our understanding of these movements.

3 Irreligious Movements in Britain and America during the Nineteenth and Twentieth Centuries

The Secularist Movement in Britain

Secularism was the pre-eminent irreligious movement of the nineteenth century. It not only predated both the positivist and Ethical Culture movements but also surpassed them in extent and exceeded them in its impact on contemporary society. Also unlike these other movements, Secularism was an intimate part of the radical tradition in political and social reform; whereas ethicists and positivists might feel obliged to engage in public service and press for reform because of their convictions, the secularists' views on religion were more likely to be an extension of the radicalism which they had already adopted in political matters. In this sense Secularism was a nineteenth-century inheritor of the tradition of total radicalism which had burst upon the European scene with the French Revolution.

The link between that revolution and mid-nineteenth-century Secularism is provided by the person of Thomas Paine, 'the virtual founder of modern democratic freethought in Great Britain and the States'.[1] The importance of Paine in sowing the seeds of anti-clerical, anti-theological and anti-Christian views can hardly be over-emphasised. In Britain, Paine's views were vigorously championed by Carlile, who, along with Robert Taylor (the 'Devil's Chaplain') and Henry Hetherington, struggled to establish a popular 'infidel' tradition. They did not establish an irreligious movement, but they did succeed, through their persistence and ready acceptance of 'martyrdom' in the 1820s and 1830s, in creating a basis for such a movement.

However, the secular movement in Britain stemmed only partly from the infidel tradition of Paine and Carlile. Robertson might claim Paine as the virtual founder of modern democratic free thought, but in reality he was only the co-founder of the secularist tradition in Britain, along with Robert Owen. Owen's contribution was more direct and constructive than Paine's, for Owenism provided the positive doctrines, and the Owenite movement provided the organisational basis, from which the secularist movement was created, and the man who created it was George Jacob Holyoake.

Holyoake was born at Birmingham on 13 April 1817. The son of a foundry worker, he himself worked as a tinner (attaching handles to lanterns) and as a whitesmith in a foundry. However, he was lucky enough to be able to attend classes at the Birmingham Mechanics' Institute and eventually, because of his impressive record, to become an instructor there, at the age of seventeen.[2] At this time Holyoake was strongly religious, but within a few years had become a convert to Owenism. This change of conviction caused Holyoake to lose his job and thus left him little choice but to devote himself full-time to the Owenite cause. He thus became a 'social missionary' for what was then known as the Society of Rational Religionists and lectured in Worcester and Sheffield. However, Holyoake's career in the Owenite movement was not due to last long, for the growth of the movement produced a reaction from the authorities and attempts were made to limit the revenue of the movement by prohibiting the collection of money by lay persons on Sundays. This forced the Central Board of the society to advise its missionaries to sign a statement to the effect that they were Protestant Christians and believers in the Gospel, a gesture which would have protected them from further interference by the authorities. Holyoake was among those Owenite missionaries who found this too much to stomach and was thus forced to resign. This first step in the direction of an explicit and avowedly anti-religious position was followed shortly afterwards by another, when he took over the editorship of the anti-theological 'Oracle of Reason', whose previous editor, Charles Southwell, had been imprisoned for blasphemy. The same fate soon overtook Holyoake as a consequence of a remark he made at a lecture in Cheltenham in 1841. The offending sentences (made in reply to a question) were as follows: 'I appeal to your heads and your pockets if we are not too poor to have a God. If poor men cost the state so much, they would be put, like officers, on half pay. I think that while our distress lasts it would be wise to do the same with the Deity.'[3]

In fact the trial and Holyoake's subsequent imprisonment did a great deal to make Holyoake known among radical opinion and to give him the aura of martyrdom which was to be a great asset in the forming of the secular movement. The period of the early 1840s was one dominated by legal prosecutions, and these stimulated the 'infidels' to form an Anti-Persecution Union to support the men and their families who were 'persecuted' for the expression of anti-religious views. By the end of the 1840s, however, the prosecutions had died away and the Owenite movement itself was rapidly collapsing. It was then that Holyoake made the first moves toward establishing a new movement; in McGee's words :

Under this combination of circumstances Holyoake cast about for new reformist opportunities. . . . Starting with the realization that in its best days the Owenite movement was essentially an ethical and social enterprise and accordingly was primarily constructive rather than critical in character, he moved on to the conception that free thought itself had a positive as well as a negative aspect-that in fact it could serve as the basis of a system of ethics under which the natural order of the freethinker would be the proper sphere of ethical goals, and the improvement of man's life here on earth by rational means the sum and substance of man's duty.[4]

Thus in the person of George Jacob Holyoake two traditions were to meet: the one - the infidel tradition, descended via Carlile and Paine from the French Revolution - was radical, democratic, republican, anti-clerical and anti-theological. The other, inherited directly from Robert Owen, was a naturalistic, ethical and social Utopian rationalism. Out of these two traditions he blended Secularism. The word 'secular' had first appeared in Holyoake's paper 'Reasoner' in 1851 and shortly afterwards Holyoake issued a statement of 'Principles and Aims' of a body he called the Central Secular Society. In this he set down the framework of a philosophical position which he was to modify but little over the next half-century. The principle was to be the 'recognition of the *Secular* sphere as the province of man' and the aims were :

1. To explain that science is the sole Providence of man. . .

2. To establish the proposition that Morals are independent of Christianity. . . .

3. To encourage men to trust Reason throughout, and to trust nothing that Reason does not establish. . . .

4. To teach men that the universal fair and open discussion of opinion is the highest guarantee of public truth. . . .

5. To claim for every man the fullest liberty of thought and action compatible with the possession of like liberty by every other person.

6. To maintain that, from the uncertainty as to whether the inequalities of human condition will be compensated for in another life - it is the business of intelligence to rectify them in this world; and consequently, that instead of indulging in speculative worship of supposed superior beings, a generous man will devote himself to the patient service of known *inferior* natures, and the mitigation of harsh destiny so that the ignorant may be enlightened and the low elevated.[5]

The influence of Owenism and Utilitarianism in the above statement is apparent enough. There is also a similarity with Comte's Positivism, but although Holyoake came to admire Comte's work greatly and was fond of quoting Comte's remark that 'nothing is destroyed until it is replaced', it does seem that Holyoake had worked out his position independently of Comte and from earlier sources.[6]

However, in many ways Holyoake's success in forming a new movement was based on his organisational rather than his intellectual skills. He had learned a good deal from his acquaintance with the Owenite and Chartist movements about the problems of organising radical opinion and, eschewing the tactics of mass agitation, he set about building a movement around the 'Reasoner' and regular provincial lecture tours. The basis of a movement began to emerge in 1851 and 1852 in London and the North-west; conferences in Manchester in May and June 1852 stimulated local societies in the North, while after much earlier activity the London Secular Society was formed in May 1853. Societies continued to grow throughout the 1850s except for short pauses in growth in 1854-5 and 1858-9.[7] Between 1851 and 1861 some sixty secularist groups appeared,[8] but it is hard to say exactly how many there were in existence at any one time. Many of these societies either developed out of, or were in fact organisationally identical with, Owenite Rational Societies. The largest number were in the North-west and the typical pattern was one where 'local societies grew and declined, were organised and suffered neglect, adopted new names and made new resolutions. The same people, by and large, figured in all of them.'[9]

By the turn of the decade the pattern changed. The radical tradition revived and with it the secular movement flourished; at the same time Holyoake's dominance over the movement waned as Charles Bradlaugh increasingly came to take over the leadership. As early as 1852-3 it had been apparent that there was no greater stimulus to the growth of the movement than clerical opposition to it, and this fact was capitalised on by Bradlaugh in a manner and to an extent that Holyoake could not have brought himself to do. Hence Bradlaugh's 'narrower, fiercer' leadership provoked more hostility, martyrdom and eventually success'.[10] Or as McGee explains it, opposition 'not only fired the Secularists to greater exertion on behalf of their programme, but helped familiarize the public with the rising secularist ideas; and the net result of all this was that the cause of Secularism was strengthened'.[11] It was on this rising tide that the National Secular Society was founded in 1866. Although there were always a number of secular societies which never affiliated to the National Secular Society (and there was for a while a rival British Secular Union[12]), for almost all of the history of the secular movement in Britain this remained the principal secular organisation.

A study of the rise and fall of support for the National Secular Society thus gives a reasonably accurate picture of the movement as a whole. In the year preceding the founding of the society there were approximately twenty-five local societies; by 1885 there were 102 branches of the N.S.S. alone, but by 1890 this had fallen back to sixty-two. This decline continued into the twentieth century and in 1946 there were only thirty-two branches.[13] What few figures there are for individual membership of the society suggest that they followed a similar pattern of rise and decline. All the evidence, in fact, points to a growth in the movement, with minor surges and lapses, up to about 1885 and then a decline, with similar ups and downs, from then to the present day.

How large and influential the movement actually was in its hey-day in the 1880s is hard to estimate. Like all movements of its kind the secularist movement seems to have had a highly mobile membership affiliated to what were often very ephemeral branches. Royle estimates the average group membership figure for the period 1841-61 as between twenty and sixty,[14] whilst McGee gives the individual membership of the N.S.S. in 1871 as 1,000 and in 1880 as 6,000." It is clear that in terms of formal membership it was a very small movement. However, the movement was rarely judged by the number of its formal adherents; clearly, if it had been, it would never have had the attention which it received from Victorian society. The strength of the movement lay much more in the number of those who sympathised either directly or indirectly with its aims, objects or predicament. Many witnesses testified to the large audiences which prominent secularist speakers, and especially Bradlaugh, were able to command, and in the 1860s the secularists in the North were able to organise massive outdoor gatherings at which up to 5,000 people attended.[16] It would be a mistake, however, to imagine that anything like a majority of those attending these meetings were committed secularists. As Royle observes, the occasions were as much recreational as anything else and comparable in some ways to a modern football match.[17] Holyoake himself claimed to have around 100,000 sympathisers but calculated that only between 20,000 and 30,000 held secularist views as 'deliberate convictions'.[18] Indeed Holyoake challenged Horace Mann's observation on the census results of 1851 that the 'masses of the working population' were 'unconscious secularists' on the grounds that to be a secularist one had consciously to consider issues and work out one's position before acting out one's convictions.[19]

Differing though the estimates of the strength and influence of the secularist movement in the nineteenth century were, all observers agreed that the bulk of its support was drawn from the working classes. It was this fact above all which accounted for the attention which the churches and the civil authorities devoted to what was only a minority movement. It was also something of a puzzle to the clergy of the time. The peripatetic clergyman Charles Davies on a visit to the South London Secular Society in the 1870s remarked that the room was full of genuine working men, 'great bearded fellows with the signs of labour on their horny hands',[20] whilst at a lecture of Bradlaugh's on the 'Existence of God' he noted that whilst the majority of the audience were 'of the tradesman and artisan class', there were also 'men-of-war's men in their naval costume, and real labourers and navvies in their working clothes; and I could not help asking myself the question, how is it that Mr Bradlaugh can get these people to pay fourpence and listen to an abstruse subject, while we cannot "compel them to come in" ?'[21]

Essentially, of course, the answer to Davies's query lay in the identification of the churches with the middle classes and 'respectable society'. There is a danger, however, in automatically assuming that, as a corollary to this, the secularist movement must have been a working-class movement, unless the latter term is given a clear definition. McGee claimed that 'Except for a few leaders, who, because of being, say, journalists or small shopkeepers, belonged to the lower middle-class, the Secularists were virtually all members of the working classes',[22] while Molesworth went so far as to say that 'Secularism was embraced by thousands and tens of thousands of the working classes'.[23] But both these statements are somewhat misleading, in the sense that the vast mass of the poor, and certainly Horace Mann's 'miserable denizens of courts and crowded alleys', never formed any real part of the membership of the movement. Horny-handed labourers such as those Davies saw at the South London Society meeting may have attended lectures, but evidence suggests that they did not form the bulk of the membership. These were drawn from the 'labour aristocracy' and small tradesmen, the 'mechanical classes', 'artisans and skilled workmen' and 'intelligent mechanics' of the time.[24] Royle[25] has estimated, from statistics taken from 'Reasoner', 'Investigator' and 'National Reformer' for the period 1841-61, that support for the movement was roughly comprised as follows :

- Men of the higher social classes   10%
- Newsagents, innkeepers, managers of temperance hotels, shopkeepers, etc.   *c. 30%*
- 'Artisans': cobblers, tailors, joiners, plumbers, hatters, hairdressers, etc. *c.* 25%
- Semi-skilled and unskilled (warehouseman, weaver, labourer) *c.* 35%

Royle also finds no evidence to suggest that support for Secularism can be identified in particular with any clearly identifiable economic or occupational groups, and concludes that although 'It might be thought that Secularism would be interpreted as an appeal to the skilled, independent, self-educated artisans or those in a state of social or economic desperation there is no real evidence for either of these'.[28] Indeed, because of this Royle argues that Secularism cut across social and economic boundaries and thus never really became a class movement.[27] The true secularist was to be distinguished more by the individualistic criteria of intelligence, energy and enthusiasm than by his membership of social or economic groupings. This may, however, be too extreme a reaction against the rather wild and loose identifications of Secularism with the working classes, because although the secularists themselves cannot be easily identified as being distinctly working-class or middle-class, it need not mean they may not have shared some common appreciation of their position on the frontier of these classes. Billington has argued that the ideology of Secularism is itself a blend of working-class collectivism and middle-class individualism and respectability, held together by a radical reformist outlook and anti-religious sentiment.[28] It may well have been the case that certain personal characteristics were essential to make a man a secularist but that he was much more likely to turn to Secularism if he came from a status group close to the 'great divide' between the working and middle classes.

The infidel tradition which Holyoake had inherited was strongly anti-clerical, less strongly anti-Christian (but anti-theological) and Deistical. Holyoake's major contribution was to develop Secularism as the 'practical side of scepticism' and thus to try to develop the movement on a constructive rather than a destructive basis. However, the constructive and destructive sides of Secularism were in a fundamental state of tension with one another. In 'working for secular improvements', whether they were in the fields of education or political and social reform, it was clearly tactically advisable to work with all those, regardless of their beliefs, who were prepared to assist. On the other hand the necessity to 'attack obstructive error' meant that one had a duty to attack such 'fellow workers' for their 'superstitious' beliefs. Nearly all secularists seem to have regarded both aims as necessary and desirable but there was no such unanimity about the priority to be accorded to each or, at a more practical level, about how the one was to be achieved without stultifying efforts to achieve the other. The clash between positive and negative outlooks seems to be a feature of all irreligious movements, but in the case of the British secular movement it combined with a clash of personalities and a struggle for leadership to produce a major schism in the movement. By intellect and temperament Holyoake was a 'constructor' and his complete dominance over the movement up to the 1860s meant that this was the emphasis most stressed at that time. Even in the 1850s, however, there had been those secularists who were critical of Holyoake's policy, and chief among these was Cooper who openly quarrelled with Holyoake over his policy of seeking common ground with Christians. In the late 1850s and early 1860s leadership of the discontented secularists was taken over by Bradlaugh - the arch-'destructor'. The clash between these two gradually became more acute and eventuated in public debates in 1870 when each presented their own policy for the movement. The Reverend Davies, commenting on the secularist schism, wrote : 'Secularists are divided into two schools of thought, as diametrically opposed to one another as Romanism and Protestantism. . . . The line of demarcation lies at the fundamental question "Does Secularism imply Atheism?" To which Mr Bradlaugh says "Yes" and Mr Holyoake, "No".[29]

In fact the conflict over the issue of atheism was really secondary to the basic conflict over tactics. By identifying the movement with atheism Bradlaugh was provoking hostility, sharpening the movement's identity, prompting opposition and thus providing the tang of martyrdom. Holyoake, by trying to remove the question of atheism to the sidelines, was hoping to gain a more respectable image for the movement and thus encourage the more 'liberal' of religious thinkers to join them. Holyoake hoped to keep the opposition to superstition separate from the implementing of a secularist programme of reform and in any case strongly believed that 'nothing would be destroyed until it was replaced'. Bradlaugh on the other hand emphasised the extent to which reform was impossible until theological error was removed. In the debates between these two great figures of the secularist movement one can find expressed all the principal arguments for the abolitionist and the substitutionist causes. As Bradlaugh in fact came to gain the ascendance in the movement, so 'abolitionism' or outright attack on religion came to be afeature of the movement, and has indeed remained so into the twentieth century. However, Bradlaugh's victory did not mean that all secularists were obliged to be atheists; it had always been the case that 'some secularists were Atheists, some were Pantheists, and some Theists',[30] and formally they were bound by their commitment to the principle that morals and conduct should be devoted to the promotion of man's welfare, not by their position on the 'theistic question'. In fact it seems unlikely that more than a minority of secularists were atheists, as Royle observes:

The difference between a Christian and a Deist was often a moral one, but that between the theist and the atheist was intellectual. It appears to have been easier for a man to lose his Christian faith than it was for him to become an Atheist. How many of those who took the first step went on to take the second cannot be calculated, but, considering the complexity of the arguments offered, it is not difficult to imagine that a considerable number did not make it.[31]

There remains the problem of identifying the forces which brought the secular movement into existence and of explaining why it should reach a pinnacle of success in the 1880s before a fairly consistent decline from that date to the present. We have already seen that the movement was built on the foundations both of a propagandist infidel tradition and on the Utopian reformist tradition of Owenism. The essential ingredient which was added to these traditions seems to have been a generalised anti-religious sentiment, sustained by a thoroughly secular world-view. As far as it is possible to date it, this ingredient appeared in the 1830s and 1840s when, as a result of clerical reaction, the 'main stream of plebeian radicalism was harshly anti-religious'.[32] Whilst previous movements of social protest had had a religious base, the spread of scepticism and a science-based rationalism now provided a non-religious base for such a protest; at the same time the reaction of the establishment supplied support for the argument that reform would not be achieved until organised religion was weakened. The organisational legacy of Owenism and Chartism, the notoriety and publicity provided by prosecutions for blasphemy and the character of George Jacob Holyoake provided the remaining ingredients.

Once the movement was in existence it was carried along by 'the strong dissatisfaction of politically and economically underprivileged groups [who] demanded a rational and convincing doctrine proving the necessity of radical social change'.[33] Support for the movement thus gained momentum during the second half of the century, stimulated both by the general radical agitation for social and political reform and from the growing weight of the cultural attack on traditional religion. Of these two trends the latter seems to have reached its apogee first, sometime in the late 1870s. Benn specifies 1877 as the year 'in which English rationalism reached its most intense expression . . . nearly every number of the "Fortnightly Review" during the second half of that year contained an attack . . . either on theology as a whole or on some generally accepted article of theological belief'.[34] After this date the cultural attack on religion slackened, largely it seems because it had been successful, although it was not until the 1880s that the effects of this change were felt in terms of the literature reaching the 'lower-strata of readers'. Benn suggests a variety of other factors which contributed to the waning of interest in theological criticism, and there seems little doubt that some of them at least, like the growing prejudice against science over vivisection, and the diversion of public interest into the Balkan problem, did help to divert attention from theological issues.

At the level of popular agitation the 1880s was the period of Bradlaugh's epic fight to take his seat in the House of Commons as the Member for Northampton and his associated battle to secure the right to affirm for non-Christians. The attendant furore and the enormous popularity of Bradlaugh at this time clearly contributed to the 'special energy' of the secularist movement during this period.[35] It was natural that interest would eventually wane after he took his seat, and within a few years he was forced to curtail his activities because of ill health. His death in 1891 emphasised the fact that the golden period of the movement was over.

The basic reason for the declining success of the movement from the 1890s onwards lies in the marked change in British society which had occurred in the previous half-century. The secular movement had gained much of its impetus from the 'harsh circumstances which had oppressed the working classes', and these had been somewhat mitigated by 1890. In addition the main force of social protest was now gathering under the banner of Socialism, and the secular movement had been fundamentally liberal from the very beginning. Holyoake regarded trade unions, like government, as a necessary evil, whilst Bradlaugh was an outspoken opponent of Socialism. Necessarily, therefore, the successful alliance which Bradlaugh had constructed between radical politics and radical free thought began to crumble. Nor could it any longer be promoted by a radical solidarity in the face of official 'persecution', as the battle for freedom of speech and expression and the right to affirm were largely over. The justice of secularisation had been accepted, at least in principle, and this very success made the impetus of the movement die away. Finally, the churches themselves had begun to respond both to the intellectual challenge of rational scepticism and secularism and the social challenge of an alienated working class. Although the fight against 'superstition' and the power of the churches was to continue well into the twentieth century, it was no longer supported by vigorous political agitation, nor were the positive principles of secularism so much in evidence.

In a broad sense the secular movement failed to achieve its aims. It did not become a mass movement but instead was always close to becoming a sect. Nevertheless, it did express the sentiments and aspirations of a large section of British society and thus was frequently able to draw upon a large body of sympathisers. It tapped the vigorous spring of anti-clericalism, the sense of moral injustice and hypocrisy and the simple desire for a better life here and now, and channelled these into an effective socio-political force for the secularisation of society. It was always an unstable mixture, and as a movement was beset by a rapidly changing membership and internal disputes, yet despite this it played a vital role in the construction of a reformed and secularised society.

Secularism in America

At the beginning of the nineteenth century the free-thought movement in America seemed, if anything, to be more favourably placed than its English counterpart. Deism and anti-Christian and anti-ecclesiastical sentiments had swept through America after the French Revolution and 'all the evidence points to a startling amount of irreligion and unbelief during this period.[36] Although there had been something of a reaction to the French Revolution, which impeded the growth of the movement just after the turn of the century, by the 1820s conditions once again favoured the 'infidels'. Unlike their brothers in blasphemy in Europe, the free-thinkers in America did not have to suffer persecution and imprisonment for the right to express their views through speech and the printed word. Although they certainly encountered hostility they could count upon the basic rights of freedom of the Press, speech and assembly, and of course they indirectly benefited from the safeguards of religious liberty in the American Constitution.[37] Also they did not have to contend with the powerful opposition of a state Church or an established aristocracy who felt the need of religion to legitimise their position. In addition to these advantages, there was, during the first half of the century, a steady influx of infidel refugees from Europe and especially from England who, anxious to escape persecution, strengthened the native free-thought movement. These advantages would suggest that the American movement might have developed with even greater vigour and success than the British one, but this was not to be.

At first the movement flourished, and by taking advantage of the freedom of the Press free-thought publications multiplied. Between 1825 and 1850 no less than twenty periodicals appeared, dedicated to the destruction of Christianity and 'superstition'.[38] New York was the main centre of these publishing activities and the leading journals were the 'Free Enquirer' and the 'Boston Investigator'.[39] Infidel societies were also started in the 1820s and flourished alongside the free-thought Press. The New York and Boston societies were the most active, but there were groups in nearly all the large towns of the North. Clearly most of the infidels' support came from the urban centres, as most of their members were to be found among lower-class radicals, 'petty tradesmen and working men',[40] although, as was the case in England, there were a few well-to-do 'reformers' who were prepared, if not actively to join the infidels, at least to finance them. Post describes the social context in which these infidel societies arose as follows:

> Part and parcel of the Jacksonian Democracy were the discontented, underprivileged workingmen who agitated in favor of political and social equality. The growth of manufacturing after the War of 1812, the domination of the means of production by the merchant-capitalist, the expansion of the market, and the efforts to reduce the cost of production went into the creation of an urban proletariat, awakening to the necessity of organization for self-preservation. It was among this class that freethought societies first appeared in New York during the 1820s.[41]

The tone of these societies Post dubs as 'crude', and certainly the periodicals were direct enough; the 'Boston Investigator' demanded nothing less than the de-Christianisation of America and was violently anti-clerical in tone. But then the secularists in America had to contend with a phenomenon almost unknown to their British counterparts of this period - a vigorous Christian anti-clerical movement. In fact during the 1820s the Christian anti-clericals had more periodicals in circulation that the freethinkers - a fact which made it that much harder for the real infidels to mobilise support and which may account for their excessive crudity of approach. Nevertheless, they did succeed in spreading unbelief and scepticism among the urban working classes, and whilst it is difficult to estimate the real extent of infidelity at this time, the evidence suggests that the masses were awoken to an interest in free thought which had never been previously manifest.

They did not, however, develop an effective national organisation (though there were several thousand subscribers to infidel papers, the national societies never mustered more than a few hundred members at most) or a careful and comprehensive missionary system. They lacked the Owenite and Chartist heritage which was open to the English secularists, and above all they lacked a George Jacob Holyoake. Thus, when interest in free thought waned in the 1850s, the movement suffered a swift reversal of fortune. The external factors contributing to the turn of the tide against free thought after the mid-century are given by Post as 'the growing preoccupation with the anti-slavery struggle and the impending crisis of civil strife, the diversion of interest to spiritualism, and the replacement of infidelity by Catholicism as the great enemy of American Protestantism.[42]

After the Civil War the free-thought movement once again revived, but now the situation had changed. One way in which things had improved for the secularists was that they were now in a position to benefit from the success of the British secular movement. There is no doubt that the British movement affected Americans in the latter half of the century.[43] Bradlaugh made a particular impact and Holyoake's writings were 'published and largely read in the United States and must be considered to have had much influence in spreading secularism as an attitude of life'.[44] The free-thought press revived, with the 'Investigator' once again prominent, but almost every large centre of population had its own journal. Local societies sprang up throughout the country from 1860 onwards and some of them became quite large. The New York State Freethinkers Association had 2,500 people present at its inauguration in 1877 and a decade later had members throughout the country.[45] However, attempts to form genuine and effective national organisations were still abortive, an unsuccessful attempt to form an Infidel Association of the United States being followed by an only slightly more successful American Secular Union.[46] Thus, although the infidel associations gained a certain amount of notoriety during the 1870s and 1880s and indeed became, for a while, the great national bogey until replaced by the anarchist and the Communist, they never had the impact as a propaganda or political pressure group which the secularists in England achieved. The one exception to this was the agitation over the separation of Church and State in the 1870s, when a move to turn America into a theocratic state provided secularists with an obvious political platform. The National Liberal League, which was established in 1876, was intended to accomplish the total separation of Church and State. Although many religious people supported the aims of the League, it was taken over almost completely by the free-thinkers and so they did not participate.[47] Eventually the League collapsed in 1884 owing to internal dissension over the question of censorship.[48]

Warren concludes that up to the period of the outbreak of the First World War, the popular free-thought movement in America never managed to make the breakthrough into respectability and indeed was never more than a 'considerable nuisance problem to the orthodox'. On the other hand its efforts were not entirely in vain:

> Thousands did hear its message and were comforted that they were not alone, that they were members of a larger brotherhood working toward a common end. How many great and little people read and were influenced by freethought literature will never be known, but undoubtedly the tremendous outpouring of atheist and other anti-religious tracts and periodicals did leave a residue in many minds.[49]

In attempting to assess why the American secularists had so little success, it is pertinent to quote from Warren:

The United States was one of the most secular nations in the world and that, in part, explains the relative weakness of the secularist movement. On the whole, there was no restriction on the practice of any religious faith. The existence of this religious liberty made it unnecessary for people to join together in remonstrances against governmental suppression. Secularists, therefore, did not have an issue powerful enough to elicit widespread support. . . . Most Americans simply took the question of separation of Church and State for granted. ... In this country, unlike elsewhere, it was not considered essential to destroy the power of the church in order to achieve enlightened reforms. The fight against the church had no place in the strategy of general reform; one was not contingent on the other.[50]

Thus, ironically enough, it was the very same conditions which appeared to favour the growth of secularism in America which in fact worked against a strong and influential movement. One feels that in the long run the secularists would have benefited from the sort of official persecution and opposition which they experienced in Britain, and they would certainly have benefited from the existence of a state Church in that there would then have been a real possibility of uniting radical, political and theological opinion.

The Positivist Movement and the Religion of Humanity

The nineteenth century is rightly known as a period of irreligious enlightenment, a time when the foundations of traditional faiths were well and truly shaken and many a fine edifice was seen to crumble. What is also true is that it was a period of religious reconstruction, and alongside the collapse of formerly imposing mansions new and less impressive houses were being built, in many cases using the rubble from the old. The century of Marx and Darwin, of Secularism, agnosticism and the higher criticism, was also the century of Joseph Smith and the Church of the Latter-Day Saints, Mary Baker Eddy and Christian Science, and Auguste Comte and the Religion of Humanity. Everywhere the old religions were tried and found wanting and there was a general feeling among enlightened opinion that they would not survive. There was no unanimity, however, over the appropriate reaction to the impending end of religion as it had traditionally been experienced. For some, and this included the secularists and rationalists in particular, this was an occasion for rejoicing, since, on the whole, religion was judged to have been a barrier to the progress and welfare of mankind. Thus, its end was not only to be applauded, it was to be hastened. For many others, however, the death of the old faiths was a serious, if not sad, occasion and this despite the fact that they were recognised to be false. True or false, the old faiths were considered to have fulfilled personal and social functions of great importance and a totally religionless future could only be envisaged with grave apprehension. Given that a sudden resurgence of the old faith was unlikely, there were only two choices open to those who took this view: either the old faith must be rejuvenated or it must be replaced by a new faith. Hence the age of irreligion was also the era of experimentation with new religions or substitutes for religion, as well as the period of strenuous attempts at religious reform. In general, the circumstances in Britain and America tended to favour the proponents of religious reform rather than the experimenters with new religions or quasi-religions, but in France the situation was reversed.

The anarchy and horrors of the French Revolution had served to warn large sections of French opinion against the dangers of irreligion, whilst the massive immobility of the Catholic Church made religious reform a somewhat forlorn hope. Thus it was in France more than anywhere else that the nineteenth century was marked by a 'vigorous proliferation of substitutes for the Christian faith . . . new creeds with new deities, new churches and rites, new concepts of immortality'.[81] Among these new creeds were several which had a marked social emphasis, and outstanding among these was Auguste Comte's Religion of Humanity.

Auguste Comte, founder of Positivism, father of sociology and originator and self-styled high priest of the Religion of Humanity, has by convention been treated as having two personas. On the one hand he is treated as a serious-minded philosopher who during the early part of his career developed his 'positive philosophy' and made valuable contributions to the theory of social science. On the other hand he is regarded during the latter part of his career as having 'gone a bit fanatic'[52] as a result of his infatuation with Clothilde de Vaux and developed an elaborate and comprehensive religion which, surrounded by 'an irresistible air of ridicule', signified the 'melancholy decadence of a great intellect'.[53] Clearly, Comte's activities as religious inventor and prophet have been a continuous source of embarrassment to all those thinkers who have been impressed by his philosophy and social theory (with the exception of the small band who embraced his religion as well). Bryson has even suggested that the attention given to the Religion of Humanity was one reason why 'sociology got off on the wrong foot in England'.[54] There is therefore a good reason for wishing to divorce his two careers and for stating extenuating circumstances for his latter 'aberrations'. However, not only is this practice rather unfair to Comte himself, who clearly saw his life's work as a unity, but it is also unfair to those who accepted the Religion of Humanity, who were far from being eccentrics or cranks. Comte recognised that if a new religion was to find acceptance in place of the old, it must be in tune with the modern world, which meant essentially that it must be in accord with science. In the first part of his life, therefore, a 'new Aristotle', he set about transforming science into philosophy; whilst in the second, a 'new St Paul', he set about transforming philosophy into religion.[55] The overall aim was the same for both parts of his life's work - the reconciliation of science and religion, with philosophy providing the link between them.

In essence, the Religion of Humanity was simple enough. There was no supernatural deity, no after-life, no immortality; all the beliefs which science could not support were swept away. To this extent Comte was in accord with the irreligious enlightenment of his age. However, this was only the starting-point, for Gomte went on to construct a new religion on this positivistic basis. The new deity was Humanity, renamed 'the Great Being', a deity that definitely existed and was as worthy of worship as any of the gods of the past. Worship of this deity was not to be separate from life, but rather everyday life itself would become religious as all thoughts are directed to Humanity, all affections focused on her and all actions in her interest. Love is to be the basis of all moral action and selfishness will be overcome by the moral influence stemming from the worship of Humanity. The objective immortality of Christianity is to be replaced by a subjective immortality in the minds of subsequent generations kept alive through special ceremonies to commemorate the dead. All spheres of social life will be subject to the overriding demands of religion in the construction of what in effect was to be a positivist theocratic Utopia. This much might well have commended itself to many of Comte's contemporaries, but Comte went on to develop his new religion down to the minutest detail, and it is here that one is conscious of Mill's 'air of ridicule'. There was to be a hierarchy of priests, all trained in medicine and science, responsible to Comte himself as high priest and exercising extensive temporal power. There was a comprehensive system of festivals, ceremonials and rites of passage, celebrating a wide variety of social relationships and personal states. The individual, for example, would be involved in no less than nine 'social sacraments' during his life, starting with Presentation (at birth), Initiation (age 14), Admission (age 21), Destination (age 28), Marriage, Maturity (age 42), Retirement (age 63), Transformation (at the approach of death) and ending with Incorporation seven years after death. There was a special calendar with thirteen months, each named after great men like Aristotle and Archimedes and containing a multitude of feast days and fast days. There were even specified shrines and pilgrimages for the devout follower of the Religion of Humanity. It is perhaps small wonder that Comte's plan to convert first Europe, then Russia, the Mohammedans, the Hindus and the Africans came to nothing, nor that in its fully developed form it was never practised anywhere.[56] Nevertheless, the Religion of Humanity did gain followers and converts both within and beyond the borders of Europe and, unlike the majority of substitute religions created in France at this time, it survived into the twentieth century. In fact positivist movements of some kind existed for a while, apart from France, in Hungary, Sweden, England, Argentina, Chile, India and Brazil, where it was first the official philosophy of the republican revolution and later virtually a state religion.[57]

Organised Positivism and the Religion of Humanity in England

That Comte's rather painfully contrived religion should have flourished in France for as long as two generations is on the face of it surprising enough, but that it should have flourished in England, if only briefly, amounts to a 'tour de force'.[58] That it was able to do so was largely due to the high quality of the converts made and thus to the disproportionate influence which they exerted. Chief among these were Richard Congreve (1818–99), tutor at Wadham College, Oxford, and three of his students, all close friends, Edward Spencer Beesly, John Henry Bridges and Frederic Harrison. These four did more than anyone else to spread the positivist message in England, being responsible for the first English translations of Comte's 'General View of the Positive Philosophy', 'Positive Polity' and the 'Catechism'. Congreve resigned his fellowship at Wadham in 1854 in order to devote himself full-time to the mastery and practice of the Comtean philosophy and religion and in 1867 founded a Positivist Society in London.[59] The positivist movement in England grew from this beginning, gaining in adherents until 1899, whereafter it rapidly declined.[60]

One of the difficulties in the way of an accurate estimate of the extent of the influence of Positivism and the Religion of Humanity in England at this time is that of determining the boundaries of the movement. Royden Harrison has suggested that three varieties of adherence to Positivism can be distinguished.

The first is the 'broad tendency' which treats Positivism as a generally influential tendency of mind, including respect for free inquiry, scepticism about beliefs which are not supported by evidence, respect for science and the like.[61] Clearly, many people would fall into this category who had no direct affiliation with Positivism as an organised movement, and indeed the main critics of Comte, such as Mill, Huxley and Spencer, would fall into this category. The second variety of adherence is through the positivist 'school'. This refers to that definite group of people whose views were based directly on the teachings of Comte and who saw it as their duty both to apply and to disseminate those teachings. Beesly, Harrison and Bridges were the principal figures in the school. Thirdly and lastly, there were the adherents who comprised the 'church' and who were primarily occupied with instituting Comte's elaborate secular religion, the principal figure here being that of Congreve. Clearly, Positivism as a 'broad tendency' was far more extensive than the positivist 'school', which in turn had more adherents of one sort or another than the 'church'. However, some people defy categorisation in these terms as their involvement with Positivism changed over time. Indeed, although Harrison's suggested varieties of Positivism have the merit of highlighting the problem of drawing boundaries around the movement, they are open to criticism. What Harrison calls the 'broad tendency' of Positivism, Simon has called Scientism, restricting the former term to 'the doctrine founded by Auguste Comte'.[62] In addition, the distinction between 'school' and 'church' is somewhat forced as the split between Congreve and his former pupils is not so easily summarised in these terms.

The positivist schism of 1877-8 was in fact a complicated affair, involving both the French and English communities, and was caused by 'a complex combination of doctrinal convictions and personal inadequacies, misunderstandings and incompatibilities'.[63] Central to the conflict was Harrison's feeling that Congreve's action in establishing a Church of Humanity was premature. Although both were committed to converting England to the worship of Humanity, Harrison felt that a significant proportion of the population had to be educated in the positivist philosophy before the practice of the religion could be implemented. To form a church when this philosophy was hardly known outside a small educated elite was necessarily to create a sect. Gongreve, on the other hand, had become more and more preoccupied with the devotional and ritualistic aspects of Comte's teaching, and had been busy preparing himself for the positivist priesthood. The split was attended by all the bitterness traditionally associated with religious schism, and for forty years the two groups went their own way, finally being reunited in 1916 after Congreve's death. It would be wrong, however, to view Harrison, Beesly and Bridges as having turned their backs on the religious aspects of Comte's teaching, for although they denied ritual the emphasis which Congreve accorded it, they too celebrated the Religion of Humanity. Indeed, the distinction seems to have been more that between 'high' and 'low' church than between a 'school' and a 'church'. The two groups were to be distinguished, however, by their degree of involvement in secular affairs, the Harrisonians being extremely active in many spheres of social, political and economic life. In this respect they played a crucial role in gaining legal recognition for trade unions, and in the feminist movement.

The positivist movement in England was never very large and in institutional terms it achieved very little success: in McGee's words, it 'made small headway in the nineteenth century, and in the twentieth declined most pitifully'.[64] The high-water mark of the movement was the last two decades of the nineteenth century, and in 1898 there were nine centres throughout the country. Groups owing some allegiance to Congreve existed in Birmingham, Liverpool, Newcastle, Leicester, Sunderland, Batley and West Hartlepool, whilst the Harrisonians had satellite groups in North London and Manchester.[65] The total number of adherents McGee estimates to have been numbered in hundreds rather than thousands, while Simon places the total of adherents in France and England combined at not more than two thousand.[66] This tiny movement was short-lived, for although it lingered on well into the twentieth century - the last positivist church closing in Liverpool at the end of the Second World War - it ceased to be an effective social movement shortly after the turn of the century. The questions which naturally arise out of a consideration of the fortunes of organised Positivism are, why did the movement flourish at all? and, having flourished, why was its death so sudden ?

That Comte's thought should have gained a certain popularity in France after the middle of the century is to some degree understandable in view of the intellectual and social temper of the times, although the reasons for its popularity in England are somewhat less obvious. What is more in need of explanation is why people in both countries were prepared to become active followers of the Religion of Humanity. Most of the converts in both countries seem to have been drawn from the 'educated middle class' and to have contained a high proportion of professional people.[67] The leaders in both countries were academics, and although there were some manual workers and craftsmen among the rank and file in France, prominent groups were doctors, civil servants, Army officers, lawyers, engineers and teachers.[68] In England, the membership was drawn largely from 'university professors and other scholars, students, physicians, attorneys *(sic)* and professional people in general'.[69] Simon writes that 'the general impression one forms of the membership is of a serious, middlebrow, rather inbred group, making up in zeal what they lacked in the way of finances and facilities'.[70] McGee argues that the appeal which the Religion of Humanity made to such people in England was that 'it offered a settlement of the great issues of the day in conciliatory terms'[71] - these 'great issues' being such conflicts as those between religion and science, capital and labour, Socialism and private property and imperialists and internationalists.[72] On these issues, Positivism offered solutions which were in themselves neither merely conservative nor radical and thus could appeal to those with liberal, moderate opinions. However, such an appeal could not last and:

> The Positivist Movement subsequently declined because in the late nineteenth and early twentieth centuries, the warring factions, though perhaps in most cases not paying much attention to the Positivists, found their way to a series of compromises, which in large measure brought this conflict to an end.[73]

This argument seems most convincing in relation to the 'great issue' of the conflict between religion and science. For although the positivist teachings on the other issues may have been influential in a few instances, they were not as generally known or as widely emphasised as the fundamental claim that Comte had reconciled 'ancient faith and modern science'.[74] At a time when the supporters of science and religion were answering the call to arms, when the battle lines were being sharply drawn and the sounds of skirmishing could be heard, the positivists refused to fight for either side. They believed that the Religion of Humanity rendered any such conflict unnecessary, since it was 'a religion which was not only scientific but which afforded an opportunity for science itself to become religious by concentrating its energies upon human welfare'.[75]

Such an argument must have had an appeal for those who, recognising merit in the claims of both of the protagonists, were therefore embarrassed by the conflict. For such people, the Religion of Humanity offered a refuge from the 'impossibilities' of traditional religion which avoided the 'mere negations' of the secularists and rationalists. In this sense it constituted one of the first compromises in what was to be a long line of attempted 'reconciliations' between science and religion.[76] Clearly those people who were most likely to feel a need for such a refuge were those whose education meant that they were in a position to appreciate the claims of science and the weaknesses of conventional doctrine and yet, because of temperament or social status, could not take the road to simple irreligion.[77] Indeed, the question of temperament seems to have been a crucial factor in determining whether the refugees from orthodox supernatural religion became worshippers of Humanity or joined the ranks of the secularists. As both groups rejected supernaturalism in all forms, the difference between them lay in the acceptance or rejection of the need for a substitute natural religion. And on this issue one either did or did not feel the need for such a substitute. Quin, who was a positivist, states quite clearly that although be became an 'unbeliever' he still wanted a 'religion', but he recognises that many unbelievers were not conscious of such a need.[78] Comte, of course, intended his religion to be a substitute for revealed religion and, in so far as the English and French positivist movement was successful, it seems to have been because that was exactly what it was.[79] At least, what evidence there is suggests that most of the recruits to the movement came from the religious rather than from the free-thinking ranks.[80] However, to imply that part of the appeal of the Religion of Humanity was that it was able to satisfy some of the individual needs which conventional religion had formerly satisfied for it adherents is not to suggest that at best it was no more than a poor substitute for the old faiths. The members of the Church of Humanity felt otherwise and Quin, when eventually forced to become a Catholic on the death of the positivist movement, clearly regarded this as second best.

There still remains the question of why the positivist movement should bloom briefly like a desert flower, and then rapidly wither away. Many contributory causes have been suggested, among them the death of the significant leaders of the movements in France and England at the turn of the century. The schism within the movement clearly damaged the movement's image severely and diverted energies from the important task of missionary work. In addition, the English positivists lacked the sort of first-rate secretarial assistance which Beatrice Webb was able to supply for the Fabians. They also lacked the support of the established intellectual community for their views, finding themselves attacked by such eminent figures as Mill, Ruskin, Spencer and Huxley. The latter in particular was known to 'fly at a Positivist with even more zeal than at a bishop'.[81]

Indeed, one of the major weaknesses of the movement was that it was open to criticism from all sides, from religious and non-religious quarters alike. As McGee observes :

Positivists were attacked by champions of religion because of their untiring praise of science. They were attacked by atheists and freethinkers for their incessant preaching of religion and scientists were frightened by their insistence that research must be subject to the discipline of an organized body of religious leaders.[82]

Clearly this was one of the inevitable penalties of occupying a 'conciliatory' position on the major issue of the day, but far more damaging were the criticisms of the content of positivist compromise rather than the criticisms of it for being a compromise. Huxley's jibe that the Religion of Humanity was no more than Catholicism minus Christianity expressed a popular view that what Positivism entailed was 'a kind of revival of Catholicism'.[83] Congreve only confirmed this view when he replied that Positivism was really Catholicism plus science. Benn helpfully suggests combining the two, so that Positivism is defined as Catholicism minus Christianity plus Science. However, it was a formula which pleased neither Catholics, Christians nor scientists, and the continued emphasis on the similarity with Catholicism aroused the suspicions of Protestants and secularists alike. Equally damaging was the growth of criticism of the scientific content of Comte's thought which, first formulated in the 1850s, was increasingly shown to be inadequate. Compromises need to be revised over time if they are to retain their character, and without the periodic revisions of the scientific and historical content of Comte's teaching it was bound to take on more and more of the characteristics of a religious doctrine and less and less of the characteristics of a scientific theory.

However, the positivist movement was first and foremost a religious movement and it was as a religion that it flourished and failed. Partly this was because it was too reminiscent of Catholicism for many Protestant Englishmen, but principally it was because it was an artificial creation. For many it was not religion at all, for others it was a religion without an Unknown or Unknowable which could be a focus of religious experience, and thus for such people it just could not function as a substitute for their traditional faith. As Bryson summarises it, 'to worship no God, yet to worship; to deny pomp and mystery, yet to talk of sacraments; to place the claims of a vague Humanity above the claims of England - all this was to mouth a religion which was no religion. It was neither fish, flesh, fowl, nor good red herring'.[84]

Nevertheless, the movement was able to make some impact on English society, and in fact, because of the quality of its supporters, it exerted an influence out of all proportion to its size. Mainly this influence was in stimulating a secular outlook and in facilitating certain social and political reforms. But it may also have played its part in helping Christianity in general to come to terms with science and to place a greater emphasis on the social mission rather than personal salvation.[85]

The Ethical Movement in America

The ethical movement in America was largely the product of one man, Felix Adler, who as the son of a rabbi was himself groomed to follow in his father's footsteps at the Temple Emanu-El in New York. However, part of his education involved him in a study of Kant under Hermann Cohen at Marburg where he came under the influence of neo-Kantian idealism. As a result he came to accept that the existence or non-existence of God and immortality could not be demonstrated and that morality could be established independently of any theological system. At the same time his period of study in Germany made him very aware of the moral problems present in contemporary society in such acute forms as the exploitation of women and of labour. These ideas became blended in Adler's mind with an intense moral righteousness which was part of his inheritance from a childhood of reform Judaism and the Emersonian vision of a religion of morality. Thus when he returned from Germany it was to find that his views on religion were too advanced even for the enlightened congregations of the Temple Emanu-El, for on 11 October 1873 he gave his one and only sermon, entitled 'The Judaism of the Future'.[86] A shocked audience signalled the end to any possibility of Felix succeeding his father in the rabbinate and thus, unwittingly, the conditions for the creation of an ethical movement were brought into existence. It was not, however, until three years later, in May 1876, that the first 'Society for Ethical Culture' was established in New York. By that time Adler had taken up an academic career and was a professor at Cornell University, but later for more than a quarter of a century he was professor of Social and Political Ethics in Columbia University.[87] The New York society flourished and by 1886 societies had also been established in Chicago, Philadelphia and St Louis.[88] Each of these early societies was autonomous, being run by a president and board of directors. Each had a regular appointed lecturer and public lectures were given each Sunday, although from time to time other eminent people would be invited to speak. A full statement of principles adopted by these societies reads as follows:

1. We believe that morality is independent of theology. We hold that the moral law is imposed upon us by our own rational nature and that its authority is absolute. We maintain that the moral life should be brought to the foreground in religion.

2. We affirm the need of a new statement of the ethical code of mankind. The formulations of duty which were given by the greatest religious teachers of the past are not sufficient for the changed conditions of modem society. We believe that moral problems have arisen in this industrial, democratic, scientific age, which require new and larger formulations of duty. Hence a new interest in ethical problems and a profounder study and discussion of them are demanded.

3. We regard it our duty as a Society for Ethical Culture, to engage in works of philanthropy on as large a scale as our means will allow. The ultimate purpose of such philanthropy should be the advancement of morality. When we contemplate the low moral condition of society and its indifference to moral aims, we feel called upon to do what we can to raise our fellow men to a higher plane of life and to awaken within them a deeper moral purpose.

4. We hold that the task of self-reform should go hand in hand with efforts to reform society. The mere fact of membership in an Ethical Society must be regarded as a tacit avowal of the desire to lead a wholly upright life and to aid in developing a higher type of manhood and womanhood than has been known in the past.

5. We believe that organization is indispensable to carrying out the aims of ethical culture and that this organization should be republican rather than monarchical. While we recognize the need of a public lecturer for the Society, we believe that the work of ethical culture in its broadest sense - the study, discussion, and the application of its principles, should be carried on as far as possible by the members themselves.

6. We agree that the greatest stress should be laid on the moral instruction of the young, to the end that in the pure hearts of children may be sown the seeds of a higher moral order, that early in life they may be impressed with the work and dignity of human existence, and that the work of social and individual perfection may be carried on with larger and nobler results from generation to generation.[89]

It is clear from these principles that the ethical movement's response to the religious crisis of the time was to enthrone morality in place of a dethroned theology. Dogmatism, ecclesiasticism and authoritarianism are all discarded and morality is revealed as the true essence of the religious spirit. The first function of these societies therefore was 'to disentangle moral ideas from religious doctrines, metaphysical systems, and ethical theories, and to make them an independent force in personal life and social relations'.[90] Thus released, the moral ideas were to become ideals interacting with reality through the medium of an ethical movement to achieve the goal of moral regeneration of individuals and of society as a whole. The primary means to this end were revealed as philanthropy and education, the 'revolutionary' solution being explicitly rejected by Adler.[91] In this respect the movement accurately reflected the attitudes of the age.

In part this can be seen as a reaction against the sterility and hypocrisy which are the concomitants of excessive creedalism in religion, reflecting a suspicion of theology which finds a responsive echo at all levels in society. In part also it can be seen as an effort to overcome the bigotry of sectarianism which so often accompanies an emphasis on creed. Part of the Adlerian vision was that ethics could provide a universal basis for fellowship for all those otherwise divided by creed. Hence:

> All ceremonial and formalism, prayer, and every form of ritualism was to be excluded, in order to exalt the movement above the strife of contending sects and parties and have it occupy 'that common ground where all may meet, believers and unbelievers, for purposes in themselves lofty and unquestioned by any'.[92]

In fact the movement did not succeed in avoiding formalism and ritual altogether, but it has maintained a consistent policy of neutrality in doctrinal matters, especially in relation to the question of belief in God. The following statement, made as recently as 1952, accurately reflects the position adopted by the movement through its history:

> Let me say at the outset that the Ethical Societies are not atheistic, and that they do not consider it their business to combat the old religions. They are not atheistic because they have no dogma at all, neither a theistic nor an atheistic one. It would not even be right to call the Ethical Movement as such 'agnostic', i.e. one that professes not to know whether there is a God or not. The Ethical Movement is simply not concerned with questions of metaphysics. It leaves it to its members to decide for themselves about their 'Weltanschauung'.[93]

In fact, it would appear that the membership has always included some atheists, agnostics and deists as well as a few orthodox theists. Naturally enough Adler himself and the movement were attacked as atheistic, a criticism which was deeply resented.

However, a stronger and more urgent reason for the need to embody the principle of the supremacy and autonomy of ethics in an ethical movement seems to have been the feeling that the moral impulse might die if left in the fatal embrace of religion. Like Comte, the early ethicists saw the destruction of conventional religion as inevitable and to an extent regrettable, though whilst he was concerned with the socially integrative and supportive role which religion performed, they were concerned with its relationship to morality. Thus while he worked to introduce a scientifically based religion to substitute for the discarded conventional one, the ethicists struggled to ensure that the ethical baby was not lost together with the theological bath-water. The very real fear was that since, by tradition, morality was sustained by religion, the collapse of religious faith would cause the abandonment of moral ideals. Adler himself spoke of morality, 'long accustomed to the watchful tutelage of faith',[94] losing this connection, and predicted dire consequences for society if no new champion of morality could be found. Eckstein, continuing this theme, refers to the 'danger' of linking ethical norms to dogma since a loss of faith in the latter may cause the former to be discarded.[95] In addition to this justification for the autonomy of ethics there was also a tendency to fall back on the presentation of morality as the one still point in a turning universe of scepticism, criticism and doubt, and the one basis on which all could agree. As Meyerhardt confidently expressed it in 1905, 'When beliefs and theories begin to crumble, the one way by which man may come forth scatheless from the struggle, is by holding fast to the simple landmarks of morality'.[96]

From the very beginning of the movement the Adlerian emphasis on 'deed not creed' meant that the ethical societies were deeply involved in social and public service activities. In 1877, immediately after the first society was formed in New York, a free kindergarten was started together with a district nursing service and a tenement-house building company. The society went on to open the 'Workingman's School' (later called the Ethical Culture School), together with a Sunday school and a 'Summer Home' for children.[97] This pattern of voluntary work in the fields of housing, education, general social welfare and politics was followed by the other societies and has remained a distinctive feature of the movement. Unlike much of the philanthropic work of the churches at this time, however, these activities were not accompanied by attempts at proselytisation. There may well have been some hope that these services would reflect to the credit of the movement, but 'there was no attempt to "convert" the people helped by Ethical Culture'.[98] This was not due so much to strong-mindedness on the part of the members of the societies as to the genuine belief that the good deed was its own justification. In fact, to begin with there was a general resistance to any form of proselytisation even outside a philanthropic context. New members had to be sponsored and women were not allowed to become members until 1893.[99] There was in addition a resistance to any efforts to formalise and institutionalise the activities of the societies, in particular toward efforts to 'professionalise' the leadership, since these characteristics, like that of aggressive proselytising, were associated in the members' minds with sectarianism. Nevertheless, circumstances demanded a certain degree of formalisation and changes were gradually introduced. What emerged toward the end of the century, however, was a pattern of activities which in its entirety resembled none of the existing denominations or faiths :

> If the Sunday meeting was reminiscent of the pulpit-centered service of Protestantism, the scholarly pursuits of the Leader were far more characteristic of Judaism. If the ethics classes were like Sunday schools, the practical works which its students undertook were more reminiscent of organized Jewish benevolence. If the form of the ceremonials at birth, marriage, or death seemed to echo tradition, the content was modem and humanistic.[100]

In time, however, even this pattern was to change as the movement adapted to the twentieth century.[101]

In 1893 the four existing ethical societies united to form the American Ethical Union and three years later they sent delegates to an International Ethical Congress at Zurich. As a result the International Union of Ethical Societies was formed.[102] The creation of this organisation indicated how far the seeds of ethical idealism had found fertile ground outside America.

Apart from the United States, England, Germany, Austria, Italy and Switzerland also sent representatives to that congress. A second congress, in 1912, drew delegates from as far afield as Argentina, China, Egypt, Haiti, the Dutch East Indies, Japan and India.[103] Outside America, however, the principal ethical movements were those in Europe, and the most significant of these was the ethical movement in England.

The Ethical Movement in England

The first British ethical society came into existence in 1886, some ten years after Adler had founded the first American society in New York. Part of the stimulus for the British society was itself American in origin, for in 1885 John Graham Brooks, an American sociologist, had distributed some pamphlets by William Salter, leader of the Chicago Ethical Society, among a group of young British philosophers. In was this group, which included J. H. Muirhead, Bernard Bosanquet and J. S. MacKenzie, which took the initiative to form a society in the following year.[104] This they did, however, only after another American, Stanton Coit -a colleague of Adler's - had stopped over in London on his way back from Germany and discussed with them the aims and principles of the American societies.[105] That Coit should have provided part of the impetus for the commencement of a British ethical movement was highly appropriate, for within a very few years he was to become an important part of that movement.[106] There were, however, indigenous influences which facilitated the emergence of organised Ethicism in England. One of these was the existence of the South Place Religious Society at South Place, Finsbury, London. This society, originally founded in 1793, had a unique tradition as a centre of liberal religious thought. Originally formed as a breakaway group from orthodox Calvinism, the society flourished first under the influence of the brilliant Unitarian W. J. Fox and then under the equally successful influence of the religious humanism of Moncure Conway.[107] By 1885, however, Conway was making preparations to retire and the society was seeking a new leader to start a new chapter in the religious evolution of the society. They found their leader in Stanton Coit and their chapter-heading was Ethical Culture.

77

The other important influence on the success of the emerging ethical movement was the existence of all small group known as the 'Fellowship of the New Life'. These people, anticipating the hippy communes of a century later, had expressed the intention of uniting 'for the purpose of common living, as far as possible on a communistic basis, realizing among themselves the higher life'.[108] Led by a Scottish philosopher called Thomas Davidson, they succeeded in establishing a centre for group living, held weekly meetings, issued a journal and sponsored a successful kindergarten. However, the fellowship itself was short-lived and its main importance lies in the fact that a split in its membership led more or less directly to the founding of the Fabian Society and the London Ethical Society,[109] many of the original members of the Ethical Society being members of the Fellowship of the New Life.[110] In addition to these two influences the nascent ethical movement was also assisted from the very beginning by the support of several eminent philosophers and academics.[111] By 1896 there were four London ethical societies combined to form the Union of Ethical Societies to which, by 1905, twenty-three official societies were affiliated.[112]

A special and distinctive part of the British ethical movement was the role played in it by Stanton Coit. As we have seen, Coit helped to provide a stimulus for the emergence of organised Ethicism in England before replacing Moncure Conway as the resident lecturer at South Place. At first it seemed that Coit was going to be as successful as Conway had been. His early lectures were well received and attendances increased. It was at his request that the society changed its name to the South Place Ethical Society.[113] However, just as the society was congratulating itself on having found such a successful replacement for Conway, a conflict arose between Coit and some of the membership which came to a head over the desirability of his being an *ex officio* member of all committees of the society. Although the membership was divided, Coit was defeated and as a result resigned on 1 January 1892.[114] He did, however, continue to be an invited speaker at South Place for several years. Nevertheless the ethical cause was still 'Coit's young bride',[115] and so he immediately took part in forming the West London Ethical Society. Here he was able to gather about him a group of enthusiastic supporters who were willing to give him the power and authority which had been denied him at South Place. In fact the society *was* Coit: he was its 'uncrowned king', occupying nearly all the offices in turn and always providing the initiative. As Spiller remarks, to 'conceive of the Society without him, would be even more confusing than to think of "Hamlet" with the Prince of Denmark left out - we would be almost entirely without a clue to the Society's development'.[116] The direction of this development was clearly indicated in 1914 when the society changed its name to the Ethical Church.

As a youth Coit had been impressed by Emerson's vision of a purely ethical religion, but unlike many others he had taken Emerson's reference to an ethical cultus involving 'a fraternity with assemblings, and holy days, with song and book, with brick and stone' very seriously indeed.[117] Although by the end of the century the ethical movement was well established on both sides of the Atlantic, very little cultus had developed. This deficiency Coit set out to remedy. In fact it was the general custom among the British ethical societies for the proceedings to open and close with a hymn and possibly a few words and for some instrumental music to be included. Coit went far beyond this token ceremonial, however, and by the time of the outbreak of the First World War the services at the Ethical Church in Bayswater were elaborate indeed. The following account is from Spiller:

> Some minutes before the Service begins, the organist plays a voluntary. On the speaker, the conductor, and the cantor (dressed in long black or red robes) entering, the congregation rises, the choir sings an introit, and the conductor then reads the Introductory Words. Then a canticle is chanted, the congregation resuming their seats, the conductor reads a Meditation, lasting some three minutes. This is followed by a two minutes period of silence.

Then, the congregation rising, the following statement of belief is intoned :

We believe —

> In the ideal of Truth, Beauty and
> Righteousness:
> It is the Principle of life,
> The benign and mighty Father of man's spirit,
> The God of reason, joy and love.
> Its service is perfect freedom,
> With promise of the lordship of man
> Over the forces of Nature,
> And over the wayward impulses
> of his own heart.

We believe-

> In those who have sacrificed
> For Truth, Beauty and Righteousness,
> And we look to them
> As saviours of the world
> From error, ugliness and sin.

We believe-

> In Man's Effort
> To establish the Ideal on earth;
> It will draw all nations
> Into everlasting brotherhood
> Of creative work.
> > The Ideal is Holy;
> > > Its servants are Holy;
> > > > Its Communion is Holy.

This is followed by an anthem, that by a lesson usually chosen and read by the speaker, that by a hymn (standing) and announcements, and that by an address of about 40 minutes duration. After this the collection is taken whilst the organist plays; an anthem follows; then an invitation is extended to visitors to join the Church fellowship; and, the congregation rising, a hymn is sung, Dismissory Words are said, the choir sings an Amen or Blessing, and the congregation disperses or individuals come forward to converse with the speaker or for general conversation. The service occupies altogether about an hour and a half.[118]

In addition, Coit had taken every opportunity to make the setting appropriate to the services and the inside of the church was richly adorned with portraits of the famous such as Milton, Tennyson and Mazzini, together with saints of the ethical movement such as Adler, Salter and Leslie Stephen. There were embroidered curtains, a bust of Pallas Athene, statues of Jesus Christ and Buddha, busts of Socrates and Marcus Aurelius, a marble altar, a porcelain statue of the Buddhist goddess Kwan-Yin and stained-glass windows containing representations of Joan of Arc, Elizabeth Fry and Florence Nightingale.[119] Coit himself was the inspiration for both the ceremonial and the adornment, the hymns, canticles, responses and anthems all being taken from his two-volume 'Social Worship'. In a sense he bears comparison with Comte as an 'inventor' of religious forms, if not of a complete religion, and, like Comte, he had a natural religion which he used as a model. For Comte this was Roman Catholicism, for Coit it was the Church of England. There, however, the similarity ends, for while Comte hoped to supplant the Roman Church with the Religion of Humanity, Coit hoped to transform the Anglican Church into a truly ethical Church. Coit's views were expressed in two books published in 1907 and 1908, 'National Idealism and a State Church' and 'National Idealism and the Book of Common Prayer', and clearly show the influence of Coleridge and Sir John Seeley. In these books Coit argues not only for the value of the ethical ideal and the importance of ethical ritual, but also for the necessity of a 'socialised' or 'socialistic' religion. Coit argues that the moral impulse derives from society itself and that some national organisation is required to stimulate, develop and apply these impulses. If there is no appropriate religious (or ethical) body capable of performing this function, then it will be taken over by the state itself. In Coit's eyes, however, there was one body ideally suited to play this role - the Established Anglican Church, the natural vehicle to represent the ideal face of the nation. All that was required was that theology should be replaced by science and philosophy with the consequent abandonment of supernatural beliefs, the Bible should be enlarged to include the ethical literature of all races, and the creeds and liturgy should be reinterpreted in ethical and psychological terms. Coit considered that the Broad Church party within the Church of England was imaginative and liberal enough to accept this reinterpretation

81

of orthodoxy and he clearly hoped that the Ethical Church would provide a pilot model to show the way. This aim is clearly expressed in the stated 'Principles and Methods' of the Ethical Church, where the intention to 'permeate all religious denominations with the foregoing principles and to influence them to revise their forms and teachings accordingly' is expressed. This was to be achieved by direct propaganda and by providing 'object-lessons in public worship adapted to modern needs'.[120]

Understandably Coit's views came in for a good deal of criticism ; many ethicists accused him of merely 'playing church' and ritualising an ethical society out of childishness and nostalgia.[121] Naturally enough the free-thinkers were annoyed by his opposition to disestablishment.[122] Coit's response was to attack the secularists for delaying the arrival of the 'ethicised' national Church by their unnecessary aggressiveness and failure to work for reform of the Established Church.[123] However, Coit's attempt to reform the Established Church from without failed; instead of expanding to become a truly national Church, it declined, and instead of abandoning theology and embracing an ethical ideal it turned in other directions. Partly his failure can be attributed to an American's natural tendency to overestimate the advantages of an established Church and to overlook its limitations, and partly to a failure to gauge correctly the psychology of the English churchgoer.[124] As it became increasingly obvious that the hoped-for reform of the Church of England was not going to occur, Coit turned his attention more and more to the nature and function of religious symbols and rituals and used the Ethical Church as a 'laboratory for experiments in the psychology of religion'.[125] Some of these views had already appeared in 'The Psychological Meaning of Churches' in 1907. At a more mundane level, Coit was active through the Ethical Church in helping to found several ethical societies, in various social and educational activities and in training a number of ethical leaders, several of whom played a significant part in the American ethical movement.[126] He died in 1944 and ten years after his death the Ethical Church was sold to the Roman Catholic Church.[127]

Coit's scheme may well appear in retrospect to be unrealistic (although his proposals for an ecumenical establishment sound highly topical), but it did have the merit of providing a clear and unequivocally distinctive purpose for the ethical movement. In particular, the significance given to ritual helped to ensure that the moral ideal remained in the centre of the stage, rather than merely playing a supporting role to a programme of philanthropic, social or semi-political action. From its very beginnings the ethical movement had spawned numerous schemes for social improvement, education or welfare and many of these quickly developed as autonomous or semi-autonomous projects retaining, at the most, tenuous links with the movement. This tendency was a continuous one, and although in one sense it was a sign of the effectiveness of the movement, it was also a source of weakness as able members were quickly lost to the movement proper. As Radest observes of the American movement, 'deed was rampant, often to the exclusion of creed and eventually to the exclusion of Ethical Culture as well'.[128] Thus, although Coit's vision of the role of the movement appeared to involve a return to some of the aspects of ecclesiasticism and sectarianism which the movement was originally founded to escape, if the gospel of social action was allowed to prevail unchallenged there was a danger that the distinctive nature of the movement would disappear altogether. This danger was apparent in the English movement's flirtation with the Labour movement at the turn of the century.[129]

The English ethical movement grew quite rapidly from its modest beginnings in 1896-7 until it reached its peak between 1905 and 1910, at which time there were over fifty societies in existence, of which seventeen were affiliated to the Ethical Union.[130] Altogether seventy-four ethical societies were started in Great Britain between 1886 and 1927. The numbers fell back slightly in 1912-13, and then rallied in 1914-16 before the steady decline during the twenties and thirties. By 1934 there were only ten societies still in existence and by 1954 this was down to four. The vast majority of these societies were in and around London and the Home Counties, although there were several Welsh societies for a brief period just after the turn of the century. One could say that when the South Place Ethical Society discussed changing its name to the South Place Humanist Society in 1969, the English ethical movement ceased to exist.

By contrast the American movement is still very much alive, with thirty societies and a membership of around 5,500 (in 1968). This compares with seven societies and a membership of 3,300 in 1930 and a membership of just over 2,000 at the turn of the century.[131] However, the American movement had hardly thrived during the twenties and thirties, and the end of the Second World War found it in a 'stagnant' position. Efforts were therefore made in 1946 to revitalise the movement and a working fund of $150,000 was raised. The American Ethical Union was resuscitated and new societies were formed in New Jersey and Washington, D.C. At the same time the Encampment for Citizenship scheme was inaugurated.[132] However, the movement which was thus brought to life differed not a little from that which was moribund at the end of the war. There was a greater concern with organisation and a more ready acceptance of bureaucracy. In addition there was a tendency toward smaller groups situated in suburban environments rather than the larger urban groups of previous decades. In many cases these groups were built around the demand for a liberal ethical alternative to the conventional Sunday schools, and in some cases 'adult activity was almost an afterthought'.[133] In general, these groups were primarily concerned with meeting the needs of their own members and thus more like the conventional church than the more outward-looking groups of former times. The educated, intelligent, self-sufficient people who had formerly constituted Adler's ethical elite were no longer available; instead the movement was recruiting middle-class people of modest circumstances who were as likely to be joining the movement for personal advice and help as much as for an opportunity to realise the ethical ideal in social service. Thus the demand for servicing the membership (and particularly its children) caused the emphasis to be placed on a pastoral service and led to the relationship between leader and members to approximate more than ever to that between a minister and his congregation.

If therefore the American ethical movement has continued to thrive even after the British movement is dead, this is largely because it no longer closely resembles the movement of pre-war days. In both countries, in fact, the tide had begun to turn against ethical idealism shortly after the beginning of the century, although organisational decline did not follow immediately. Two world wars and the rise of the social gospels of Marxism and Socialism together with anti-rationalist Freudian-ism created a climate hostile to the optimistic and individualistic teachings of the ethicists. At the same time the ethical message of 'deed not creed' no longer seemed novel in a climate of moderated creedalism and liberal religion. Internal inadequacies also helped to weaken the movement. In America the failure to create an effective national organisation clearly mitigated against the development of a large and effective social movement; in both countries persistent secto-phobia hampered efficient organisation and aggressive proselytising.

There is no doubt, however, that a major source of weakness for both movements was their ambiguous attitude toward their relationship with conventional religion. In general the movement was sympathetic toward religion and saw itself as doing the work of religion, yet it renounced that element which for most people was the very essence of religion, the belief in God. It could therefore only offer itself as a substitute for conventional religion for those people anxious to escape conventional doctrine or for those defining religion as essentially an ethical commitment. However, an inter-war and post-war falling away from religion caused the demand for such substitution to decline, and in Britain at least the moral was clear: 'Church membership and church attendance as social habits are in decline, and an alternative which too closely resembles this pattern is likely to share the disfavour'.[134] In America, however, these same habits did not go into a decline and so the emulation of the conventional religious model remained a real option. Thus it was that by the late 1950s the ethical movement in Britain had given way to an emerging humanist movement, whilst in America the ethical movement was increasingly taking on the characteristics of a church-like body.

Free Religion in America

Some of the difficulties in distinguishing between irreligion and radical, unorthodox or reformist religion encountered in Chapter 2 are well illustrated by the American nineteenth-century movement for free religion. This movement of religious liberalism was a 'secession' from the Christian camp and was quite deliberately discredited by the orthodox through being confused with secular anti-Christian or atheistic movements.[135] Yet the movement itself was a counter-attack upon scepticism on behalf of the religious values which the Christian churches appeared to be in no position to defend,[138] and as such it did blunt the edge of irreligious attack as well as make an appeal to the great group of the unchurched in the nineteenth century.[137] It was, nevertheless, sandwiched between orthodoxy and outright irreligion and had difficulty in maintaining its own distinctive ground.

The Free Religious Association was founded in 1867 by an ex-Unitarian minister called Francis Ellingwood. The basic idea of the association was 'the application of free thought to religious problems with the consequent emancipation of religious belief and life from allegiance to all authority save that of truth as determined by rational human intelligence'.[138] It was therefore fiercely anti-authoritarian and anti-ecclesiastical and sought to promote freedom of religious conscience in all spheres. Naturally it found some support from free-thinkers, but the majority of members were liberal Unitarians, Universalists, progressive Quakers and Jews.[139] There was no agreement on the content of religious belief but a general endorsement of the 'universality of the religious sentiment'.[140] Persons describes free religion as 'the theistic crust of late nineteenth-century humanism'.[141]

The Free Religious movement represents a significant minority cultural tradition in America and Britain. This is the liberal religious tradition which, eschewing the confines of the Christian tradition and Theism, places its faith in a universal and unconfined religious impulse. This tradition has been consciously continued in contemporary America by, among others, the religious humanists. The Fellowship of Religious Humanists was in fact modelled on the Free Religious Association and stands for much the same principles. In recent years this tradition has come to have increased official recognition as a legitimate component of the plural religious establishment in American society and is thus perhaps less unorthodox and radical than it once was.[142] Clearly there is little merit in forcing a sharp distinction between unorthodox radical religion and liberal irreligion, but one feels that in the case of contemporary America the Fellowship of Religious Humanists must be very close to this arbitrary line.

The Rationalist Press Association

The declining influence of the secular movement during the late 1880s made some secularists feel that the changing times required a corresponding change in the aims and methods of free-thought propaganda. Under Bradlaugh the secular movement had promoted the cause of Secularism side by side with radical politics, and the consistent policy of the 'National Reformer' had been 'Republican, Atheistic and Malthusian'. But now, the radical cause was itself split by the rising tide of Socialism, and those free-thinkers who had always felt concerned to advocate free thought for its own sake, and who indeed felt that the association with politics was a hindrance to successful free-thought propaganda, came into their own. These were the secularists who held:

> that the association of Freethought propaganda with political campaigns was a serious dissipation of missionary strength and who believed that ordinary men and women, though differing on matters of politics, were ready and eager to share in the debates upon the fundamental problems of religion, science, and philosophy hitherto conducted exclusively by the elect.[143]

As well as eschewing politics these secularists rejected the tactics of political agitation; they turned away from oratory, debates and mass meetings, which had been the secularists' stock-in-trade for so long, and turned instead to publishing. The secularists who did this were very clearly in the Holyoake mould (and indeed he was one of them) in that, enamoured of respectability, they were reacting as much from the 'tone' of previous secularist activities as from their recent lack of success. Thus they preferred to speak of Rationalism rather than Secularism and agnosticism rather than atheism, and in general 'The new Agnostics condescended to the old secularists. They recoiled from the old vulgarity, the poorly paid and pompous speakers, the ill-bred audiences'.[144] Whatever the real

87

combination of motives may have been, this group of men formed the Rationalist Press Association in 1899.[145]

The association was to fulfil a specialised function, which was to publish and distribute books which established publishers and booksellers were afraid or unwilling to handle because of their anti-religious associations. The immediate impetus to form the association was provided by Charles A. Watts, who, as printer and publisher, was responsible for the 'National Reformer' and for most of Charles Bradlaugh's books and pamphlets. Watts issued a 'publisher's circular' in 1885 in order to make contact with readers who wanted to buy the kind of heretical books not normally on sale. Then in 1889 he formed the R.P.A. as a company limited by guarantee, as a means of publishing and distributing such books. Members of the association who subscribed 5s. or more annually received books to the value of their subscriptions. By this means Watts succeeded in bypassing the unwilling booksellers. The association really came into its own in 1902 when Watts published paper-cover 6d. reprints of serious scientific works. In that year over 155,000 copies were sold from a list of eight titles which included Huxley, Haeckel and Matthew Arnold.[146] Even greater success was achieved in this direction by Watts's son, Frederick, who succeeded in selling over one million copies of books in the Thinker's Library series.

However, the association was more than just a successful book club. It was an organisation committed to the cause of Rationalism, defined as 'the mental attitude which unreservedly accepts the supremacy of reason and aims at establishing a system of philosophy and ethics verifiable by experience and independent of all arbitrary assumptions or authority'[5].[147] Thus the association's membership was not merely an indication of those who wished to study Rationalism, it was an indication of those who had 'zeal for the Rationalist movement'. The membership (and subscribers) had reached 556 by 1903, 2,150 by 1910, 3,015 by 1927, 3,802 by 1939 and then its highest peak (5,010) in 1947,[148] The number of members and subscribers then fell steadily from 1947 to 1957. In a sense the very success of the R.P.A. had helped to bring about this decline. Books of a 'heretical' character began to be published by many established firms and the large publishing empires embarked on the paperback revolution. Thus the demand for books published by the R.P.A. fell away and the association, in common with many small publishers, began to experience economic difficulties. By the 1950s it was experiencing both a decline in membership and a steep rise in costs. However, although the association had almost lost its publishing role, it still acted as a propaganda agency for Rationalism. It published the monthly 'Literary Guide' (now 'Humanist') and an annual, the 'Rationalist Annual' (now 'Question'), and organised conferences.

The Humanist Movements

The nineteenth century was the time of the irreligious reformation, when opposition to religion in many forms, but especially in the form of an aggressive and politically conscious militancy, was most apparent and most widespread. But when the new century dawned, the irreligious movements were clearly on the wane. Referring to London, Smith comments that 'after 1919 the heretical movements are hard to find'.[149] The movements did not disappear, nor did their philosophies die, but they became increasingly ignored. It was one of the fascinating contradictions of the Victorian age that it had been at the same time both very religious and very irreligious; now it seemed that both positions had begun to succumb to a muted and secularised indifference toward all religious questions. This change has led some commentators to assume that irreligion itself was a creation of the nineteenth century, a special feature of a unique historical situation, and now that that situation had passed, irreligion too would disappear.[150]

However, the position taken here is one which sees the irreligious response as an ever-present one in society (at least until such time as religion itself ceases to exist as a social phenomenon) and thus one which will always be taken up. It may well exist as a submerged or suppressed tradition and it will in many cases be a minority tradition, but it will always be there. Thus it does not seem likely that such a tradition would flower in one century and disappear in the next. It seems much more likely that it has changed its form in response to a changing social and cultural environment and to the changes in religion itself. This indeed is what has happened, and the change itself is well summarised as the 'humanist revolution'.[151]

The humanist movement in the contemporary world has taken over the mantle of the secularists and free-thinkers, and to a lesser extent the ethicists, as the principal propagandists of the irreligious response and the main political force for secularisation.

Humanism in America

Organised Humanism began to emerge in America in the late 1920s when a group called the Humanist Association, centred on the Meadville Theological Unitarian School at Chicago, was formed to launch a magazine entitled the 'New Humanist' They then renamed themselves the Humanist Press Association and tried to distribute pamphlets and books in addition to publishing the magazine. Many of the activists in this group were students studying for the Unitarian ministry who had been influenced by A. Eustace Haydon's humanistic interpretation of world religions.[152] This group did a great deal to promote the cause of Humanism when they published the 'Humanist Manifesto' in 1933. Much discussed, the manifesto helped to rally liberal, theological and humanistic opinion and stimulated a strong reaction from conservative theologians. The declaration itself was a frontal attack on orthodox theology in the name of religious humanism and stressed the danger of identifying the word 'religion' with 'doctrines and methods which have lost their significance and which are powerless to solve the problem of human living in the twentieth century'.[153] The manifesto attacked the notion of creation, rejected the traditional dualism of mind and body, upheld the theory of evolution, dismissed supernaturalism and defined religion merely as 'those actions, purposes, and experiences which are humanly significant'.[154] In 1941 the Humanist Press Association was reincorporated as the American Humanist Association. By the beginning of the 1950s the leadership of the association was passing from the professors of philosophy and ministers of liberal churches, who had been the signatories of the Manifesto, to secular humanists who, having no 'professional' interest in theology, were concerned to develop a programme of social action. By 1955 there were some twenty-five local chapters of the association supporting regular regional conferences.[155] By January 1962 the individual membership was in excess of 4,500, about one-tenth of whom were students; by 1968 the total membership had declined somewhat but the proportion of students had risen to one-fifth. (There were seventy-five local groups in 1962.)[156] About half the total membership was not connected with any local group.

Humanism in Britain

The editor of 'Humanist News' wrote of the formation of the British Humanist Association in 1963 that it was 'an event which can be said to signal the formation of the Humanist Movement in this country'.[157] However, he went on to qualify his statement by adding : 'As with the birth of all movements, there was something which went before. There were already humanist town and university societies and the sponsoring bodies, the E.U. and the R.P.A., had been reaching out to Humanism for some time.'[158]

In fact the formation of the British Humanist Association was a somewhat belated recognition of the reality of a national humanist movement, which had come into existence in the previous decade. The details surrounding the emergence of the humanist movement are less clear-cut than those for any of the movements already discussed because Humanism was not the 'creation' of any one man. Indeed as as 'idea-system' or 'attitude of mind' it is none too easy to delineate, as its popularity as a word has led to its use in many diverse contexts. All that can clearly be said is that, although its use in an irreligious context predates the middle 1950s, it was during those years that it became popular as a label for those who had turned their backs on traditional religion altogether. For some time both the ethical and rationalist movements had been suffering a reversal of fortunes, and propaganda in the names of these time-honoured banners drew little response. However, both the Ethical Union and the Rationalist Press Association found that advertising in the name of Humanism did produce a public response. For both organisations this discovery was very welcome, for by the middle 1950s the future of neither of them was any too assured. The Ethical Union had declined from its peak in 1905-6 when it had had twenty-six affiliated societies to a mere four at the end of 1954. The R.P.A. was in no happier position. Its total number of members and subscribers had fallen consistently for the previous seven years, forcing the management to conclude that 'demand for rationalist publications of the sort which formerly appealed has greatly diminished', and as a result the membership of the R.P.A. was no longer 'an economic unit'.[159]

Then in 1954 the Ethical Union embarked on a policy of trying to create new groups; this policy was successful and several new groups were formed in the following years, especially in the London and Home Counties region. However, these new groups owed comparatively little to the ethical tradition which had inspired the union itself. The 'new generation' of non-believers was not principally interested in philosophical and ethical issues and certainly was not attracted to the ceremony which had been a feature of the traditional ethical societies. They were interested in 'practical matters of fact in regard to things like education, delinquency and other matters of general social concern'.[160] By 1956-7 these new groups came to adopt the name 'humanist' to identify and describe their own practical and non-religious concern with the problems of living.

By this time too, the Rationalist Press Association had realised that there was a new generation of non-believers likely to be sympathetic to their aims, and in 1957 the association launched a large membership drive and made an intentional shift of emphasis from Rationalism toward Humanism. The 'Literary Guide' was renamed the 'Humanist' and announced that there would be a shift in editorial policy 'from the things we do not believe in, or condemn, to a positive affirmation of what we do believe in and are willing to support'.[161] As the editor observed, what people were worried about in the twentieth century was not the authorship of the Pentateuch but 'antiquated laws which hold up common-sense reforms in regard to divorce, euthanasia, abortion and so on'.[162] This campaign was very successful and removed the immediate threat to the continued existence of the association.

However, it now became apparent that the Ethical Union and the Rationalist Press Association were appealing to the same audience and in the same name - that of Humanism - and thus there developed a move to bring the two historically distinct traditions into some permanent association with one another. There were obstacles to a simple merger between the two organisations and difficulties arising from that proportion of their memberships which was still basically committed to the older ethical or rationalist position. Nevertheless, in 1963 the two organisations launched the British Humanist Association as a 'common front' body which was principally intended to avoid wasteful competition for members between the parent bodies and which took over all advertising, publicity and public relations. The new body was an immediate success. Launched in May 1963, the association had 824 members by the end of the year and had received approximately 4,000 inquiries over the eight months. Under the impetus created by the formation of this body the humanist movement continued to expand.[163]

The British Humanist Association was the focus for this expansion as most groups were affiliated to it and it had the major responsibility for the creation and maintenance of groups. At the individual level it provided a counselling service 'to help people face their difficulties and solve their personal problems', supplied a humanist funeral service and worked through the Humanist Housing Association to accommodate homeless old people.[164] At the social level the association acted directly to realise the humanist goal of fulfilled individuals and fulfilled societies. This it did by supporting social reforms 'in the general areas of the penal system and of civil liberties' and by working for the reform of the law relating to marriage, abortion, euthanasia and homosexuality.[165] It also acted as a pressure group to represent the interests of humanists in public affairs. In particular it tried to secure greater representation of humanist views in broadcasting and the Press, but it also presented memoranda to Royal Commissions and other national bodies.

In fact the British Humanist Association was not the first national humanist organisation.[166] For in December 1959 the University Humanist Federation was formed to consolidate the growth of Humanism in the universities which had occurred in the preceding two years. For several reasons the growth of Humanism in the universities had occurred somewhat earlier than that in the towns, and the initiative for a national organisation came from an Oxford undergraduate, A. F. M. Brierley. With support from the R.P.A. and the E.U. he succeeded in organising a conference in Birmingham in 1959. As a result the University Humanist Federation was brought into existence and by the time the British Humanist Association was formed it had seventeen affiliated societies.[167]

Humanism bears an obvious kinship with the other irreligious philosophies and styles of life which were its nineteenth-century forebears. Like Secularism, Humanism tends to see science and education as a kind of providence, regards the possibility of an other-worldly existence with complete scepticism and finds the purpose of life in the fulfilment of man's secular hopes in the present world. Like Ethicism it sees disinterested service of mankind as more moral than doing good for the purpose of gaining after-worldly rewards. It is, however, a fresh response to a changed socio-cultural environment and is thus not adequately presented as merely the continuation of the nineteenth-century tradition under a new name.[168]

For the secularists of the last century, evolution was principally a stick with which to beat scriptural religion and the notion of divine revelation. For the contemporary humanist, however, it is more a prop to support his basic structure of beliefs. Whether or not individual humanists accept the elaborated view of evolutionary humanism which Julian Huxley has presented, Humanism in Britain has clearly been influenced by his views.[169] The world-view of Humanism is based upon the picture of reality which science reveals, and central to this picture is the concept of evolution as 'a process in time that is self-transforming, irreversible, long enduring, and generates novelty, increasing variety, and higher degrees of organisation'.[170] It is this concept which provides the humanist with an image of the universe as monistic, impersonal and subject to change and an image of himself as related directly and indirectly to all forms of life and as the principal agent for further evolution on this planet. It is against this background that the possibility of progress is emphasised and the goal of self - and societal fulfilment are set. The emotional response contained in the humanist prescription for living is one of a ready acceptance of the real conditions of life, whilst the moral responsibility for all mankind which each man possesses is heavily underlined. Also contained in Humanism is a traditional irreligious concern for the democratic values of freedom of speech, civil liberties, pluralism and anti-authoritarianism. Governing the whole of the specific content of the humanist value-orientation there is a practical and confident attitude toward the problems of like which emphasises the claim that 'Humanism is a new way of life rather than a system of philosophy. Humanists may belong to different philosophical schools, but they are more concerned with changing the world than describing it.[171]

Unlike the other movements discussed in this chapter, the humanist movement is not one which can conveniently be discussed in terms of its origin, ideology, social significance, decline and consequence. For as yet it remains a vigorous social movement with at least as much future as it has past. There are signs that it might have passed its apogee as measured by the number of affiliated groups and individual members, but even this assumption may well prove false. Without the peculiar advantage of historical hindsight, therefore, it is necessary to make the most of the advantage of sociological insight.

What a study of the contemporary humanist movement in Britain reveals is a small movement, comprised very largely of professional people, particularly teachers, doctors and welfare workers and in which men outnumber the women and the young outnumber the old — a young movement which represents a respected and influential philosophical and moral tradition but yet one which lacks an unambiguous organisational ideology. Lacking the unifying mark which Adler set on Ethicism and Holyoake (later Bradlaugh) on Secularism, the humanist movement remained for some time undecided whether its principal role was propaganda, support and succour for the irreligious, acting as a pressure group for a disadvantaged minority, or some form of socio-political action aimed at bringing about the 'humanist society', or as a welfare agency. All these aims received some support from within the movement, but lack of resources, organisational exigencies and the need for an unambiguous public image meant that a single aim had to dominate. Eventually the decision was made in 1967 to concentrate efforts in the direction of a programme of socio-political action. However, by no means all humanists saw their commitment in these terms, and even those who did were not agreed on what the content of that programme should be. Thus the movement, as a social movement, still appears ineffective in attaining its own declared goals. However, it exercises an influence quite disproportionate to its size through the high status and prestige of many of its members and of the philosophical stance which it represents.

4 Irreligion and Society

Religion and Morality

There are various ways in which a discussion of irreligion tends to involve a discussion of religion and morality. In the first case a discussion of the boundaries of the phenomenon of religion as well as that of irreligion involves distinguishing morality from religion. This, as we have seen, is a special problem when considering those non-supernatural belief systems like Positivism, Ethical Culture and Humanism in which the moral or ethical issues are the primary ones. In the second place there is the whole question of the relationship between religion and morality. Assuming that we can distinguish between them, what is their relationship? This question involves irreligion mainly because of a traditional and widely asserted view that, since religion fosters morality, irreligion fosters immorality. This argument will be considered at some length in this chapter.

In theory there are several possible relationships between religion and morality.[1] Yinger outlines four of these: morality as an inseparable part of religion; morality and religion separate and unrelated; morality and religion as identical; morality and religion closely related, only with morality as 'senior partner'. Nevertheless, in practice, as Yinger himself observes, 'to the majority of the adherents of the "world religions" morality is an inseparable part of religion'.[2] He could well have added 'and immorality is an inseparable part of irreligion'.

It is historically true, therefore, that the emergence of irreligion as a distinct cultural and social phenomenon in the societies of Western Europe and North America in the nineteenth and twentieth centuries has been accompanied by prophecies of associated moral doom on the part of religious spokesmen. Bishop Berkeley's statement that 'nothing leads to vice so surely as irreligion' summed up the feelings of successive generations of religiously-minded individuals. Indeed the association of irreligion and immorality was so widely accepted that a term like 'atheist' was often employed in a derogatory way to denote the immoral.[3] Correspondingly, the religious was the moral and since morality was in general viewed as the basis of social order and harmony, religion was regarded as the very essence of a stable social life; as the Roman Catholic

97

journal 'The Tablet' expressed it in 1883, 'When religion goes the foundation of all civilized society is a hempen rope.'[4]

This natural assumption of an intrinsic relationship between religion and morality meant that whoever espoused an irreligious position would be open to an accusation of immorality. In the fervent battles of the nineteenth century between religionists and irreligionists, this position distinctly favoured the supporters of religion who rarely missed an opportunity of associating infidelity and immorality. Post observes that one of the most 'potent' arguments used against American free-thinkers in the first half of the nineteenth century was that they were 'naturally immoral and depraved.[5] Most of the popular free-thought leaders of the period suffered attacks on their personal character and various charges of immorality if not depravity. A particularly popular charge was that free-thinkers favoured, if not actually practised, free love.[6] It was also very common for the supporters of religion to cite the French Revolution as evidence of the horrors which might follow from the spread of infidelity.

Much has happened since the end of the nineteenth century to make such arguments appear quaint and slightly ridiculous to the ears of modern man. And yet not only is the relationship of religion to morality very much still an open question, but the association of irreligion with immorality has not been lost. One suspects that for the great majority of people morality is still seen as an inseparable part of religion, and the public opinion poll material concerning the teaching of religion in schools seems to support this view.[7] Among the more educated sections of society it is far more difficult to continue to hold such a view, since one is more likely to be aware of the existence of non-religious people who appear to be no less moral than everyone else. However, proponents of the 'irreligion equals immorality' thesis still exist, although the form of the thesis has changed somewhat since the turn of the century.

The original nineteenth-century account of the relationship between irreligion and immorality was that the rejection of the Christian religion and belief in God in particular meant that, as Dostoevsky put it, 'anything is permitted'. In other words it was belief in the supernatural sanctions of Christianity which was the prime reason for leading a moral life. That this argument no longer survives in this simplistic form is largely due to the fact that the non-religious sections of the populations of contemporary societies are not noticeably more immoral than any other. However, the thesis still survives in a modified form. The basic link between religion and morality is still asserted, but it is no longer claimed that irreligion will *immediately* be associated with immorality. The first generation of irreligionists, that is those non-believers of believing parents, will not necessarily be less moral than their parents in their behaviour because they have, inevitably, 'absorbed' a Christian moral ethic. However, since they have not carried forward the Christian beliefs which sustain this morality, the morality will not be an effective force for their children but will also eventually disappear. Thus, in effect, there is a timelag between the appearance of irreligion and the onset of immorality, morality being sustained in the interim by the 'spiritual capital' which has been accumulated. This was the view taken by Rowntree and Lavers of the state of British society in 1951:

> The Christian ethic is instinctively regarded today as the standard of values over wide spheres of public and private life, because for long periods in the past those values were accepted as having the supernatural sanction of Christianity as a revealed religion. We are in fact living on the spiritual capital of the past.[8]

They then go on to express their fears about what fate might befall society when the Christian ethic has ceased to be its guide. The inter-generational argument is specifically presented by Sperry in his discussion of religion in American society. The first generation of 'irreligionists' will have enough 'moral money in the bank', since they have preserved and continued to practice the Christian ethic. The second generation, however, 'have no religious memories and traditions behind them'. This generation Sperry dubs as 'happy, healthy, admirable, altogether lovable pagans' who are as innocent of theology and ethics as if 'all ecclesiastical institutions from the time of Moses had never existed'.[9] (Sperry seems to view the new irreligious as approximating to noble savages rather than to the Victorian conception of the depraved 'fallen' people.)

Clearly some consideration of the popular claim that irreligion and immorality are related is necessary. The evidence for their association needs to be examined, as does the possible manner of their association. Before proceeding, however, it is interesting to note how this popular argument about irreligion and immorality has, as an academic counterpart, the thesis (discussed above) that religion promotes societal integration. The popular argument is that irreligion leads to immorality which, if unchecked, leads to societal disintegration. The academic argument emphasises the corollary of this, which is the role which religion plays in upholding the common system of moral norms which in turn maintain an adequate level of integration in society. It would seem that the two arguments are to some degree mutually supporting, and the persistence of the latter despite the paucity of corroborative material for industrial societies might well be due in part to the continued existence of the former argument at a more popular level in society.

Evidence about the relationship of irreligion and immorality comes mainly from two sources, the psychological investigations of a small group of American and British research workers and the statistics for rates of criminal and delinquent behaviour of religious and non-religious populations. In neither case is the evidence without considerable difficulties of interpretation, and it cannot be said that sufficient information exists to warrant a definitive statement about the relationship, but the data can be treated as suggesting probable relationships. It is necessary to discuss the relationships of irreligion and immorality in the plural rather than the singular relationship because neither religion nor morality (and hence their opposites) can be treated as unitary entities. In addition to this, we have already noted that several relationships between religion and morality can, and do, exist at the cultural level, so it is not unreasonable to assume that this is true at the behavioural level also.

It would greatly simplify an examination of the relationship of morality and religion if we could assume that both of these were single dimensions of human behaviour in which people varied merely in the degree and not in the character of their involvement. Unfortunately we can make no such assumption. Whilst there may be disagreement over the number of dimensions involved in 'religiosity', there is no longer any disagreement about the fact that more than one exists.[10] Similarly Wright has identified four different types of variable involved in the measurement of morality, and he comments that 'the interrelationship between these different measures, and between each and religion, is likely to be very complex'.[11] With respect to religion one can distinguish the primary dimensions of belief, practice, experience and knowledge, whilst for morality one can distinguish between overt behaviour (transgression of moral injunction or 'good deeds'), internal responses to acts (e.g. guilt), moral insight and moral beliefs.[12] There are therefore at least four separate measures of both religion and morality and therefore presumably no less than sixteen separate relationships. Only a few of these have actually been examined.

By far the most common manner of examining the relationship of irreligion and immorality has traditionally been the procedure whereby statistics for rates of criminal and delinquent acts have been taken as the indices of immorality, and non-affiliation to religious organisations has been taken as an index of irreligion. Sorokin employs this approach in his examination of Western religion and morality and states that 'for the period 1897-1909 in Holland and 1924-34 in the United States criminality and delinquency rate of persons without any religious affiliation and membership happened to be lower than that of persons affiliated with Catholic, Protestant and Jewish religions'.[13] From this evidence he concludes that the association of immorality with irreligion is not valid, at least for the times and places quoted. Although other studies seem to confirm the generally law-abiding character of those people without religious affiliations, it is necessary to be cautious in the interpretation of this fact. Not only is criminal behaviour not the same thing as immoral behaviour, but those people who lack religious affiliation may not be irreligious. Even if these qualifications are overlooked, it remains the case that only one measure of immorality - overt behaviour of a transgressional kind - is being related to one measure of religiosity - practice, in so far as this is indicated by affiliation. It is also relevant to observe that the differences in overall incidence and type of crime by religious faith and denomination are as significant as any recorded differences between the religious and the non-religious; as Argyle observes, 'there is no incompatibility between religion and crimes of all sorts'.[14]

Crime statistics can only indirectly be regarded as an index of morality, whereas psychologists have attempted to relate direct measures of morality like cheating and lying to religious adherence. The classic study of this kind was that conducted by Hartshorne and May in 1928. In this study measures of moral transgressions were related to the dimension of religious practice in the form of churchgoing, and the general result was that there was no overall difference between churchgoers and non-churchgoers.[15] Other studies of delinquency and of the conscience motive either seem to indicate that there is no relationship between religion and morality on the measures used, or else provide conflicting evidence. In general Sorokin's rather sweeping generalisation on this subject must be said to have a great deal of truth. He summarised a variety of these studies as indicating that:

> .. there is no relationship of any consequence between Biblical information, church membership, attendance of Sunday schools and religious services, knowledge of moral precepts of Christian ethics on the one hand, and delinquency, criminality, actions of cheating, or such personality traits as honesty, service, co-operation, self-control and moral conduct, on the other.[16]

However, one cannot help feeling that Sorokin's rather off-hand dismissal of this body of research is due, at least in part, to the fact that he was looking for evidence of the relationship between religion and morality. Once one accepts the premise that the various facets of religiosity and morality may vary independently of one another, one is forced to abandon the search for the single relationship between religion and morality. Seen in this context, the results of these studies may be less inconclusive and contradictory than they are seen to be from Sorokin's perspective.

Public and Private Morality

One of the difficulties involved in any attempt to investigate religion and morality is the problem of determining what constitutes moral and hence immoral behaviour. It is partly because of this difficulty that evidence concerning criminal behaviour, which is much more easily determined, is frequently used instead. This, however, is a dangerous practice for it causes the differences between criminal and moral behaviour to be overlooked. Criminal behaviour is easy to determine simply because there are agreed social definitions of crimes; moral behaviour becomes difficult to define because there may not be general social agreement on what are moral acts. Whereas a society can have only one criminal code it may have several moral codes, and this is particularly likely to be true of modern pluralistic societies. Measurement of the degree of immorality of various groups in society thus becomes a very slippery exercise in which there is a real danger of projecting the morality of a dominant ethnic or class group on to a nonconforming minority and hence 'defining' immorality into existence. Even where all groups in society are agreed on the acts which are to be regarded as immoral, they may attach a very different emphasis to the degree of immorality involved. Thus a Nonconformist may consider gambling and drinking to be as immoral as stealing, whilst an Anglican would consider them to be less so. These considerations would seem to suggest that the efforts to compare believers and non-believers, or indeed any groups in society, on the basis of some constructed general morality index is a dubious practice. A more realistic procedure would be to determine the nature and strength of the moral beliefs of the various groups in society and then examine the extent to which they appear to live up to their own moral standards.

Seen in the light of these considerations, some recent research in social psychology appears to offer the hope of determining some meaningful relationships between religion and morality after all. A fairly consistent result of studies of the religious and the non-religious has been the fact that religious people report that they engage in fewer 'immoral' sexual activities such as masturbation, homosexuality and premarital intercourse than do non-religious people. Although there are several possible explanations of these results, one of the simplest would be that the non-religious are less inclined to view these actions as wrong and therefore less likely even to try to avoid them. As Wright observes, the differences may merely reflect 'differences in moral judgement rather than differences in capacity for self-control'.[17] This interpretation receives confirmation from the results of a study of moral attitudes among university students.[18] Here it was discovered that the religious reported much less involvement in sexual behaviour, gambling and drinking than the non-religious, but when the moral evaluation of these actions was held constant, the non-religious who thought an action was wrong were no more likely to report engaging in it than the religious who thought it equally wrong. Here we have direct confirmation of the above suggestion that in a plural society what at first sight may appear as a difference in rates of immorality between social groups might well prove in fact to be an instance of moral pluralism. In the study mentioned, both groups seemed to be equally moral in the sense that they reported an equal incidence of infringing their own moral code.

There is another aspect of the Putney and Middleton study which is significant in the context of the present discussion. This is the fact that the immoral acts considered in the investigation were classified into two groups according to whether the consequences of the acts were felt mainly by the individual or by others. Acts of the former kind were said to constitute 'ascetic' or 'private' morality, whilst acts of the latter kind were identified as constituting 'social' morality. In fact ascetic morality referred to forms of sexual activity, gambling, smoking and drinking whilst social morality referred to stealing, cheating and aggression toward others. Their results showed that there was no difference in the extent to which believers and non-religious upheld the social morality, but that believers were much more likely than non-believers to support the ascetic morality. This general conclusion was confirmed by a British study of 2,276 grammar-school children in which it was also found that the 'more ascetic the moral issue, the stronger the association with religious belief and practice'.[19]

It can be seen from this evidence that it is possible to maintain that a relationship exists between religion in general (at least a certain form of Christianity) and a particular form of morality. Conversely, it can be argued that the irreligious do reject a certain form of morality, that is an ascetic personal morality, whilst upholding a general social morality to the same extent as the religious.

One of the implications of this conclusion is that the growth of irreligion may well be bringing about a change in the nature of moral behaviour in contemporary society. The change is not that which the Victorians feared - the disintegration of an ordered social life - but a shift in the focus of moral concern from the sphere of personal and primarily ascetic acts to the sphere of public and anti-social acts. If this is indeed the case it is not difficult to see why this might be, for even if religion in general has not declined, religion as a source of supra-social sanctions has clearly lost ground. If, therefore, one distinguishes between acts which primarily invoke a supernatural sanction and those which merely invoke social sanctions, the decline of belief in the supernatural will remove the primary justification for the former but not the latter.

There seems to be little doubt that one of the most significant changes in the religious climate of contemporary society over the past hundred years has been the decline in the role of religious belief as a negative sanction controlling behaviour. McIver and Page have emphasised that since religion implies a relationship between man and some higher power, it normally invokes a sanction which can be called 'supra-social', 'whether it be primitive ghost fear or the present wrath of God' or the penalties of an after-life of torture in hell or merely the sense of being 'out of tune with the "infinite" when its supposed laws are disobeyed'.[20] Such sanctions were an integral part of the Victorian form of evangelical Christianity which hinged on beliefs in an after-life of rewards and punishments.[21] However, ever since the 1880s and 1890s these beliefs have been in decline and thus their role as sanctions on behaviour has also diminished. Of particular importance has been the decline in the number of people believing in hell, since a number of old negative supernatural sanctions are built on the premise of its existence.

> Although the evidence from the past is not strictly comparable it seems reasonable to suppose that the belief in hell, and consequently, of possible damnation, was held by a much larger proportion of the population than the 18 per cent of today. With its virtual disappearance it could be argued that the major supernatural sanctions of Christianity have also disappeared, for, implicitly, if there is no belief in hell the concept of Judgement also becomes

meaningless; and then all that is left of Christianity is a system of ethics. . . [22]

The above observation of Gorer echoes an earlier one of Rowntree and Lavers who similarly found that 'only a handful of people believe in hell, whether with or without everlasting flames'.[23] They, however, go on to observe that the decline of this belief has the most profound practical consequences since it means 'that people can no longer be frightened into conversion'.[24] Equally, of course, they could no longer be frightened into attending church or behaving in an ascetic manner in their private life. Even earlier confirmation of the fading role of religious belief as a negative sanction comes from an observation on the religious attitudes of soldiers in the First World War. Comparing the present situation with that of the pre-war days, an anonymous reporter remarks that 'The fear of the Lord has vanished like the morning mist'.[25] In this case the practical implication is reported to be the fact that the soldiers see no good reason why they should listen to the padre if they don't want to.

Tentatively, therefore, we may conclude that the rise and spread of irreligion has indeed been associated with a change in the nature of morality. We ought, however, to be very cautious before making any simple assumptions about causality. For although it may seem at first sight that since theology legitimates morality a change in the former will lead to a change in the latter, there are, as has been observed, many possible relationships between the two. Indeed, it is argued elsewhere that one of the main sources of the attack on established theology in Victorian England was the growth of a new moral sense. In addition, it would be a grave mistake to examine changes in religion and morality without reference to developments in the general social and cultural milieu in which they exist. Hopefully, however, we may at last be able to leave the crude Victorian assumptions of causality behind us and move nearer to an understanding of the mechanisms which relate the various forms of morality to the religious and irreligious perspectives.

Irreligion and Politics

It has frequently been maintained that irreligion and a radical political outlook are to be found in association with one another. Like the 'irreligion equals immorality' thesis, with which it is often coupled, this argument has a long history and can be traced easily as far as the early nineteenth century and the reaction to the French Revolution. That event, probably more than any other, convinced the propertied classes in England that the alliance of conservatism and piety stood opposed by an alliance of infidelity and radicalism. Like the association of irreligion and immorality, however, the link between irreligion and radical politics was an argument of great tactical advantage to the conservatives, who could use it to cast doubt on the piety of reform-minded politicians, or to frighten a radically-minded congregation away from Socialism. Conversely, leaders of free-thought organisations had all forms of extreme political views attributed to them, in much the same way that, in the McCarthy era in the United States, atheists were naturally taken to be Communists. The relationship between irreligion and politics has thus more often been propounded than explored, and despite the confidence and frequency with which the assertion is made it still awaits definite confirmation.

There are three levels at which this problem can be examined. Firstly, at the individual level, the political views and voting habits of individual atheists, agnostics, humanists and others can be ascertained. Secondly, the political outlook and commitment of irreligious organisations can be studied, and thirdly, the irreligious philosophies of Secularism, Rationalism, Ethicism and Humanism, together with the specific positions of atheism and anti-clericalism, can be examined in their relationships to various political ideologies. Although these levels are related, it cannot be assumed that the same relationship between the irreligious response and political opinion will hold for all three. Even if the majority of members of an irreligious organisation hold left-wing views, there may be organisational or strategic considerations which prevent that body adopting a formal commitment to a Socialist position. Similarly, if logic seems to demand that Marxists should be atheists, or rationalists egalitarians, one should not be surprised to find such links denied in reality.

All the evidence seems to suggest that, at the first level at least, the association of irreligion and political radicalism is justified. Budd has gone on record as stating categorically that as far as the membership of British irreligious organisations is concerned, 'the majority of members . . . have been left-wing'.[26] Certainly, what evidence there is supports her conclusion, but in itself it is hardly sufficient to bear the weight of such a general statement. A survey of the membership of the Leicester Secular Society revealed that 81 per cent regularly voted for the Labour Party,[27] whilst a questionnaire sent to the members of the Rationalist Press Association in 1961 showed that 55 per cent of the members were prepared to describe themselves as 'left-wing'. Of the remainder, 33 per cent were 'middle of the road' and 11 per cent 'right wing'.[28] The results of this questionnaire were also reported as showing that there was 'a high correlation between Left Wing and Atheists, Middle of the Road and Agnostics'.[29] A more recent survey of the political outlook of humanists in New South Wales reveals that 'about two-thirds of humanists hold political views ranging to the left, with about one-third of humanists placed relatively to the right'.[30] Although these results endorse the general view that the irreligious tend to be left of centre in their political outlook, they also support Tribe's opinion that 'the membership of the freethought organisations today probably includes a far from negligible proportion of Conservatives, particularly in the R.P.A.'.[31] Indeed the above figures indicate only a bare majority of left-wing members in the R.P.A. Obviously, the right-of-centre rationalist and the conservative humanist should not be regarded as mere freaks of nature or 'the exception which proves the rule', but as a very real category of the irreligious, even if they are usually in a minority position.

The other conclusion to be drawn from these surveys is that there may be very real differences in the political outlooks of the memberships of the various irreligious organisations. Although the different surveys are not strictly comparable, there is a suggestion that the membership of secularist organisations is more solidly left of centre than the membership of humanist ones, which, in turn, is more solidly left of centre than rationalist organisations. At the same time there is a hint, in the results of the R.P.A. survey, that the further left one is in religious terms, then the further left one will be in political terms also. These are only intriguing suggestions, but they do support the view that it is unreal to treat the irreligious as a single group when considering their political outlook and affiliations.

Historically too, the evidence suggests that it was rare for an irreligious organisation to possess a membership unanimous in its political persuasions. In nineteenth-century Britain the leaders of the secular and rationalist movements were almost all Liberals, as in all probability were the majority of the early members of these movements, but the spread of Socialism soon destroyed all possibility of unanimity. Prior to the emergence of Socialism as an effective political doctrine there was a real possibility that the irreligious would share one common radical political outlook. Of the two existing political parties it was virtually unthinkable for a secularist or free-thinker to align himself with the Tory Party, in view of the latter's close identity with the Church of England and the propertied classes. Holyoake was a Liberal, Bradlaugh stood for Parliament as a Liberal M.P., the founders of the R.P.A. were all Liberals. The subsequent generation of free-thinkers, however, were more likely to count themselves Socialists than Liberals. But in this respect there was even less likelihood of unanimity among the irreligious. For although the forces of social revolt might run parallel to the revolt against the old faith, there was no unanimity. There were secular Socialists and deeply religious Socialists. 'There were secularists who regarded any socialism as anathema.'[32] The situation was little different in America where the free-thought movement was also paralleled by a young but vigorous Socialist movement. However, 'while many socialists were infidels, comparatively few free thinkers were socialists; socialists always remained a minority among freethinkers'.[33]

In many ways the nineteenth-century free-thinker was temperamentally opposed to Socialism. Typically a self-made and self-taught man, he supported the doctrines of self-help and cooperation, but was opposed to large-scale governmental intervention to improve the conditions of life.[34] In addition, hisradical political outlook was most likely the by-product of his irreligiosity, so that for him the elimination of religion was the primary problem. The Socialist's irreligiosity by contrast was typically a derived one.

The essential difference between the socialist and the 'organisational' freethinker was that the former viewed religion in the context of a whole social pattern and not as an isolated phenomenon. The socialist was anti-religious in so far as religion in his eyes was a bulwark of that system which he endeavoured to destroy. The 'dogmatic' freethinker, on the other hand, condemned religion, not because it was an impediment to the achievement of any specific political and economic system, but because it resulted in the enslavement of man's mind. In short, the one possessed an integrated view of life based upon a clearly defined analysis of society of which anti-religion was one facet. The other was interested in the struggle against religion as the be-all and end-all of his ideological crusade.[35]

When the free-thinker and the Socialist agreed in their condemnation of religion, therefore, this was despite a difference in premises.

Politics and Organised Irreligion

'All the organisations in the free thought movement have traditionally been non-party.'[36] Although Tribe made this comment with reference to free thought in Britain, it is equally true of America. None of the major irreligious organisations in either country has ever affiliated or declared itself to be in favour of any political party. This is true despite the fact that proposals for declaring a political bias have been made - and considered - by several free-thought organisations from time to time.[37] In all instances the general opinion has been against any formal statement of support for a particular party. Similar recurrent proposals for the inauguration of a 'free-thought party' as a rival to the existing parties have rarely even been given serious consideration, although an attempt to form such a party was made in America in 1879 using the National Liberal League as a base.

That attempt, however, 'died at birth'.[38] In addition there have been attempts to persuade the irreligious organisations to sponsor their own Parliamentary candidates, if not with a view to forming a party, at least with the object of publicising the movements' aims.[39] These proposals have also never been taken up. On top of all this there is considerable evidence that the leaders and representatives of the various organisations have frequently taken precautions to ensure that their actions in no way compromised the non-party image of their movements. Thus Foote, from the moment he became president of the N.S.S. in 1890, 'ceased to side with any political party or to share in any direct political action. He has never written or spoken *for* or *against* any political party whatever for nineteen years.'[40] This constitutes an impressive record of successful resistance in the face of continuing temptation to enter the party-political arena, and it raises the question of why none of the organisations has ever succumbed.[41]

Although all the major irreligious movements carefully avoided any party-political commitment, it would be grossly misleading to assume that they were not involved in politics. The very nature of the aims of these movements meant that some form of involvement in politics was inescapable. Only political action could remove the penalties which the irreligious suffered, erase the privileged position accorded to the Christian faith, introduce a secular system of education, and bring about all the other changes which were involved in the general platform adopted by the irreligious movements. This form of involvement in politics, however, is clearly different from that of a political party with its explicit goal of exercising power through government; this form of involvement is incidental to the primary aims of the movement, which are seen as intellectual, moral, ethical or merely cultural. It is this fact which provides the primary justification for avoiding party politics, whilst at the same time justifying political action in general. *Some* form of political activity must be undertaken if the irreligious cause is to prosper, but at the same time if political activity itself is allowed to become the dominant activity, then the higher cultural goal is likely to be compromised. Most members of these organisations seem to have accepted the force of this argument, which helps to explain why there have been no instances of commitment to individual political parties. There have, however, been considerable differences of opinion over the extent to which involvement in politics is itself required in order to realise the higher ends. These differences have existed and still exist both between the various organisations and within their memberships.

At the one end of the scale are those organisations which, like the Rationalist Press Association, have virtually turned their backs on political activity entirely. Formed at the end of the nineteenth century, the R.P.A. was founded by a group of freethinkers who were of the opinion that 'the association of Free-thought propaganda with political campaigns was a serious dissipation of missionary strength' and who therefore deliberately 'eschewed politics' when framing the aims and objects of the association.[42] This clearly represented a reaction from the very political character of the secular movement at this time, which under Bradlaugh's leadership had become a republican, atheistic and Malthusian brand of Secularism. In an early brief statement of the aims and objects it was made clear that the association did not bind itself to the advocacy of any particular social or political views, although it recognised the need for political reform and expressed the hope that individual rationalists would be active in this sphere. The main reason for adopting this position was that 'the great principle of Rationalism must not be compromised by identification with opinions which are shared only by certain sections of liberal thinkers as the main objects of the Association are philosophical, ethical, and educative'.[43] There was, in addition, 'ample machinery' in existence for political action, but insufficient for the dissemination of rationalist and free-thought views.[44] In consequence, the association pursued a policy of scrupulously avoiding all obvious political issues as a means of ensuring neutrality in party politics. They were careful to avoid publishing books of a partisan political character and tried to ensure that representatives of every political party were members of the board of directors. Political differences were held to be irrelevant, in theory and practice, to the work of the association. This policy, although frequently attacked by members of the association, has always appeared to have the support of a majority of the membership, who are very quick to complain if they detect the slightest hint of political bias in the journal 'Humanist'. It has also been defended, by the directors of the association, on the grounds that partisanship would split the membership and that the policy of neutrality has clearly been to the benefit of the association.[45]

The ethical movements in Britain and America had their origins in movements for the reform of traditional religion, and while mounting a sustained critique of religion, they remained fundamentally sympathetic toward the religious outlook. This gave the ethical societies an advantage over the rationalist and secularist organisations when it came to the thorny problem of political commitment. Since, traditionally, religion had become quite divorced from politics, the identification of the ethicist's position as basically religious meant that there was no expectation of political involvement. To a large extent, therefore, the ethical societies were free from the considerable pressure to 'go political' which was constantly experienced by secular societies and to a lesser extent by the R.P.A. Indeed they were able to capitalise on their 'religious' image by presenting themselves as more politically conscious than the churches.

Like the other irreligious organisations they were formally 'non-party', but unlike the R.P.A. they were not indifferent to political questions:

> Ethical Societies have no Party in Politics. Political questions, when dealt with from their platforms, are treated from the Ethical standpoint regardless of party. Members are urged to take their share as citizens in the work of the Municipality in which they live, and to show an active interest in the larger political questions of the State. Questions affecting the health of the people, the welfare of the working classes, the status of women, the care of children, temperance and education, are most frequently dealt with, and an effort is made to show the direction in which reform should be sought.[46]

As the above quotation indicates, the ethical commitment required more than the propaganda activities of the R.P.A.: social action necessarily arose from the emphasis on 'deed not creed' and that action frequently meant some involvement with politics. Unlike the secular movement, the ethicist's concern with socio-political action was not the privileges accorded to religion, but the application of a liberal, ethical and humanitarian ideal to all spheres of social life. The principal stamping-grounds of ethical culture have been education, discrimination by sex or colour, youth, penal reform and international relations. In all these areas, however, the tactics have been those of a pressure group, not those of a political party. The attempt has been to create a climate of opinion favourable for reform, to educate,

113

to enlighten, to experiment and in general to 'ethicise'. This effort to ethicise all areas of life led 'inevitably into the muddy waters of politics'.[47] Politics was itself considered to be one of the areas of life most in need of the application of ethical idealism, and Adler himself was foremost among those who attempted to bring an end to political corruption in New York City in the 1880s. Adler even went so far as to hold a 'political ethics circle' 'to meet the difficulties experienced by independent citizens in determining . . . how they ought to vote'.[48] Nevertheless such activity was never much more than a small part of the programme of the movement and does not appear to have compromised its non-party position.

One can place the nineteenth-century British secular movement at the opposite end of the spectrum from the non-political Rationalist Press Association. Although the movement was never primarily a political one it was certainly a political force, especially under Bradlaugh's effective leadership. Undoubtedly significant as a factor enabling the movement to enter the wider field of politics was the fact that, prior to 1880 at least, the political outlook of members appears to have been comparatively uniform. Thus the leaders could count on the membership as a whole supporting them in their political forays — something which does not appear to have been true of the other irreligious movements. The way in which the political force of Secularism was employed in the nineteenth century has been summarised by Eros:

> Both Holyoake and Bradlaugh . . . took part in the historical task of reassembling the scattered Owenites and Chartists and of leading them under the flag of freethought away from the sectarian and Utopian socialism of Owen and the hopeless isolation of Chartism towards a co-operation with middle-class radicals. Their aim was the democratization of English politics and their final goal a republic. But on their way they worked for co-operation, suffrage and legislative reform alongside radicals like Bright and Mill.[49]

Most irreligious movements have seen politics as a secondary matter, the primary concern being with the removal or replacement of the traditional religion. Political means might be employed to achieve this goal, which itself could be considered to have political implications, but the supremacy of the irreligious ideal is not necessarily compromised in either event. Since this ideal is a radical one, there is bound to be some kinship between it and other radical ideas, including political ones, and so it is not surprising that when irreligion emerges as a political force it is usually in a radical form. The relationship with political radicals is likely to be a somewhat uneasy one in view of the tendency of both sides to feel that the other party has their priorities reversed. The real problem for the irreligious movement is that posed by the 'social gospels' of Socialism and Communism. For the Anglo-American forms of irreligion are basically doctrines of individual salvation, worked out as alternatives to the traditional Protestant teachings about personal salvation. The basic belief is that of the perfectibility of human beings as individuals through individual action. It is a doctrine of *self-realisation* with the state and society performing a secondary role. It is thus in the very nature of the irreligious philosophy that it should be congruent with a radical liberal political outlook but tend to conflict with the collectivist outlook of Socialism and Communism. However, the decline of Liberalism as a political tradition, together with the decreasing influence of the Protestant conception of individual salvation, has exacerbated the conflict between the irreligious tradition and the political religions which offer a social gospel. The new generation of unbelievers are as likely to have been weaned on Socialism as on Protestantism and are notably unconvinced with the traditional argument that politics is a secondary matter.

This growing pressure from the young for a greater political consciousness can be seen in the recent history of the British humanist movement. In July 1965 the Ethical Union, one of the sponsoring bodies of the British Humanist Association, lost its charitable status because the Charity Commissioners felt that its aims could be interpreted as implying political activity. Since this change in status carried with it the threat of a loss of tax rebate and a consequent annual deficit of over £3,000, there was an immediate move to regain charitable status. However, when the suggestion was made that the aims of the association should be altered to facilitate this, the objection was raised that this was 'risking preventing effective Humanist participation in political affairs'.[50] The ensuing debate revolved around the value of involvement in political action and was decisively settled in January 1967 when an overwhelming majority of members voted against seeking to regain charitable status. In fact this vote merely gave concrete expression to a sense of dissatisfaction with the

115

prevailing attitude toward political action which had been growing for almost a decade. This issue had first been debated fully in the pages of 'News and Notes' in 1958-9 and 1960-1, where the policy of only engaging in 'marginal political action' was attacked. This was in fact the traditional policy of the British ethico-humanist movement, and involved the definition of political action as something of concern to the movement only when 'political' obstacles stand in the way of the realisation of its aims:

> For the most part, organised humanists are concerned with what is open to them to do under existing laws and public policies, in so far as what they are trying to do is obstructed by existing laws and policies. This is likeliest to happen in societies without established rights and liberties safeguarding freedom of conscience, printing and speaking, association and meeting; and in those areas where traditional religious views are deemed to be identical with the public interest, such as questions touching the family (divorce, abortion, adoption, birth control).[51]

This marginal involvement was now under attack by those who felt that a 'more radical and thoroughgoing approach is required', an approach which outlined a policy on all social and political issues.[52] Following the decision not to seek to regain charitable status, the way was open for these members to press the association to develop just such a comprehensive policy, and this was accomplished at the annual conference in 1967 when a general statement of policy was formulated. Although this did represent a marked shift in policy, the central concerns of the association remained those specific to an irreligious organisation. Indeed the efforts to broaden the political consciousness of the movement do not seem to have produced any real response from the membership in the way in which Bradlaugh and others were able to do in the nineteenth century.

Whether the policies formulated refer to marginal or central political matters, the tactics adopted by the irreligious movements are the same. Basically they consist 'in the humdrum but important and cumulatively effectual daily vigilance demonstrated by public meetings, deputations, letters to the Press, and the like'.[53] Also, since the 1960s, there has been a systematic attempt to organise a group of Members of Parliament who will support a humanist platform. Regular meetings are held at which M.P.s are provided with information and briefings on issues such as the abortion law and religion in schools. There are about forty M.P.s definitely committed to the humanist position (all of them Labour), but something nearer 200 could be said to be generally sympathetic to the aims of the movement.

Recently the American Ethical Union has explored a new avenue of semi-political action through which to promote its cause. This has been the practice of legal intervention in cases which seemed to have a particular relevance to the movement's philosophy and programme.[54] It did this first in the McCullum case in 1946 concerning religious instruction during school time and has done so since in a series of cases concerning the right to hold public office without a religious test (1960), the elimination of prayer as a regular exercise in public schools (1961), the elimination of Bible readings as a regular exercise in public schools (1962) and the rights of non-theists to conscientious objector status (1965).[55]

Thus, as with our previous discussion about irreligion and morality, so in relation to the above discussion of irreligion and politics we must emphasise, in conclusion, that no simple relationship exists. The question of the relationships between the various philosophies of irreligion and the different brands of political ideology is one which cannot be explored in its full subtlety here. On the other hand we have seen that the majority of irreligious organisations have officially stood aloof from party politics, though not from political issues. The picture is more complicated at the individual level, where although a general association of radical politics and irreligion is discernible, the exceptions are far from insignificant.

The Functions of Irreligion

To conceive of such ideologies and associated social movements as Secularism or Humanism as functional equivalents of traditional religions is necessarily to equate the functions of religion and those of irreligion. What needs to be considered, however, is not the functions of the 'isms' which may be found in association with rejection of established religion, but the functions of the rejection itself. What personal or social functions are fulfilled by the individual or collective manifestations of reaction against established religion?

Perhaps the best-known answer to this question is that which attributes a positive role to unbelief in helping to 'purify' or strengthen religious belief itself. This argument has a very ancient pedigree but has naturally come more to the fore as irreligion itself has become a more apparent feature of contemporary life. It is an argument which has many variations. At a simple level it can be argued that the visible existence of unbelievers can function to remind the believer of his commitment to his faith, or alternatively act as a rallying-point for the faithful, much as the Muslim 'infidels' were for the Crusaders. At a more sophisticated level, it can be argued, as Marty does for nineteenth-century America, that the churches may use the existence of the infidel to help them advance their own factional interests.[56] Thus one denigrates one's more radical fellow believers by attacking their supposed 'infidelity' or by defining infidelity in terms of their beliefs. This sort of usage, however, does not really depend upon the existence of the irreligious so much as on a belief that the irreligious exist, and thus it is more relevant to consider the forms of this argument which are concerned with the role which the presence of an irreligious counterculture can play in benefiting religion.

In this context irreligion is clearly fitted to play a role in 'purifying' religious belief of any inadequate or unnecessary elements. This is a theme which Catholic thinkers have developed in recent years with respect to atheism. Whereas, by tradition, the Catholic Church has condemned atheism *in toto,* there is now a tendency to distinguish between 'good' and 'bad' atheism and to commend the former for performing just such a role. Maritain was one of the first to distinguish between 'positive atheism [as] an active struggle against anything that reminds us of God' and 'negative atheism, [as] a casting aside of the idea of God'.[57] Luijpen is another of those who has developed this distinction and writes of 'a good kind of atheism - the kind that discards pseudo-gods'.[58] He instances Socrates as a 'good atheist' because he rejected the pseudo-gods of Athens and continues: 'As a negation of a pseudo-god atheism is good and has a purifying value.'[59] In relation to contemporary faith Luijpen demonstrates how many theists hold beliefs about God that are unjustifiable and suggests that the atheists' objections to these beliefs are to be welcomed. Atheism in this respect serves as a purgative, playing the part of negative judgement in the knowledge of God. How far he is prepared to go in rehabilitating at least one form of atheism is indicated in the following passage:

> We do not maintain that all 'atheists' are merely intent on discarding pseudo-gods and are in reality theists who fail to understand themselves. But we agree with Jean Lacroix when he says that whereas formerly it was the custom to emphasize the implicit faith of unbelievers, the time has come for pointing out the implicit unbelief of believers. Contemporary atheism can make an inestimable contribution to the task of unmasking this unbelief and purifying faith.[60]

It is in this context that Lacroix can speak of his gratitude to his atheist friends for having taught him 'not to cheat'.[61] But, as he observes, atheism may well purify the idea of God at the expense, for some believers at least, of making him more remote.[62] One can, in fact, find similar arguments in the writings of many Christians of different nationalities and persuasions. Langmead Casserley refers to the 'proper contribution which [anti-Christian thought] may make to the dialectic process which conducts Christian thought itself deeper and deeper into the profounder exploration and understanding of its own bottomless faith',[63] whilst the Reverend Stewart D. Headlam actually tossed a bouquet to the secularists: 'we Christians owe much to the National Secular Society: it has helped us to overthrow many idols and sweep away much rubbish'.[64] This argument is, nevertheless, only very indirectly a claim that irreligion performs a positive cultural function, for basically it is merely an extension of the traditional claim that religion is functional and thus whatever promotes the cause of religion is by implication functional too. In reality, of course, the relationship between religion and irreligion is mutual and complex and the positive benefit which irreligion brings to religion is only a small part of the total relationship. This relationship will be taken up more fully in Chapter 5.[65]

There remains the central question of what functions irreligion might perform directly, either for individuals, sub-groups or for society in general. As some of the many difficulties which surround functional analysis have been referred to earlier, we will concentrate in the following discussion upon establishing a probable case for specific functions, rather than attempt a thorough critique of particular propositions. The emphasis is on establishing that such functions might exist.

We are so accustomed to the functionalist emphasis upon the role of religious belief in maintaining the psychological health of the individual that it is easy to overlook the fact that there is also a reverse side to the coin. If, under some circumstances, religion reduces guilt, then, under others, it has the effect of inducing it. If, under some circumstances, religious belief and ritual help to alleviate anxiety, under other and even similar circumstances they may actually help to create that anxiety.[66] If religion helps to provide solutions to the basic problems of meaning, it also creates those problems and in some cases is unable to provide the solutions. The rejection of religion may thus have entirely beneficial consequences for the psychological health of the individual. This phenomenon is best illustrated by the numerous accounts of relief and joy which attended the rejection of the Victorian doctrine of everlasting hell-fire. Budd records that some 'Freethinkers who described their loss of fear of death and hell, felt an initial euphoria and freedom analogous to the Christian's joy at conversion',[67] and Janet Courtney records how a belief in a 'burning hell' was a burden on many a heart.[68] Clearly, for many of those who partially or totally reject a conventional religion, this act may well be functional by resolving emotional conflict, or alleviating anxiety.

At a level of analysis above the individual, one can point to the possibility of irreligion functioning as a class or status-group ideology. Billington has argued that Holyoake's brand of Secularism functioned, at least for one secular society, to validate the status of its members.[69] As a group the members were drawn from the labour aristocracy and had a degree of common consciousness of their class interests, which included both the recognition of their conflict of interest with the middle classes and their superior status in relation to the mass of working people. Secularism provided an ideology which was sufficiently radical to use to attack the *status quo* above them, but also sufficiently individualistic, with an emphasis on 'respectability', to justify their superior status in relation to those below them. In this sense Secularism could be said to be an alternative to sectarianism for the elite of the working class, but 'with the exception of the Labour Church, the Christian Socialists and perhaps the Primitive Methodists, secularism was more politically and socially Radical than the sects'.[70]

Langmead Casserley has also suggested that irreligion functions as a group ideology for the new middle class. Commenting on the fact that the new middle classes of the late nineteenth and early twentieth centuries seem to have imitated the working class's habitual indifference toward religion, he suggests that:

> various intellectualized forms of the retreat from Christianity originally emerged and flourished as the group ideology of a new middle-class intelligentsia, anxious to vindicate its right to possess and enjoy the inheritance of the mediaeval clerical elite and to enter what, in our civilization, are the prestige-bearing occupations.[71]

Competition with the clergy for such prestigious occupations as teaching and public administration is seen by Casserley as the crux of the new middle classes' hostility toward religion, since their anti-clericalism was a ready base for a wider anti-religious feeling.

The irreligious movements of the nineteenth and twentieth centuries assisted in the secularisation of society in the sense that they promoted and accelerated the disengagement of various social institutions and activities from the legitimation and control of religion. This process had already developed to the point where most economic and political activity had been secularised, but the contribution of these movements was to extend the areas of autonomy from religious control to include education, social welfare and the sphere of private morality. In this sense the irreligious continued to perform the role of helping to create a secular state which the Dissenters had been instrumental in achieving before them. This process is not yet complete, for religion still sometimes claims a special prerogative over some areas of public or private life which thus provides a focus of agitation for existing irreligious movements. In addition, of course, it has been the special contribution of the irreligious movements to force societies based merely on freedom of religious worship, but committed to upholding religion in general, toward the 'purely' secular position of upholding the right of all citizens to freedom of religious *or* non-religious expression. This process is certainly not complete, but has been a steady if not spectacular one over the last two centuries. A major milestone in Britain was the introduction of the right of affirmation in courts of law, whilst the recent Supreme Court recognition of non-theistic religion may prove to be a similar milestone in America.[72]

At the cultural level of analysis irreligious movements have also clearly assisted the processes of secularisation in the sense of promoting desacralisation. We have already seen how the secular movement, in particular, mounted an attack on the Bible and then on the whole belief-system of Christianity. The rationalist movement then continued this process by widely disseminating the results of scientific and philosophical speculation critical of traditional theology. This process of cultural attack has been often discussed, but what is not so often mentioned is that this was associated with an attack on the sacred as it was manifested in social life. Thus the attack on the Book of Genesis, etc., was matched by an attack on the sanctity of the Sabbath, the Bible as a special object of reverence (rather than its teaching) and the clergy themselves. This process was an essential one in the further introduction of a totally secular state.

Another major function of irreligion is to cause expressions of discontent and frustration to be diverted away from religious channels of expression, as is instanced by the perfectionist sects, and toward socio-political channels. Sorokin has observed that the trend to express dissatisfaction through non-religious secular movements rather than sectarian movements can be traced back to the eighteenth century.[73] In nineteenth-century Britain the last major religious sectarian protest was Primitive Methodism. Thereafter the forms of expression become more and more secular in form, going through the borderline phenomenon of the Labour Church to the Labour movement itself. Clearly the secularists' insistence on the purely speculative character of an after-life, added to their insistence on the possibility of reforming the 'here-and-now', was instrumental in bringing this change about. It can also be argued that irreligious evangelism helps to 'create' protest, as well as merely diverting it into secular channels by presenting the present state as not 'God-given' but mutable.

At an individual level also, there is evidence that the irreligious movements help to transform mildly a-political people into radical protesters. Budd mentions the fact that for some radicals 'militant atheism was merely a transient interest' before moving on to other fields of social or economic radical agitation.[74] This would seem to be a common experience. A person interested in theological controversy becomes interested in an irreligious movement, joins, becomes confirmed in his irreligion and then moves off to some specific field of radical reform. However, it has been suggested that the opposite might sometimes occur, that is, that irreligious movements might divert attention from pressing social and economic problems to the 'sterile' field of theological controversy. The evidence would seem to suggest that in most instances the reverse is more likely to be the case.[75]

This argument naturally leads on to the general thesis that irreligion is but a transitional phase in societal development from a state of a dominant traditional religion to one where 'messianic mass movements of modern socialism or nationalism' have taken over from religion.[76] Or, in a less wide-ranging thesis, that the irreligious phenomenon is but a stage in the shift of popular interest and public concern from the realm of the religious to that of economic concerns and politics. It must be conceded that this latter point has a good deal of historical validity and that, ironically enough, the very success of irreligious movements brings about their own decline. In so far as the irreligious convince the population at large that secular concerns are of prior importance, then the shift of interest manifests itself, among other ways, by an indifference to the truth or falsehood of religion. As, therefore, theology ceases to be an issue, the irreligious message is ignored as much as the religious. However, a shift of interest to social and political matters does not in itself necessarily meant that some substitute messianic faith of a secular variety will replace traditional religion. That argument is predicated on the assumption that such faiths are functional alternatives to traditional religion and that some such alternatives are in some sense 'needed' after the demise of religion. Whether this is a meaningful assumption to make, and if so with what qualifications, is a question which will be taken up in the concluding chapter. First, however, we will turn briefly to the problem of the origins of the irreligious impulse.

The Springs of Irreligiosity

What are the sources of irreligion? What factors are conducive to the reaction against religion which is the subject of this investigation? Certain of the contributory factors have been mentioned in the course of tracing the fortunes of the various irreligious movements. Persecution was one factor which, although inhibiting the immediate actions of the irreligious, certainly seemed to strengthen the irreligious impulse itself. We have noted too how there appears to have been irreligious reactions to periods of intense revivalism. The revival of the free-thought movement in America in the 1820s, for example, has been partly accredited to a 'reaction against excessive evangelical emotionalism',[77] whilst Budd remarks that 'after the South Wales revivals of 1904-5 . . . many people in the revival area had become secularists, and at least ten branches of the National Secular Society were formed there in 1905-6, only to disappear as rapidly as the other effects of the revival had done'.[78]

It is traditional, however, to see the upsurge of irreligion in Western civilisation as part of a general intellectual process which, starting with the Enlightenment and stimulated by the French Revolution, culminated in the great intellectual debate of the late nineteenth century. One thinks of T. H. Huxley and Bishop Wilberforce, the impact of Darwin, and the higher criticism. No doubt it is true to see the process of the spread of irreligion as associated with these changes, but it could well be a gross over simplification if these cultural events were presented as necessarily the causes of the growth of irreligion. There is considerable danger here of over-intellectualising what is in reality a complex process of transition, in which not only are political, economic and social factors involved, but there is also a likelihood of considerable emotional investment. Thus it is necessary to be on our guard against rationalisations as well as wary of over-generalising from the experiences of the intellectual and articulate few. In fact there is a considerable body of evidence to suggest that the actual transition from religious commitment to religious rejection is much more a matter of moral outrage and ethical rebellion than one of intellectual doubt and rational persuasion.

Thus Murphy argues that the explanation of the decline of Victorian orthodoxy in terms of Lyell, Darwin and the higher criticism is implausible because it obscures 'the fact that the Victorian religious crisis was produced by a fundamental conflict between certain cherished orthodox dogmas . . . and the meliorist ethical bias of the age'.[79] By analysing the rejection of orthodoxy by the representatives of their age, Murphy concludes that it was the attempt to reconcile this meliorist bias with orthodoxy which brought them to the point of 'rebelling against these doctrines as ethically outrageous'.[80] Once this rebellion had occurred, then the idea of evolution and the higher criticism were available as a suitable substitute *Weltanschauung*. A very similar argument, but in relation to a different section of Victorian society, is advanced by Budd who emphasises the importance of moral outrage as a factor leading people to abandon their belief and join the secularists:

> The weight of feeling behind the attack on Christianity was not that it was untrue but that it was wicked. One Freethinker said; I lost my faith in Christianity because it conflicted with my own standards of right and wrong. In short it wasn't good enough for my conscience'.[81]

This view is also endorsed by Royle, who states that:

> Just as Christian belief can be, and often is, founded on an emotional response in a given situation, to be confirmed later by intellectually satisfying 'evidences', so Infidelity seems to have frequently been inspired by disgust with the Church and moral revulsion against the Christian doctrines, and then sustained by a growing intellectual conviction of the Tightness of such a rejection, a conviction perhaps hastened by an uncritical handling of the so-called facts of the matter.[82]

Certainly the groundswell against Christianity was well under way before the Darwinian revolution and higher criticism were able to make their impact, and for the working classes these esoteric ideas never really penetrated at all. Nevertheless, the rejection of Christianity and also of religion in general is a continuing feature of these classes and takes the form of an emotional and moral rejection of something which is alien if not threatening. Thus an officer reporting on the religious attitudes of the men in the trenches in the First World War wrote that:

> the majority have not the foggiest notion of what Christianity is all about; their opposition to it is emotional and instinctive, not reasoned. Perhaps because Christianity is expressed in a form they think insincere (e.g. it has a language of its own not readily understood by the outsider) and is bound up with a social system they dislike.[83]

Clearly, in reality, there are doubtless as many possible causes of irreligiosity as there are for religious commitment itself, and it is only really possible here to enumerate some of those which have been noted or reported. Basically, one looks for one or more alienative experiences which provide the trigger for the irreligious response as well as for the supportive agency which provides the cultural 'materials' (evidence, argument, justification) to maintain such a stance. Such experiences may be personal and poignant, like Holyoake's memory of the death of his baby sister Eliza whilst his mother was out paying the church rates and the Easter dues, or Bradlaugh's experience when reporting his difficulties in studying the Gospels to his vicar, who responded by suspending him for three months and writing to his father about the boy's 'atheistical' tendencies and then following this with a course of 'persuasion' for the boy which amounted to persecution. At a more general level, a soldier's experience of random death and destruction may cause him to revolt against the very notion of God. Experiences like these which are alienative in consequence are in all probability always available in society, although they may be more prevalent under regimes of authoritarian orthodoxy. Although there are comparatively few reports of instantaneous conversions to irreligion, it would appear that irreligious experiences are probably almost as widespread and as diverse in form as are religious experiences. Charles Southwell reported being instantaneously converted to irreligion in his 'Confessions'. He wrote that on reading Timothy Dwight's 'Sermons' he experienced 'a feeling like an electric shock [which] struck my frame; all my thoughts and feelings underwent a change, and I became involuntarily, and without any choice of my own, what I am now - an Atheist'.[84]

Fundamentally, however, the irreligious response, where it is widespread enough to identify as a distinctive socially-based phenomenon, is associated with the identification of religion as itself class-based and class-supported. The interests of the clergy and the Church are not those of large sections of society who regard religion as alien and exploitative. Frequently religion is seen as unintelligible, dull and feminine, while churchgoers are viewed as hypocritical and snobbish. All these responses are quite widespread and commonplace among the working classes in Britain. Typically, the working classes see the churches as standing for 'a dull, tame, almost negative and altogether unattractive standard of comfortable and complacent respectability, a respectability quite compatible with flagrant inconsistency and selfishness'.[85]

5 Conclusion: Irreligion and the Functionalist Perspective in the Sociology of Religion

Although there is no one functional theory of religion, there is a dominant tradition in social anthropology and sociology which emphasises the consequences, as opposed to the purposes, of religious beliefs, practices and organisations for the maintenance and continued existence of societies, groups or individuals. The dominant emphasis in this tradition has been upon the positive function which religion performs in the integration of societies, but a variety of other functions have been postulated. O'Dea, in reviewing these functions, summarises the role ascribed to religion in functional theory as one which:

> identifies the individual with his group, supports him in uncertainty, consoles him in disappointment, attaches him to society's goals, enhances his morale, and provides him with elements of identity. It acts to reinforce the unity and stability of society by supporting social control, enhancing established values and goals, and providing the means for overcoming guilt and alienation. It may also perform a prophetic role and prove itself an unsettling or even subversive influence in any particular society.[1]

Even though the suggestion is made in the last sentence that religion might have dysfunctional consequences, the burden of the above quotation is clearly that religion is considered to play a dominantly functional role. The fact that the functionalist perspective thus tends to overlook the dysfunctions of religion is not, however, the principal point at issue here, although one of the consequences of this is the tendency to ignore the possibility of there being positive consequences of irreligion. The more basic objection to the functionalist perspective is that it overlooks the phenomenon of irreligion altogether, either by pretending that it doesn't exist, or by defining it out of existence. It is therefore necessary to look more closely at the functionalists' treatment of irreligion.

128

A comment which could be described as a hardy perennial of functionalist literature on religion is the observation that religion is a universal feature of human society. It is a comment which has been repeated so often that one is inclined to forget that it is, or should be, an empirical observation and not a sociological theorem. As an empirical observation, however, it can only be confirmed or refuted if the writer concerned gives a fairly full substantive definition of religion. In the nature of the case, however, functionalists provide functional and not substantive definitions. As Geertz has observed:

> The oft-heard generalization . . . that religion is a human universal embodies a confusion. It is probably true . . . that there is no human society which totally lacks cultural patterns that we can call religious under the present definition or one like it. It is surely untrue that all men in all societies are, in any meaningful sense of the term, religious.[2]

This, nevertheless, is a distinction which is hardly ever made. It is indeed quite remarkable that while sociologists of a functional persuasion are so very quick to observe that religion of some sort can be found in every society, even the most secular, they refrain from mentioning that some irreligious people can be found in all societies, even the most religious.[3] Of course, this form of selective perception is theoretically prompted, as the ascription of important societal functions to religion necessarily leads to the assumption of its universal distribution. This view is then reinforced by a careful selection of material from pre-literate or small-scale societies. It nevertheless remains a somewhat amazing oversight on the part of contemporary sociologists. For several sociologists of a functional persuasion, irreligion is not overlooked. It is seen and even described, but redefined as a religious phenomenon, thereby helping to maintain the impregnability of the assumption that religion is a universal feature of human societies. Thus, Lenski refers to Communism and 'contemporary humanism of the type espoused by such men as Bertrand Russell and Julian Huxley' but chooses to define religion in such a way that he can include these as systems of belief.[4] He indeed recognises that his definition of religion as 'a system of beliefs about the nature of the force (s) ultimately shaping man's destiny, and the practices associated therewith, shared by the members of a group' means that 'every normal adult member of any

129

human society is religious. . . . Only small children and persons of subnormal intelligence are non-religious in our sense of the term.' But he clearly does not feel that this might be an argument against his definition.[5] Indeed Lenski represents an interesting case of the extension of the postulation of religion as a universal feature of human societies from the status of an inter-societal statement to an intra-societal statement. Lenski is not alone in defining religion in such a broad functional manner that it becomes possible to suggest that irreligious people cannot really exist. Arnold Toynbee has said very much the same thing:

> To have religion is one of those distinctively human characteristics of mankind that differentiate us from our non-human fellows on the face of this planet. This assumption implies that every human being has religion: in fact, that one cannot be human without having it in some form.[6]

Although one's immediate reaction to such statements might be to rush and produce the writings of Charles Bradlaugh or Colonel Ingersoll, or even to round up a posse of members of a contemporary humanist group, one knows that these statements are not made out of ignorance of the existence of people who specifically repudiate every form of religion. If such statements came merely from theologians or people with deep religious commitment, one might feel inclined to dismiss them on the ground that they are polemical rather than descriptive, but when they originate from sociologists presumably speaking *qua* sociologists and not *qua* religious persons, they cannot be dismissed in such a fashion. How, therefore, is it possible for sociologists to make such statements, and what, if anything, can they mean?

The initial suspicion is that these statements are based on the postulation of a religious instinct or faculty in all human beings. At one time such a view was widely held, but it has to be stated quite categorically that on present evidence such a view is un-supportable. In any case psychological reductionism of this kind would hardly be acceptable in contemporary sociology. It may be the case, nevertheless, that some sociologists still harbour the inclination to fall back upon the postulation of a universal human instinct for religion.[7] It is more probable, though, that sociologists would postulate a basic social religious faculty, asserting that

130

the religious response is an intrinsic ingredient in the very nature of human social relationships. This seems to approximate to Luckmann's position where he describes socialisation as an essentially religious process.[8] Luckmann's ground for making this assertion is that it is through the socialisation process that man transcends the sensate immediacy of his biological constitution, and thus by identifying transcendence with religion he is able to suggest that a religious process is involved in the warp and weft of social life.

The central point at issue here is the value of a broad inclusive functionalist definition of religion. In general the argument in favour of a functionalist definition is that it avoids the obvious pitfalls of ethnocentrism whilst at the same time drawing attention to the central social role of religion as a basic 'process' on a par with those in the realms of economics and politics. These advantages, however, are likely to be more apparent than real, or at least they must be offset against the very real disadvantages of such a definitional approach for research in contemporary societies. For it remains the case that there is little unanimity over what the functions of religion are, or rather over what are the essential functions. All that is really known is what functions a particular religion or religious belief fulfil under particular conditions, and one can only speculate on what general 'competence' religions may indeed possess.[9] At the same time a religion is a complex of beliefs, actions, attitudes and organisation and is thus capable of fulfilling a wide variety of functions at the societal, groupal or individual level. For convenience of definition, however, it is probable that only a few of these will be singled out. There is therefore plenty of scope for bias, whether it be theoretically inspired or a product of cultural or religious ethnocentrism. In this respect functionalist definitions are rarely less 'biased' than the substantive definitions which they condemn. This can be seen from an examination of the current vogue for functionalist definitions of religion in terms of its reference to things 'ultimate'.

'Ultimate Confusion'

The use of the concept of ultimacy is very widespread in current attempts to define the primary function of religion. There are, nevertheless, several variations in the usage of the term 'ultimate'. In those instances where sociology is most obviously theologically inspired, one may come across a reference to religion as a system of beliefs concerning a sacred entity which is described as *the* ultimate, as a 'beyond', a 'ground of being', in which the sociologist, no less than the practitioners of the religion he is studying, seems to accept the objective reality of such an ultimate. This then becomes simply a substantive definition of religion in which the rather *démode* term 'God' is supplanted by the more fashionable term 'ultimate reality'. However, it is more usual to find the word 'ultimate' as an adjective rather than as a noun, as in references to 'ultimate problems', 'ultimate solutions', 'ultimate commitment', 'ultimate concern', 'ultimate relevance', 'ultimate meaning' and 'ultimate significance'. The former of these is particularly popular, being used by such well-known functional theorists as Parsons, Bellah and Yinger. In general, this tradition of usage derives from Weber via Parsons; focusing on the tension which man experiences between his expectations and his experiences, it suggests that religion fulfils the function of providing 'solutions' to what are perceived of as the ultimate problems of life. Thus Yinger refers to religion as 'a system of beliefs and practices by means of which a group of people struggles with these ultimate problems of life'.[10] A third usage of 'ultimate', which often in practice appears in an association with ultimate problems, but is logically distinct, is the notion of religion as concerned with ultimate solutions to problems. Partly the implication here is that religion is a more basic solution to the problems of life than any secular alternatives and hence is more 'ultimate' in that sense, but more frequently the implication is that religion is the 'final' solution to the problems of life. When all else has failed, one turns 'ultimately' to religion. Benson implies that this is also one of Yinger's usages of the term.[11] Finally, there is the usage of the term 'ultimate' which goes outside the framework of problems and their solution altogether and is merely concerned with the issue of saliency. Here one finds reference to religion as that which relates to issues of ultimate 'concern' or ultimate 'significance'.[12] It is important in this context to examine the cogency of each of these usages, since the manner in which religion is defined in relation to some conception of 'ultimacy' is in turn directly related to the way in which functional theorists approach the question of functional alternatives and secular 'equivalents' to religion.

The first point which needs to be made is that although the reliance on 'ultimacy' can be made to relate to Weber's approach to the study of religion by linking it to the problem of theodicy, it does seem in fact that its current vogue among sociologists is due more to its widespread use by theologians. Tillich in particular has been an obvious influence on contemporary American sociologists of religion and, at the least, his usage of 'ultimacy' has reinforced its use within sociology. However, it is hard to see how one can justify the uncritical importation of theological concepts into sociology, especially if they are contrary to widespread conventional usage. Tillich himself contrasts his definition of religion as 'being grasped by an ultimate concern' with what he recognises as the more conventional notion of 'an organized group with its clergy, scriptures, and dogma'.[13] This contrast is emphasised by him for polemical reasons, because he wishes to draw attention to what he takes to be the universal and basic ground for the religious response. In addition, however, his usage of the term 'ultimacy' is deliberately ambiguous, referring as it does both to the notion of an objective ultimate reality and to our subjectively experienced ultimate concern. These facts alone should make the sociologist wary of too readily resorting to Tillich for an avenue of escape from the definitional dilemma.

The more fundamental problem, however, lies in attempting to translate the generalised notions of 'ultimacy' into specific statements about the content and nature of religion so that one can construct hypotheses and derive generalisations which relate to particular religions and social contexts. The most promising usage in this respect would appear to be that which identifies religion as concerned with ultimate problems and then tries to specify exactly what these ultimate problems are. Yinger has indeed attempted to list these, and although recognising that there might be disagreement over some, he claims that 'a great many would accept [his list] as among the fundamental concerns of human societies and individuals'.

133

The list he gives is as follows:

1. How shall we respond to the fact of death?

2. Does life have some central meaning despite the suffering and the succession of frustrations and tragedies?

3. How can we deal with the forces that press in on us, endangering our livelihood, our health, the survival and smooth operation of the groups in which we live - forces which our empirical knowledge is inadequate to handle?

4. How can we bring our capacity for hostility and our egocentricity sufficiently under control that the groups within which we live, without which, indeed, life would be impossible, can be kept together?[14]

If it could be demonstrated that this list is an accurate and comprehensive statement of the central, ultimate and universal concerns of human beings, then the problem of identifying and delineating religion would indeed be solved. Unfortunately this is a long way from being established, and even others who share Yinger's approach to the definition of religion seem to favour a somewhat different list of ultimate problems.[15] It is obvious that the chances of one's successfully drawing up a list of 'universal ultimate problems' is not great and, short of a quite massive cross-cultural and historical research programme, the end result is likely to reveal more about one's own religious predilections than those of mankind in general. In any case the attempt is likely to founder in the effort of distinguishing between 'ultimate' and 'non-ultimate' problems. One would expect that sociologists of culture would take the view that what are presented as 'problems' within any given society or sub-culture is a cultural variable, just as what are treated as 'ultimate' and 'non-ultimate' problems would be a cultural variable. It would therefore only be possible in a very vague and general way to hope to predicate in advance what these might be prior to the establishment of the facts from a thorough investigation. However, this is not the procedure followed. Instead a list of problems is postulated which, as in Yinger's case, usually focus on death, frustration and despair, and evidence is selected to justify the list. In this case most evidence is taken from pre-literate societies which emphasise such problems. Clearly this list is inspired less by comparative and historical research in sociology and anthropology than by theological considerations,

134

and Yinger at least is honest enough to confess this when he declares that he 'agrees with William James and with the great majority of theologians who hold that a religion that does not grapple with the pessimistic aspects of life is a truncated, incomplete system'.[16] Thus it transpires that the attempt to specify universal ultimate problems is in fact little more than a specification in sociological garb of the view of the human situation currently held by Christian theologians, with the inevitable consequence that religions which deviate markedly from this model are judged in a *sociological* context to be in some way incomplete as religions. Could we not draw up a list of 'ultimate human problems' which, instead of being inspired by William James's religion of the 'sick-soul' variety, is derived from his religion of 'healthy-mindedness', in which the central problems are those of life, not death, expressing joy, not enduring suffering, and the like? Would not such a model deserve the title of a 'religion' as much as Yinger's?

If we turn from the use of ultimacy in relation to problems to its use in relation to solutions, we find ourselves dogged by very similar difficulties. An attempt to cope with experienced human problems by postulating a supernatural or superempirical world beyond that of sense-experience is clearly a very different response compared with attempts which are limited to mundane empirico-rational experimentation, but in what sense is it necessarily more 'ultimate'? Similarly, why should one necessarily suppose that if rational-empirical methods of solution fail, men will 'ultimately' turn to religion for an answer, rather than, as Benson suggests, 'psychotherapy or drink'.[17] It must be concluded that recourse to notions of ultimacy hardly seems to have helped the cause of delineating religion for sociological purposes, but has in the process obscured the very real fact of the existence of irreligious phenomena.

There is, of course, the tendency when faced with some of the above objections for proponents of the use of ultimacy to fall back on to a position of complete cultural relativity and assert that religion is *whatever* the respective individuals regard as ultimately important or problematical. This, of course, amounts to a complete semantic take-over bid on the part of the concept of religion and is so totally divorced from common usage and reality as to be a barrier to research. In addition to which it logically excludes the question of any functional alternatives to religion.

135

The 'Adequacy' of Irreligion

One of the major disadvantages of the functional approach to religion discussed above is its tendency to present religion in the role of (at least in part) a problem-solving mechanism. It is a cultural device which, it is suggested, provides 'solutions' to perceived human problems. Or in Yinger's more careful formulation, it is an attempt to solve such problems. This perspective thus disguises the extent to which religion itself creates problems of meaning. This is true at two levels.

In the first place it is necessary to accept that there are no universally 'given' human problems. What is identified as a problem is dependent on the cultural tradition of the individual or society concerned. Necessarily, therefore, we learn to identify problems (and as a corollary not to identify other experiences as problematical), and since religion is usually a very important part of our culture, religious considerations will enter into what we do and do not define as such. In this basic sense, therefore, religion identifies problems for us (and thus to an extent, subjectively speaking, creates them) and then, of course, goes on to suggest 'solutions' to these problems. It was in this sense that Hocking wrote of religion as 'the healing of a breach which religion itself has made'.[18] Secondly, at a less general level, specific religious culture-systems may become so resistant to change that they become out of tune with the majority of the life-experiences of their adherents. In such a situation the religion may, instead of helping the solution of problems, actually exacerbate them.

Once it is recognised that religion sometimes performs a problem-creating function in either or both of the above senses, then it becomes possible to see that the irreligious response might be the cultural form in which the attempt to solve problems of meaning is expressed. Very simply, we may conceive of all societies (and possibly all individuals, but there is a danger of over-rationalising man) as possessing over-arching cultural forms or value-orientations, conceived of as 'a generalized and organized conception, influencing behaviour, of nature, of man's place in it, of man's relation to man and of the desirable and non-desirable as they may relate to man-environment and inter-human relations',[19] but that, as Glock and Stark suggest, such orientations can themselves be subdivided into the religious and the 'humanistic' 'perspective realms', depending on whether or not some statements affirming the existence of 'a supernatural being, world or force are included'.[20] Such value-orientations attempt to cover the full range of man's experiences and to offer a coherent and integrated 'solution' to these. But in the very nature of the case they cannot do this; some experiences remain unexplained and some part of the proffered 'solutions' will itself be problematical. Value-orientations, in other words, are successful in presenting a meaningful account of some part of man's experience, only at the expense of rendering some other portion meaningless, ambiguous or mysterious. This fact, however, is frequently disguised from the acceptors of the value-orientation by the way in which the problems which their orientation does deal with are presented as *the* problems of life. Thus, to take an example, most forms of Protestant Christianity leave the area of political life 'uncharted', whilst Marxism and Communism leave areas of personal ethical life similarly 'uncharted', but these 'weaknesses' are disguised to the extent to which both present the areas which they do explain as *the* life issues. It is therefore meaningless, in any general way, to refer to any one value-orientation or even type of orientation as more adequate than any other. All have their inadequacies which are to be judged only in the context of the life-experiences of given human societies. We are therefore forced to conclude that what are spoken of as the secular alternatives to traditional religion, such as Communism, Nationalism and Humanism, can in no way be judged to be either more or less adequate as value-orientations than religion itself, since they focus on different areas of human experience. In a general sense they are merely different. This, however, is rarely the position adopted by sociologists who discuss these 'secular alternatives'.

There is a notable lack of unanimity as to whether those ideologies or 'faiths' can justifiably be treated as functional equivalents to traditional religions. It is very common to find Communism, Nationalism and Humanism mentioned in this context, but there is little consensus as to what others should be included. Among a wide and sometimes bizarre range of candidates the following are a typical selection : Fascism, Socialism, internationalism, Freudianism, democracy, Scientism, science, psycho-analyticalism and baseball.[21] Rarely, however, are the grounds for inclusion in this list stated with sufficient clarity to allow a detailed examination of the validity of the claim that these 'isms' are functional equivalents to traditional religion. Where the statement merely means that these ideologies are value-orientations just as religions are, then one cannot object to them, although one could judge them to be platitudinous. It is where there is a suggestion that they fulfil the same needs as religion that one enters the murky and confused area of the meaning of functional alternatives.

Marion Levy has written of the 'great deal of nonsense [which] is talked and written as a result of misunderstanding the problem of functional substitutability', and it is hoped that it will not be added to here.[22] It would seem that general statements of the kind 'Communism is a functional alternative to Catholicism' are virtually meaningless. Functionalist statements need to specify the related needs, the specific items and the social and temporal context of applicability. Thus one would prefer a statement to the effect that Comte's Religion of Humanity served the same intellectual and emotional needs for a section of the English middle classes in the late nineteenth century as Roman Catholicism fulfilled for Catholics of the same socio-economic position. Even this statement possesses many ambiguities, but at least it is potentially an empirical statement capable of refutation.

The central problem here is like that encountered in the earlier discussion of ultimacy, the tendency for the functionalist framework to include a common and universal set of assumptions. Previously it was the assumption of common universal human problems, here it is common universal human needs. In the above example it is only possible to speak of the Religion of Humanity and Catholicism as functional alternatives if one assumes that Catholics and Comptists had the same needs. If one starts to think in terms of different patterns of needs, then in what sense can one talk of functional alternatives? If one suggests that the personal needs which religion satisfies are not fixed and universal, but partly the product of the religious tradition itself, then the discussion of irreligious responses as functional alternatives to religion becomes complex. For there are two possibilities open with respect to those individuals who lose their religious faith. The one - that of the true functional equivalent -is that they will seek other ways of satisfying the needs which religion fostered and satisfied for them. The other path - which cannot be conceived of as that of a functional equivalent - is that where the needs are lost along with the faith. The Victorian honest doubter who loses his faith may not lose his need to feel that in some way he will continue to 'exist' after his death and may find a surrogate for physical immortality in the ethicists' belief in vicarious ethical immortality. On the other hand he may lose this need along with his faith, in which case he could well join the secularists and be as scathing about the ethicists who 'play at church' as about the straightforwardly religious. Of course, in both cases he is likely to need a value-orientation, but the real question is how far will the specific needs, like the need for the alleviation of guilt, for some form of personal immortality, for communal celebration and the like, continue. It is quite clear from the vigorous debates between those irreligionists who were abolitionists and those who were substitutionists that the total of those who lost their faith was equally divided between these two types. The substitutionists based their arguments on the premise that the needs will continue and that traditional religion will not therefore be replaced until alternatives are offered. The abolitionists, on the other hand, based their arguments on the premise that the needs need not continue and that to dispense with religion is to dispense with unnecessary needs (like the need to alleviate guilt which religion itself has created).

This debate lives on, and Julian Huxley is a good example of a contemporary substitutionist who is alarmed by the fact that what he sees as the decline of religion is leaving a vacuum of unfilled needs.[23] As a consequence he proposes that evolutionary humanism should be presented as a 'religion' in order to satisfy the emotional as well as the intellectual needs which are being neglected. Over against this view one has to set the argument that the 'death of religion' only results in a sense of bereavement for some and then only for a short while. In time the sense of loss is overcome and adjustment is made to the new circumstances. There is thus no need for the self-conscious introduction of a new faith which is modelled on the old and aims to be a substitute or surrogate for it. Rather the changed situation means that such substitutes will fail to gain support just as the model on which it is based failed; only a value-orientation which caters for different needs as well as containing different beliefs can expect to prosper. As Luckmann has observed, this is particularly likely to happen in periods of rapid social change when:

> the everyday concerns of the fathers are no longer those of the sons
> and many of the concerns of the sons were unknown to the fathers. In

the context of such changing concerns even the major and 'invariable' biographical crises and their solutions, including death, will appear in a different perspective to the sons. In general we may say that matters that come to be of 'ultimate' significance for members of later generations are likely to be congruent only to a limited extent with matters that were of 'ultimate' significance to earlier generations.[24]

This latter point is well illustrated by the dialogue between humanists and Christians where some of the lack of understanding (on both sides) is clearly due to the failure to realise that the respective 'faiths' are not addressed to the solution of the same problems. Thus the Christian objection that Humanism is inadequate because it does not deal with problems of death and suffering rather misses the point since by its nature Humanism does not present such 'experiences' as essentially problematical. The humanist position does not present Time and Death as the ultimate problems; on the contrary they are accepted as 'essential human resources of life and living', whilst the Absolute and the Eternal are seen as the equivalents to Time and Death.[25] Thus in Blackham's own words, 'the humanist [is not] the fox without a tail; if he has no tail, it is because he is a different breed of fox. He is not looking at the Christian world without faith and hope. He has turned completely round and sees another scene'.[26]

The moral is clear. Traditional religions like Christianity, and what are usually called secular alternatives like Humanism and Marxism, cannot meaningfully be judged to be any more or less adequate than each other than introversion can be judged to be a more adequate personality type that extroversion. They are merely more or less appropriate to given personalities and societies, just as one could argue that introversion might prove a more appropriate personality type for success in the academic world, whilst extroversion leads to success in politics. Unfortunately, sociologists of religion have made comparisons of adequacy between the two forms, and as one would expect from the history of the sub-discipline, they are mostly in favour of traditional religion. Thus Glock and Stark, and Yinger, both suggest that 'secular systems of value-integration' may well prove 'inadequate' 'because of their inability to achieve their proclaimed goals'.[27] Glock and Stark ask:

Are humanist perspectives more likely to commit themselves to determinate statements about the empirical world and hence be more prone to disconfirmations ? One supposes that predictions of a 'Thousand Year Reich' would be considerably more fragile than those concerning 'a thousand year Invisible Rule of Christ'.[28]

Presumably, of course, they may also prove to be 'more adequate' because they are more prone to 'confirmation', something which does not appear to be true of the many examples of 'determinate statements' made within religious perspectives.[29] However, the issue is simply that such observations miss the point. It might be true that in a particular social context traditional religion functions more successfully in value-integration than say Humanism. It may also be the case that in a different context Humanism functions more successfully in adaptation to the environment than traditional religion, as Hoult implies when he says that 'Religions which stress the here-and-now, such as naturalistic humanism and Ethical Culture, encourage behaviour believed to ensure the best chance of survival in this world.'[30] But on what overall criterion can the one form be judged to be inferior or superior to the other? The really relevant problem which needs to be considered is the examination of the actual conditions which are associated with each type of 'perspective realm', and here we may do well to follow Yinger's suggestion that the difference lies in the extent to which the actual experience of a society is 'punishing'.[31] The more punishing the experience, the greater the likelihood that the culture-system will emphasise supernatural means and/or ends.[82]

Religion and Irreligion: Confrontation or Symbiosis?

Finally, we may turn to a consideration of the present and possible relationships between irreligion and religion. In Chapter 2 we defined irreligion as, in essence, a reaction against conventional religion, whilst we had earlier made the point that the widespread distribution of irreligion throughout society was a comparatively recent phenomenon. For the vast majority of human history it has been religion which has held dominance over man and society whilst irreligion was regarded as either a trivial nuisance or a small but disturbing problem. Now irreligion has become democratised and is being incorporated into the cultural and social establishment of many Western European societies. There is no longer any real possibility therefore of irreligion itself being ignored or discarded as a minor irrelevance. For it would appear that for the immediate future at least religion and irreligion are likely to continue, and an important part of their respective environments will be the existence of the other. How will they view each other? What form will their relationship take? Indeed what significance will this relationship have for the development of Western civilisation? Very large questions indeed, but important enough to warrant raising. .

It is customary to consider religion and irreligion as standing in a relationship of confrontation, of truth against counter-truth, and such a picture has real support in historical fact. Much of the confrontation may well have been bogus, serving the interests of parties within one or other camp or based upon ignorance of the true nature of the enemy, but the nature of the relationship as understood by both parties was certainly that of animosity.

Both, to some degree, served the function of negative reference groups for each other, so that whatever smacked of religion was automatically anathema to the irreligionist and vice versa. This is the relationship which has been widely identified and described and is epitomised in the title of A. D. White's book 'A History of the Warfare of Science with Theology in Christendom'.[33] But as we have seen, there was a strong subsidiary tradition in which the irreligionists' attitude toward religion was one of sympathy and not hostility. They did not see themselves as 'confronting' religion but as reforming it, even though this sympathy was rarely reciprocated from the religious side.

Much has happened to irreligion as well as to religion since the confrontations of the later nineteenth century. There is now an irreligion 'ancient and modern' as well as a religion ancient and modern, and the traditional relationship of confrontation has given way to something approaching a creative symbiosis. Of course the old-style confrontation still persists and can be observed in the propaganda literature of the 'old guard' on both sides. To a greater extent, however, the myth of confrontation is maintained by 'false' confrontations in which 'modern irreligion' or 'modern religion' attacks 'ancient religion' or 'ancient irreligion'. As Professor Hamilton has observed, 'many secular modern men like their theological foes to be as orthodox as possible so they can be rejected as irrelevant'.[34] And the reverse is equally true. The truly significant relationship is that between modern religion and modern irreligion, and this is as yet still emergent, but it would appear to approximate more to one of sympathetic symbiosis than anything approaching confrontation. We have already seen how Catholic theologians and philosophers are busy finding good in irreligion and rehabilitating atheism, and how there has long been a tradition of irreligious sympathy for religion. Other factors now seem to be facilitating a greater sense of sympathy for the old 'enemy' on both sides, and although a critical stance is not abandoned, the criticism is more considered and informed than formerly. Such a situation would appear to favour the development of both traditions more than the former relationship of outright confrontation.

Whether this will continue to be true is uncertain, and if it is, what paths the two great traditions will take is a fascinating issue on which to speculate. However, not only would such speculation carry one outside the permitted arena of sociological commentary, it would not be appropriate to end a study of irreligion by indulging in prophecy. The temptation will thus be resisted this time.

Notes

1 Prologue: Toward a Sociology of Irreligion

1. S. Mayor, 'The Churches and the Labour Movement' (Independent Press, 1967) pp. 77-8.
2. Perhaps in this respect we should be far more critical of the Victorians than we have been. Instead of praising them for their manifest devoutness and conscientiousness in all things religious and thus by implication denigrating ourselves in this respect, we should criticise them more for their unseemly excess of religious zeal, the fanaticism with which they indulged in the cults of the Bible and the Sunday as well as their uncritical acceptance of dogma and custom. Perhaps we should even criticise them for their failure to doubt and, in relation to religious practice, their failure to rebel and deny the pressures of conformity.
3. J. M. Robertson, 'A Short History of Freethought, Ancient and Modern', 3rd ed. (Watts, 1915) ii 391.
4. E. J. Hobsbawm, 'Primitive Rebels' (Manchester U.P., 1959) chap. viii. Hobsbawm's discussion of the 'labour sects' is particularly relevant to this process of social change.
5. H. P. Becker, 'Through Values to Social Interpretations' (Duke University Press, Durham, N.C., 1950) p. 275.
6. L. Shiner, 'The Concept of Secularization in Empirical Research', in 'Journal for the Scientific Study of Religion', vi 2 (1967).
7. H. J. Blackham, 'Modern Humanism', in 'Journal of World History', viii 1 (1964) 117.
8. T. Parsons, 'Sociology and Social Psychology', in 'Religious Perspectives in College Teaching' (Ronald Press, New York, 1952); G. Lenski, 'The Religious Factor' (Anchor Books, New York, 1963).
9. P. Sorokin, 'The Western Religion and Morality of Today', in 'International Yearbook for the Sociology of Religion' (Cologne, 1966) ii 9-44.
10. C. Glock and R. Stark, 'Religion and Society in Tension' (Rand McNally, Chicago, 1965) p. 85.
11. See discussion in Chapter 2, pp. 39-40 below.

12. At the International Symposium on the Culture of Unbelief, Rome, March 1969.
13. Cardinal Franz Konig, 'The Second Vatican Council and the Secretariat for Non-Believers', in 'Concurrence', no. 1 (spring 1969) p. 37.
14. Ibid.
15. See, for example, N. J. Demerath III and Victor Theissen, 'On Spitting against the Wind: Organisational Precariousness and American Irreligion', in 'American Journal of Sociology', Lxxi 6 (May 1966) 674-87.
16. See, for example, Millett's comment that 'Although our immediate object of study is religious institutions, a functional approach requires that such institutions be situated in the total social context, non-religious as well as religious, in order to be fully understood'. D. Millett, 'A Typology of Religious Organisations Suggested by the Canadian Census', in 'Sociological Analysis', xxx 2 (summer 1969) 118.
17. N. J. Demerath, 'Program and Prolegomena for a Sociology of Irreligion', in 'Actes de la X Conference Internationale' (Conference Internationale de Sociologie Religieuse, Rome, 1969).

2 *The Nature and Forms of Irreligion*

1. A.Kellett, 'Isms and Ologies' (Epworth Press, 1965) p. 142.
2. A.W. Benn, 'The History of English Rationalism in the Nineteenth Century', 2 vols (Russell & Russell, New York, 1962; 1st ed., 1906) p. 4.
3. See, for example, J. E. Courtney, 'Freethinkers of the Nineteenth Century' (Chapman & Hall, 1920).
4. See Chapter 3, p. 55, below.
5. See M. R. Cohen, 'Baseball as a National Religion', in L. Schneider (ed.), 'Religion, Culture and Society' (Wiley, New York, 1964).
6. See Leslie Weatherhead's arguments for Christian agnosticism in 'The Christian Agnostic' (Hodder & Stoughton, 1965).
7. H. J. Blackham, 'The Ethical Movement during Seventy Years', in 'The Plain View', no. 6 (Jan 1946), and W. Eckstein, 'The Need For Ethical Reconstruction' in 'Proceedings of the First International Congress on Humanism and Ethical Culture' (Humanistisch Verbond, Utrecht, 1953).
8. As an example of this debate see Julian Huxley, 'The Coming New Religion of Humanism', in 'The Humanist', xxii 3 (Jan-Feb 1962) and the

reply by Harry Elmer Barnes and Herbert T. Rosenfeld, 'Is Humanism a New Religion?', in 'The Humanist', xxii 4 (1962).

9. Kellett, `Isms and Ologies', pp. 12-13; Robertson, 'A Short History of Freethought, Ancient and Modern', p. 21.

10. W. L. Courtney, 'Do We Believe? A Record of a Great Correspondence in the "Daily Telegraph", October, November and December, 1904' (Hodder & Stoughton, 1905).

11. Demerath appears to choose to emphasise the ideological dimension of irreligion for his own purposes, whilst recognising that the other dimensions exist; see 'Program and Prolegomena for a Sociology of Irreligion', pp. 162-3.

12. See Chapter 4, pp. 124 ff. below.

13. 'The Army and Religion: An Enquiry and its Bearing upon the Religious Life of the Nation' (Macmillan, 1919).

14. Rev. C. M. Davies, 'Heterodox London: or Phases of Free Thought in the Metropolis', 2 vols (Tinsley Bros, 1874).

15. This distinction has also been made by Demerath; see 'Program and Prolegomena for a Sociology of Irreligion'. The intention is to use the term 'a-religious' with the same connotations in the religious sphere which 'a-political' has acquired in the realm of politics.

16. P. Aldane, 'The Problem in East London', in R. Mudie-Smith (ed.), 'The Religious Life of London' (Hodder & Stoughton, 1904).

17. Mayor, 'The Churches and the Labour Movement', p. 23.

18. J. Lofland and R. Stark, 'The Concept of Seekership', in 'American Sociological Review', xxx (1963) 868 ff.

19. Glock and Stark, 'Religion and Society in Tension', p. 27.

20. Lofland and Stark, 'The Concept of Seekership', p. 870.

21. M. Quin, 'Memoirs of a Positivist' (Allen & Unwin, 1924) p. 41.

22. Charles Y. Glock, 'The Study of Non-belief: Perspectives on Research' paper read at the International Symposium on the Culture of Unbelief, Rome, March 1969.

23. Universalists and Unitarians were frequently condemned as 'infidels' in America during the nineteenth century; see A. Post, 'Popular Free-thought in America, 1825-1850' (Columbia U.P., New York, 1943) p. 195. Also, for a discussion of how the branding of religious opponents as irreligious was employed as a strategy for advancing the aims of one Church against its rivals, see M. E. Marty, 'The Infidel: Free-thought and

American Religion' (World Publishing Company, Cleveland and New York, 1961).

24. Another difference between the irreligious and the religious reformer may be that the latter is trying to add to the religious tradition, not just to subtract from it. Attempts to introduce 'alien' components into an established religious tradition (i.e. spiritualism, polygamy) may of course provoke as violent a reaction as the attempts of the irreligious to eliminate components of the tradition.

25. In one sense one could, of course, talk of the state Marxism of countries of Eastern Europe as established irreligious orthodoxies.

26. J. V. Langmead Casserley, 'The Retreat from Christianity in the Modern World' (Longmans, 1952) p. 8.

27. Mayor, 'The Churches and the Labour Movement', p. 400.

28. The fact that the nature of one's irreligious commitment may be conditioned by the character of the religion that one was formerly committed to is well illustrated in the lives and writings of many 'honest doubters' of Victorian society. The moral earnestness of the evangelical was a characteristic of free-thinkers as it was of the devout. In addition, although the former no longer seriously believed in religion, they believed that it should be taken seriously. This attitude is in sharp contrast to that of many contemporary irreligionists who, not having formerly been seriously committed to religion, do not now feel that it ought to be taken seriously.

29. For further discussion of this debate with reference to particular irreligious movements, see Chapter 3 below.

30. See G. Gorer, 'Exploring English Character' (Cresset Press, 1955) p. 109.

31. A.Post, 'Popular Freethought in America, 1825-1850', p. 188.

32. The popular stereotype of the atheist is detected easily enough by the frequency with which he is described by the qualifying adjectives 'dogmatic', 'aggressive', 'arrogant' and the like. A good illustration of this stereotype is Warren's description of D. M. Bennett, the editor of 'Truth Seeker': 'like most atheists, [he was] defiant, belligerent and aggressively hostile'. S. Warren, 'American Freethought, 1860-1914' (Gordian Press, New York, 1966) p. 191.

33. Glock and Stark, 'Religion and Society in Tension', p. 65, and Charles Glock and Rodney Stark, 'Christian Beliefs and Anti-Semitism' (Harper & Row, New York and London, 1966) p. 216.

34. The suggestion that the non-religious lack visibility as an organised group in American society is made by Vernon. See Glenn M. Vernon, 'The Religious "Nones": A Neglected Category', in 'Journal for the Scientific Study of Religion', vii 2 (fall 1968) 219-29.
35. The Dutch humanists, for example, who are highly organised, have an estimated 15,000 members.
36. W. L. Sperry, 'Religion in America' (Beacon Press, Boston, 1963) p. 256; S. Budd, 'The Humanist Societies: The Consequences of a Diffuse Belief System', in B. R. Wilson (ed.), 'Patterns of Sectarianism' (Heinemann, 1967) pp. 377-405 Demerath and Thiessen, 'On Spitting against the Wind', pp. 674—87.
37. H. B. Radest, 'Toward Common Ground: The Story of the Ethical Societies in the United States' (Frederick Ungar, New York, 1969); Blackham, 'The Ethical Movement during Seventy Years'.
38. Post, 'Popular Freethought in America', p. 170; Warren, 'American Freethought, 1860-1914', p. 117.
39. Budd, 'The Humanist Societies', in Wilson (ed.), 'Patterns of Sectarianism'.
40. This fear is well illustrated by Harrison's reaction to Gongreve's move in forming a positivist church when Positivism had hardly begun to establish itself in England. Harrison feared that this would necessarily create a sect and he fervently disliked the 'small-town pettiness' of sects. Thereafter he consistently referred to the members of Congreve's church as 'the brethren'. W. M. Simon, 'European Positivism in the Nineteenth Century: An Essay in Intellectual History' (Cornell U.P., Ithaca, N.Y., 1963) pp. 57-8.
41. There was among the working classes a feeling that there was more brotherhood in the public-house than in the average church.
42. Lenski, 'The Religious Factor', p. 331 n.
43. There is also the possibility of irreligious communities. Although on the face of it the irreligious have no rationale for withdrawal from the world as have the religious, communities which were justifiably defined as irreligious by the consensus of opinion of their age have existed. Robert Owen's New Harmony community in Indiana falls into this category. Usually, however, as in this case, there is some powerful positive bond that holds the community together.

3 Irreligious Movements in Britain and America during the Nineteenth and Twentieth Centuries

1. Robertson, 'A Short History of Freethought, Ancient and Modern', ii 383.
2. J. E. McGee, 'A History of the British Secular Movement' (Hadleman-Julius, Girard, Kans., 1948) ii 12.
3. Ibid., p. 13.
4. Ibid., p. 14.
5. E. Royle, 'George Jacob Holyoake and the Secularist Movement in Britain, 1841-1861', Ph.D. thesis (Christ's College, Cambridge, 1968).
6. Ibid., p. 187.
7. Ibid., pp. 216-17.
8. G. H. Taylor, 'A Chronology of British Secularism' (National Secular Society, 1957) p. 8.
9. Royle, 'Holyoake', p. 213.
10. Ibid., p. 227.
11. McGee, 'British Secular Movement', p. 72.
12. Ibid., p. 42.
13. Ibid., p. 42.
14. Royle, 'Holyoake', p. 268.
15. McGee, 'British Secular Movement', p. 73.
16. Royle, 'Holyoake', p. 243.
17. Ibid.
18. Ibid., p. 266.
19. Ibid.
20. Davies, 'Heterodox London', i 221.
21. Ibid., ii 119.
22. McGee, 'British Secular Movement', p. 9.
23. Royle, 'Holyoake', p. 264.
24. Ibid., p. 270.
25. Ibid.
26. Ibid.
27. Ibid., p. 273.
28. R. Billington, 'Leicester Secular Society, 1852-1920: A Study in Radicalism and Respectability', unpublished dissertation (University of Leicester, 1968).
29. Davies, 'Heterodox London ', i 366—7.

30. McGee, 'British Secular Movement', p. 36.
31. Royle, 'Holyoake', p. 116.
32. J. Eros, 'Organised Freethought in Mid-Victorian England', in 'Sociological Review', ii 1 (July 1954) 99.
33. Ibid.
34. Benn, 'The History of English Rationalism in the Nineteenth Century', p. 387.
35. Robertson, 'A Short History of Freethought, Ancient and Modern', ii 401.
36. Post, 'Popular Freethought in America, 1825-1850', p. 16.
37. Although Woodbridge Riley observed that the free-thinking societies in early nineteenth-century America suffered from being identified in the public mind with Freemasonry and as a result were attacked for their secrecy and presumed foreign allegiances. W. Riley, 'Early Free-Thinking Societies in America', in 'Harvard Theological Review', xi 3 (July 1918) 247-84.
38. Post, 'Popular Freethought in America', p. 34.
39. Ibid.
40. Ibid., p. 94.
41. Ibid., pp. 75-6.
42. Ibid., p. 234.
43. N. R. Burr, 'A Critical Bibliography of Religion in America', 2 vols (Princeton U.P., 1961) ii 1143.
44. Ibid.
45. Warren, 'American Freethought, 1860-1914', pp. 196, 204.
46. Ibid., p. 175.
47. Ibid., p. 160.
48. The furore surrounding the Comstock Postal Laws was in fact the occasion for its collapse: ibid., p. 162.
49. Ibid., p. 230.
50. Ibid., pp. 179-80.
51. D. G. Charlton, 'New Creeds for Old in Nineteenth Century France', in 'Canadian Journal of Theology', iii 4 (1962) 260.
52. G. Bryson, 'Early English Positivists and the Religion of Humanity', in 'American Sociological Review', i 3 (June 1936) 344.
53. Charlton, 'New Creeds for Old', p. 263.
54. Bryston, 'Early English Positivists', p. 344.
55. Charlton, 'New Creeds for Old', p. 263.

56. D. G. Charlton, 'Secular Religions in France, 1815-1870' (Oxford U.P., 1963).
57. J. E. McGee, 'A Crusade for Humanity: The History of Organised Positivism in England' (Watts, 1931); Simon, 'European Positivism in the Nineteenth Century'; Charlton, 'New Creeds for Old', p. 264. In sharp contrast to this success in South America, the story of the Religion of Humanity on the North American continent is dismal indeed. The only American group devoted to the Religion of Humanity seems to have been that founded by an Englishman, Henry Edgar, in the Utopian community of Modern Times on Long Island. This could hardly be described as a success for after five years of effort he had made only ten converts, four of whom were his wife and children. See R. L. Hawkins, 'Positivism in the United States (1853-1861)' (Harvard U.P., Cambridge, Mass., 1938) chap. 3.

The following delightful little vignette of Comte in his house at 10 Rue Monsieur-le-Prince is by an American Unitarian minister, the Rev. Joseph Henry Allen, who visited Comte in 1857:

> In one of those quiet suites of rooms, so pleasant to the memory of the visitor in Paris, with their grave, antique furniture, and their cool floors of polished chestnut, a few steps from the Odeon and the Luxembourg, dwells this self-chosen Pontiff of the human race. He is a man of not quite sixty, with the short stature, the large black eye, and the dark features of southern France; his manner simple and courteous; his conversation rapid, impatient, and very trying to the unpractised ear; his recreation music, of which he is passionately fond. He imperiously disclaims all halfway discipleship, and is unsparing in his charges of hypocrisy on those who have followed his method but criticized his results.

From Hawkins, 'Positivism in the United States', p. 73.
58. Simon, 'European Positivism', p. 68.
59. Bryson, 'Early English Positivists', p. 351.
60. McGee, 'Crusade for Humanity', pp. 184-5.
61. R. Harrison, 'Professor Beesly and the Working-Class Movement', in Asa Briggs and John Saville (eds), 'Essays in Labour History', rev. ed. (Macmillan, 1967) pp. 205-41.
62. Simon, 'European Positivism'.
63. Ibid., p. 60.

64. McGee, 'Crusade for Humanity', p. 227.
65. Ibid., pp. 129-51, 178.
66. Ibid., p. 184; Simon, 'European Positivism', p. 69.
67. McGee, 'Crusade for Humanity', p. 43; Simon, 'European Positivism', p. 70.
68. Simon, 'European Positivism', pp. 69—70.
69. McGee, 'Crusade for Humanity', p. 41.
70. Simon, 'European Positivism', p. 70.
71. McGee, 'Crusade for Humanity', p. 168.
72. Ibid., pp. 233-4.
73. Ibid., p. 186.
74. Quin, 'Memoirs of a Positivist', p. 9.
75. McGee, 'Crusade for Humanity', p. 42.
76. Christian Science, Scientology, etc. (see above, Chapter 4).
77. Quin, 'Memoirs of a Positivist'.
78. Ibid., p. 42.
79. Simon, 'European Positivism', p. 70.
80. Ibid.; Robertson, 'A Short History of Freethought', i 484.
81. Bryson, 'Early English Positivists', p. 361.
82. McGee, 'Crusade for Humanity', p. 229.
83. Ibid., p. 94.
84. Bryson, 'Early English Positivists', p. 362.
85. McGee, 'Crusade for Humanity', p. 231.
86. Radest, 'Toward Common Ground'.
87. C.S. Braden, 'These Also Believe' (Macmillan, New York, 1949).
88. Radest, 'Toward Common Ground'.
89. M. W. Meyerhardt, 'The Movement for Ethical Culture at Home and Abroad', in 'American Journal of Religious Psychology and Education', iii 1 (May 1905) 78.
90. Blackham,'Modern Humanism', p. 110.
91. Radest, 'Toward Common Ground', p. 40.
92. Meyerhardt, 'The Movement for Ethical Culture', p. 76.
93. Eckstein, 'The Need for Ethical Reconstruction', p. 81.
94. Meyerhardt, 'The Movement for Ethical Culture', p. 76.
95. Eckstein, 'The Need for Ethical Reconstruction', p. 82.
96. Meyerhardt, 'The Movement for Ethical Culture', p. 75.
97. Ibid., p. 79.

98. Radest, 'Toward Common Ground', p. 39.
99. Ibid., p. 144.
100. Ibid., pp. 51-2.
101. See below, pp. 84—5.
102. Meyerhardt, 'The Movement for Ethical Culture', pp. 80-1.
103. Radest, 'Toward Common Ground', p. 92.
104. G. Spiller, 'The Ethical Movement in Great Britain' (Farleigh Press, 1934).
105. Ibid., p. 2.
106. See below, pp. 79-83.
107. S. K. Ratcliffe, 'The Story of South Place' (Watts, 1955).
108. W. S. Smith, 'The London Heretics, 1870-1914' (Constable, 1967) p. 134.
109. 'International Humanist and Ethical Union and its Member Organisations' (Utrecht, Oudegracht, 1962) p. 15.
110. Smith, 'The London Heretics', p. 125.
111. Blackham,'The Ethical Movement during Seventy Years,pp.137-149.
112. Meyerhardt, 'The Movement for Ethical Culture', p. 81.
113. Spiller, 'The Ethical Movement in Great Britain', pp. 26-7.
114. Ibid., p. 32.
115. Ibid., p. 27.
116. Ibid., pp. 68-9.
117. Ibid., p. 68.
118. Ibid., p. 80.
119. Ibid., p. 83.
120. Ibid., p. 77.
121. H. Blackham, 'Stanton Coit 1857-1944' (Favil Press, n.d.).
122. T. Tribe, 'One Hundred Years of Freethought' (Elek Books, 1967) p. 39.
123. Ibid., p. 38.
124. Radest, 'Toward Common Ground', p. 76.
125. Blackham, 'Stanton Coit 1857-1944', p. 16.
126. Spiller, 'The Ethical Movement in Great Britain', p. 91; Radest, 'Toward Common Ground', p. 75.
127. Tribe, 'One Hundred Years of Freethought', p. 39.
128. Radest, 'Toward Common Ground', p. 131.
129. Ibid., p. 86.
130. Spiller, 'The Ethical Movement in Great Britain', p. 115.
131. Radest, 'Toward Common Ground'; 'Yearbook of American Churches'.
132. Radest, 'Toward Common Ground', p. 290.

133. Ibid., p. 293.
134. Blackham, 'Modern Humanism', p. 102.
135. J. W. Smith and A. L. Jamison, 'The Shaping of American Religion' (Princeton U.P., 1961); Burr, 'A Critical Bibliography of Religion in America'.
136. S. Parsons, 'Free Religion' (Beacon Press, Boston, 1963) p. 153.
137. Ibid.
138. Ibid., p. 148.
139. Radest, 'Toward Common Ground', p. 58.
140. Burr, 'A Critical Bibliography of Religion in America', i 263.
141. Persons, 'Free Religion', p. 107.
142. In the Torcaso decision of 1961, the Supreme Court recognised that there are non-theistic religions in America and accepted in principle that adherents of these religions had the same rights as adherents of theistic religions. Secular Humanism and Ethical Culture were among those specified as non-theistic religions.
143. Gowans Whyte, 'The Story of the R.P.A., 1899-1949' (Watts, 1949) p. 12.
144. Smith, 'The London Heretics', p. 70.
145. The background to this decision was given in F. J. Gould, 'The Pioneers of Johnson's Court: A History of the Rationalist Press Association from 1899 Onwards' (Watts, 1929).
146. Gowans Whyte, 'The Story of the R.P.A.', p. 54.
147. 'Memorandum and Articles of Association of The Rationalist Press Association Limited' (May 1899) p. 3.
148. Gowans Whyte, 'The Story of the R.P.A.', p. 55.
149. Smith, 'The London Heretics', p. 279.
150. See Marty, 'The Infidel: Freethought and American Religion'.
151. This is the title of a book by Hector Hawton (Pemberton Publishing Co. Ltd, 1963).
152. Blackham, 'World Humanism', p. 113.
153. Reprinted in 'Religious Humanism', iv 2 (spring 1970) 61.
154. Ibid., p. 62.
155. Private correspondence with Edwin H. Wilson.
156. 'Humanist' (U.S.A.), xxv (Jan-Feb 1968) 34.
157. 'Humanist News' (May-June 1964) p. 1.
158. Ibid.
159. 'Rationalist Press Association 57th Annual Report' (1955) p. 9.

160. Ford, 'The New Groups', in 'News and Notes' (Aug 1955) pp. 3-4.

161. 'Literary Guide' (Feb 1956) pp. 32-3.

162. Ibid.

163. Sources: 'Humanist News' ('News and Notes') and the B.H.A. Annual Reports.

164. 'The British Humanist Association' (pamphlet, n.d.).

165. Ibid.

166. 'News and Notes' (Apr 1959) p. 3. There had been a 'Humanist Council' in 1950, established by the Ethical Union, the R.P.A. and the South Place Ethical Society as a general umbrella organisation for public relations purposes, but the word 'humanist' was adopted when no other single word was found which could apply to all three organisations.

167. F. M. Brierley, 'Report on University Humanist Groups' (Oct 1963, mimeographed).

168. Budd is one of those who has rather misleadingly presented the contemporary humanist movement as if it was merely an extension of the nineteenth-century irreligious movements rather than as an essentially 'new' movement with a distinctive ethos. See Budd, 'The Humanist Societies', in Wilson (ed.), 'Patterns of Sectarianism'.

169. Among his many works on this theme, perhaps the most influential has been 'Religion without Revelation' (Parrish, 1957).

170. J. Huxley, 'The Humanist Revolution', in 'The Human Crisis' (Univ. of Washington Press, Seattle, 1963) p. 5.

171. 'The Humanist Alternative' (pamphlet, n.d.) p. 3.

4 *Irreligion and Society*

1. The following discussion is based largely on J. M. Yinger, 'Religion, Society and the Individual' (Macmillan, New York, 1957) pp. 24 ff.
2. Ibid., p. 24.
3. Warren, 'American Freethought, 1860-1914', p. 185.
4. 'The Tablet' (Jan 1883) p. 8.
5. Post, 'Popular Freethought in America, 1825-1850', p. 200.
6. The vast majority of these charges were without any foundation in fact, although free-thinkers frequently held liberal positions on moral and sexual matters. The only free-thinker who seems to have explicitly advocated free love was Ezra Heywood, who established his New England Free Love League in 1873. Persons, 'Free Religion', p. 119.
7. Although there is a good deal of controversy over whether parents really want religious education for their children or merely moral education, it would seem that most parents are not accustomed to making this distinction. See the survey reported in 'New Society', 27 May 1965, and the N.O.P. survey 'Moral and Religious Education: What the People Want', published by the British Humanist Association in April 1969.
8. B.S. Rowntree and G. R. Lavers, 'English Life and Leisure: A Social Study' (Longmans, 1951) p. 372.
9. Sperry, 'Religion in America', p. 257.
10. See the various works of Glock and Stark, especially 'Religion and Society in Tension'.
11. D.Wright, 'Morality and Religion: A Review of Empirical Studies', in 'Rationalist Annual' (1967) p. 27.
12. Ibid., pp. 28 ff.
13. Sorokin, 'The Western Religion and Morality of Today', in 'International Yearbook for the Sociology of Religion', ii 16.
14. M. Argyle, 'Religious Behaviour' (Routledge & Kegan Paul, 1958) p. 99.
15. H. Hartshorne and M. A. May, 'Studies in Deceit' (Macmillan, New York, 1929).
16. Sorokin, 'The Western Religion and Morality of Today', p. 16.
17. Wright, 'Morality and Religion', p. 29.

18. S. Putney and R. Middleton, 'Ethical Relativism and Anomia', in 'American Journal of Sociology', lxvii 5 (1962) 430-8.
19. D. Wright and E. Cox, 'Religious Beliefs and Co-education in a Sample of Sixth-form Boys and Girls', in 'British Journal of Social and Clinical Psychology', no. 6 (1967).
20. R. M. McIver and C. H. Page, 'Society: An Introductory Analysis' (Holt, Rinehart, New York, 1949) p. 168.
21. R. C. K. Ensor, 'England 1870-1914' (Clarendon Press, Oxford, 1936) pp. 137-43.
22. Gorer, 'Exploring English Character', p. 253.
23. Rowntree and Lavers, 'English Life and Leisure', p. 354.
24. Ibid.
25. 'The Army and Religion', p. 196.
26. Budd, 'The Humanist Societies', in Wilson (ed.), 'Patterns of Sectarianism', p. 391.
27. Billington, 'Leicester Secular Society, 1852-1920', Appendix.
28. 'The Humanist' (Feb 1961) p. 54.
29. Ibid.
30. G. Fairbanks, 'The Humanist Political Spectrum', in 'Australian Humanist' (Oct 1968) p. 47.
31. Tribe, 'One Hundred Years of Freethought'.
32. Smith, 'The London Heretics', p. 17.
33. Post, 'Popular Freethought in America, 1825-1850'.
34. Tribe, 'One Hundred Years of Freethought', p. 86.
35. Warren, 'American Freethought, 1860-1914', p. 136.
36. Tribe, 'One Hundred Years of Freethought', p. 81.
37. A proposal that the Humanist Association should declare a political bias was made in 1958: ibid., p. 82.
38. Warren, 'American Freethought, 1860-1914', p. 166.
39. Suggested to the Humanist Council in 1957 and the British Humanist Association in 1966. See Tribe, 'One Hundred Years of Freethought', p. 82.
40. Ibid., p. 81.
41. There are, however, some qualifications to be made to this general rule. Some of the Welsh ethical societies at the turn of the century had very close links with the Independent Labour Party, and Blackham reports that Merthyr Tydfil Ethical Society resolved itself into a branch of the

Independent Labour Party and returned Keir Hardie. Blackham, 'The Ethical Movement during Seventy Years', p. 149. The ethical movement as a whole, however, did not develop such links. In addition, the Labour Church movement and the associated Socialist Sunday School movement could be regarded as quasi-irreligious movements which had very definite ideological and organisational links with the Labour movement. For details of these movements, see K. S. Inglis, 'The Labour Church Movement', in 'International Review of Social History', iii (1958) 445-60, and F. Reid, 'Socialist Sunday Schools in Britain, 1892-1939', in 'International Review of Social History', xi (1966) 18-47.

42. Gowans Whyte, 'The Story of the R.P.A.', p. 12.
43. Ibid., p. 39.
44. Ibid., p. 44.
45. Ibid., p. 42.
46. 'A Few Points about Ethical Societies' (pamphlet, n.d.).
47. Radest, 'Toward Common Ground', p. 176.
48. Ibid.
49. Eros, 'Organised Freethought in Mid-Victorian England', p. 115.
50. 'Humanist News' (Sep 1965) p. 4.
51. Blackham, 'Modern Humanism', p. 116.
52. 'News and Notes' (Apr 1962) p. 51.
53. 'News and Notes' (Apr 1961) p. 2.
54. Radest, 'Toward Common Ground', p. 301.
55. Ibid.
56. Marty, 'The Infidel: Freethought and American Religion'.
57. Quoted in Kellett, 'Isms and Ologies', p. 13.
58. W. A. Luijpen, 'Phenomenology and Atheism' (Duquesne U.P., Pittsburg, 1964) p. xiv.
59. Ibid., p. 80.
60. Ibid., p. xiv.
61. J. Lacroix, 'The Meaning of Modern Atheism' (Gill, Dublin, 1965) p. 63.
62. Ibid., p. 23.
63. Casserley, 'The Retreat from Christianity in the Modern World', p. 41.
64. McGee, 'A History of the British Secular Movement', p. 81.
65. See below, pp. 142-4.
66. It has indeed been long recognised that the relationship between ritual and anxiety is a complex one and that ritual may well arouse anxiety

before alleviating it. The crucial question, however, is, as O'Dea puts it, 'To what extent do institutionalized religion and magic represent a net gain for men with respect to the alleviation of anxiety?' T. F. O'Dea, 'The Sociology of Religion' (Prentice-Hall, Englewood Cliffs, N.J., 1966) p. 10. The position taken here is that for some irreligious people at least institutionalised religion and magic represented a net loss with respect to such alleviation.

67. S. Budd, 'The Loss of Faith: Reasons for Unbelief among Members of the Secular Movement in England, 1850-1950', in 'Past and Present', no. 36 (1967) pp. 106-25.
68. Courtney, 'Freethinkers of the Nineteenth Century', p. 7.
69. Billington, 'Leicester Secular Society, 1852-1920'.
70. Ibid., p. 64.
71. Casserley, 'The Retreat from Christianity in the Modern World', p. 130.
72. See W. G. Katz and H. P. Southerland, 'Religious Pluralism and the Supreme Court', in 'Daedalus', xcvi (1967) 180-92.
73. Sorokin, 'The Western Religion and Morality of Today'.
74. Budd, 'The Loss of Faith, 1850-1950', pp. 108-9.
75. The former argument is one presented by Warren at the conclusion of his study of free thought in America in the latter half of the nineteenth century. Warren, 'American Freethought, 1860-1914', p. 229.
76. Eros, 'Organised Freethought in Mid-Victorian England', pp. 98-120.
77. Post, 'Popular Freethought in America, 1825-1850', p. 231.
78. Budd, 'The Loss of Faith', p. 123.
79. H.R. Murphy, 'The Ethical Revolt against Christian Orthodoxy in Early Victorian England', in 'American Historical Review', ix (July 1955) 800.
80. Ibid., p. 816.
81. Budd, 'The Loss of Faith', p. 114.
82. Royle, 'George Jacob Holyoake and the Secularist Movement in Britain, 1841-1861', p. 103.
83. 'The Army and Religion', p. 62.
84. Royle, 'George Jacob Holyoake', p. 38.
85. 'The Army and Religion', p. 207.

5 Conclusion: Irreligion and the Functionalist Perspective in the Sociology of Religion

1. O'Dea, 'The Sociology of Religion', p. 16.
2. Clifford Geertz, 'Religion as a Cultural System', in Donald R. Cutler (ed.), 'The Religious Situation: 1968' (Beacon Press, Boston, 1968) p. 664.
3. O'Dea is one of the few sociologists of religion who recognises this oversight and he chides his colleagues for it:
   '. . . functionalist theorists are not justified in neglecting an examination of the functional significance of doubt itself, and the reasons for its appearance in certain societies and certain periods of history. Doubt as well as belief, is subject to social conditioning, and like belief, has positive or negative functional significance.'
   O'Dea, 'The Sociology of Religion', p. 18.
4. Lenski, 'The Religious Factor', p. 331.
5. Ibid.
6. A.Toynbee, preface to John Cogley, 'Religion in a Secular Age: The Search for Final Meaning' (Pall Mall Press, 1968) p. vi.
7. F. Zweig, 'The Quest for Fellowship' (Heinemann, 1965) p. 121.
8. Thomas Luckmann, 'The Invisible Religion' (Macmillan, New York, 1967) chap. 3.
9. The use of competence rather than 'function' is deliberate and follows Nadel's usage, thereby avoiding the implication of religion as some form of inherent functional requisite. See Worsley's discussion of Nadel in P. Worsley, 'The Trumpet Shall Sound' (MacGibbon & Kee, 1968) pp. xxx-xxxii.
10. Yinger, 'Religion, Society and the Individual', p. 9.
11. P. H. Benson, 'Religion in Contemporary Culture : A Study of Religion through Social Science' (Harper Bros, New York, 1960) p. 162.
12. Luckmann, 'The Invisible Religion'.
13. D. Mackenzie-Brown, 'Ultimate Concern: Tillich in Dialogue' (S.C.M. Press, 1965) p. 4.
14. Yinger, 'Religion, Society and the Individual', p. 9.
15. Talcott Parsons, for example, gives a central place to the problem of justice. See 'Sociology and Social Psychology', in 'Religious Perspectives

in College Teaching', pp. 286-337. Another notable omission from Yinger's list is the problem of ethics and morality.

16. Yinger, 'Religion, Society and the Individual', p. 81.
17. Benson, 'Religion in Contemporary Culture', p. 162.
18. W. E. Hocking, 'The Meaning of God in Human Experience' (Yale U.P., New Haven, 1912) p. 238.
19. C.Kluckhohn *et al.,* in Talcott Parsons and E. A. Shils (eds), 'Toward a General Theory of Action' (Harper, New York, 1961) p. 411.
20. Glock and Stark, 'Religion and Society in Tension', pp. 10-11.
21. The following are a few samples of the lists of 'functional alternatives' to traditional religion mentioned in some well-known texts in the sociology of religion: communism, nationalism, humanism, internationalism and science (T. F. Hoult, 'The Sociology of Religion' (Holt, Rinehart & Winston, New York, 1958)); communism, nationalism, fascism and socialism (E. K. Nottingham, 'Religion and Society' (Random House, New York, 1954)); communism, nationalism and humanism (Yinger, 'Religion, Society and the Individual'); communism, humanism and Freudianism (Lenski, 'The Religious Factor'); communism, humanism, nationalism and fascism (G. M. Vernon, 'Sociology of Religion' (McGraw-Hill, New York, 1962)); communism, humanism and psychoanalytism (R. Robertson, 'The Sociological Interpretation of Religion' (Blackwell, Oxford, 1970)).
22. Marion Levy, 'Structural-Functional Analysis', in 'Encyclopaedia of Social Science' (1968) iii 27.
23. Julian Huxley, 'Evolutionary Humanism', in 'Proceedings of the First International Congress on Humanism and Ethical Culture' (Amsterdam, August 1952) pp. 12-30.
24. Luckmann, 'The Invisible Religion', p. 82.
25. H. J. Blackham, 'The Pointlessness of it All', in Blackham (ed.), 'Objections to Humanism' (Constable, 1963) p. 103.
26. Ibid., p. 108.
27. Yinger, 'Religion, Society and the Individual', p. 70; Glock and Stark, 'Religion and Society in Tension', p. 11.
28. Ibid.
29. Glock and Stark seem to overlook the many examples of determinate statements arising from religious perspectives that have been dis-confirmed. The forecasts of the Second Advent are an obvious case in

point. It is surely debatable whether predictions deriving from 'humanist perspectives' have, in fact, been 'more fragile' than those deriving from religious perspectives. Festinger's study of unfulfilled prophecy is surely pertinent here (Leon Festinger *et al,* 'When Prophecy Fails' (Univ. of Minnesota Press, Minneapolis, 1956)). This is not to say that, in principle, religious perspectives may not have a greater potentiality for avoiding such fragility. But this potentiality is acquired at the loss of the possibility of confirmation.

30. Hoult, 'The Sociology of Religion', p. 387.
31. Yinger, 'Religion, Society and the Individual', p. 16.
32. Ibid.
33. Macmillan (1896) 2 vols.
34. Quoted by M. E. Marty, 'The Religious Situation: An Introduction', in Cutler (ed.), 'The Religious Situation: 1968', p. xxxviii.

Bibliography

P. Aldane, 'The Problem in East London', in R. Mudie-Smith (ed.), 'The Religious Life of London' (Hodder & Stoughton,1904).

Michael Argyle, 'Religious Behaviour' (Routledge & Kegan Paul,1958). 'The Army and Religion : An Enquiry and its Bearing upon the Religious Life of the Nation' (Macmillan, 1919).

Franklin L. Baumer, 'Religion and the Rise of Scepticism' (Harcourt, Brace, New York, 1960).

H. P. Becker, 'Through Values to Social Interpretations' (Duke University Press, Durham, N.C., 1950).

Alfred William Benn, 'The History of English Rationalism in the Nineteenth Century', 2 vols (Russell & Russell, New York, 1962; 1st ed. 1906).

Purnell Handy Benson, 'Religion in Contemporary Culture : A Study of Religion through Social Science' (Harper Bros, NewYork, 1960).

Rosamund Billington, 'Leicester Secular Society, 1852-1920: A Study in Radicalism and Respectability', unpublished dissertation (University of Leicester, 1968).

Harold J. Blackham, 'Stanton Coit 1857-1944' (Favill Press, n.d.). 'The Ethical Movement during Seventy Years', in 'The Plain View', no. 6 (Jan 1946) pp. 137-49.
'The Pointlessness of it all', in Blackham (ed.), 'Objections to Humanism' (Constable, 1963).
'Modern Humanism', in 'Journal of World History', 1 (1964).

Charles S. Braden, 'These also Believe' (Macmillan, New York, 1949).

D. Mackenzie Brown, 'Ultimate Concern: Tillich in Dialogue' (S.C.M. Press, 1965).

Gladys Bryson, 'Early English Positivists and the Religion of Humanity', in 'American Sociological Review', 3 (June 1936).

S. Budd, 'The Loss of Faith: Reasons for Unbelief among Members of the Secular Movement in England, 1850-1950', in 'Past and Present', 36 (1967) pp. 106-25.
'The Humanist Societies: The Consequences of a Diffuse Belief System', in Bryan R. Wilson (ed.), 'Patterns of Sectarianism' (Heinemann, 1967) pp. 373-406.

N. R. Burr, 'A Critical Bibliography of Religion in America', 2 vols (Princeton U.P., 1961).

Colin B. Campbell, 'Humanism and the Culture of the Professions : A Study
    of the Rise of the British Humanist Movement 1954-63', Ph.D. thesis
    (University of London, 1967).
    'Humanism in Britain : The Formation of a Secular Value-Oriented
    Movement', in David Martin (ed.), 'A Sociological Yearbook of Religion in
    Britain: 2' (S.C.M. Press, 1969) pp. 157-72.
Julian Victor Langmead Casserley, 'The Retreat from Christianity in the
    Modern World', the Maurice Lectures for 1951 (Longmans, 1952).
D. G. Charlton, 'New Creeds for Old in Nineteenth Century France', in
    'Canadian Journal of Theology', 4 (1962) pp. 258-69.
    'Secular Religions in France, 1815-1870' (Oxford U.P., 1963).
O. J. Cockshut, 'The Unbelievers' (Collins, 1964).
John Cogley, 'Religion in a Secular Age : The Search for Final Meaning' (Pall
    Mall Press, 1968).
Morris R. Cohen, 'Baseball as a National Religion', in Louis Schneider (ed.),
    'Religion, Culture and Society' (Wiley, New York, 1964).
Janet E. Courtney, 'Freethinkers of the Nineteenth Century' (Chapman &
    Hall, 1920).
W. L. Courtney, 'Do We Believe? : A Record of a Great Correspondence in
    "The Daily Telegraph", October, November and December, 1904' (Hodder
    & Stoughton, 1905).
Donald R. Cutler (ed.), 'The Religious Situation : 1968' (Beacon Press,
    Boston, 1968).
Rev. Charles Maurice Davies, 'Heterodox London : or Phases of Free
    Thought in the Metropolis', 2 vols (Tinsley Bros, 1874).
N. J. Demerath III, 'Social Class in American Protestantism' (Rand McNally,
    Chicago, 1965).
    'Program and Prolegomena for a Sociology of Irreligion', in Actes de la X
    Conference Internationale, Conference Internationale de Sociologie
    Religieuse (Rome, 1969).
    and Victor Theissen, 'On Spitting against the Wind: Organisational
    Precariousness and American Irreligion', in 'American Journal of
    Sociology', 6 (May 1966).
Rudolf Dreikurs, 'The Programme of Humanism', in 'Proceedings of the First
    International Congress on Humanism and Ethical Culture' (Humanistisch
    Verbond, Utrecht, 1953) pp. 106-11.

Walter Eckstein, 'The Need for Ethical Reconstruction', in 'Proceedings of the First International Congress on Humanism and Ethical Culture' (Humanistich Verbond, Utrecht, 1953) pp. 80-5.

R. C. K. Ensor, 'England 1870-1914' (Clarendon Press, Oxford, 1936).

J. Eros, 'Organised Freethought in Mid-Victorian England', in 'Sociological Review', ii 1 (July 1954) 98-120.

G. Fairbanks, 'The Humanist Political Spectrum', in 'Australian Humanist' (October 1968).

Clifford Geertz, 'Religion as a Cultural System', in Cutler (ed.), 'The Religious Situation : 1968'.

C.Y. Glock, 'The Study of Non-belief: Perspectives on Research', paper read at the International Symposium on the Culture of Unbelief, Rome, March 1969.

and R. Stark, 'Religion and Society in Tension' (Rand McNally, Chicago, 1965).

and 'Christian Beliefs and Anti-Semitism' (Harper & Row, New York and London, 1966).

Geoffrey Gorer, 'Exploring English Character' (Cresset Press, 1955).

F. J. Gould, 'The Pioneers of Johnson's Court: A History of the Rationalist Press Association from 1899 onwards' (Watts, 1929).

M. Guyau, 'The Non-Religion of the Future: A Sociological Study' (Schocken Books, New York, 1962).

Royden Harrison, 'Professor Beesly and the Working-Class Movement', in Asa Briggs and John Saville (eds.), 'Essays in Labour History', rev. ed. (Macmillan, 1967) pp. 205-41.

Hugh Hartshorne and Mark A. May, 'Studies in the Nature of Character', vol. i: 'Studies in Deceit'; vol. ii: 'Studies in Service and Self-control' (Macmillan, New York, 1929-30).

Richmond Laurin Hawkins, 'Auguste Comte and the United States (1816-1863)' (Harvard U.P., Cambridge, Mass., 1936). 'Positivism in the United States (1853-1861)' (Harvard U.P., Cambridge, Mass., 1938).

W. Herberg, 'Protestant, Catholic, Jew' (Doubleday, New York, 1960).

E. J. Hobsbawm, 'Primitive Rebels: Studies in Archic Forms of Social Movement in the 19th and 20th Centuries' (Manchester U.P., 1959).

William Ernest Hocking, 'The Meaning of God in Human Experience' (Yale U.P., New Haven, 1912).

Thomas Ford Hoult, 'The Sociology of Religion' (Holt, Rine-hart & Winston, New York, 1958).

Julian Huxley, 'Evolutionary Humanism', in 'Proceedings of the First International Congress on Humanism and Ethical Culture' (Amsterdam, 21-26 Aug 1952) pp. 12-30.

'The Human Crisis' (University of Washington Press, Seattle, 1963).

K. S. Inglis, 'The Labour Church Movement', in 'International Review of Social History', iii (1958) 445-60.

'Churches and the Working Classes in Victorian England' (Routledge & Kegan Paul, 1963).

'International Humanist and Ethical Union and its Member Organisations' (Utrecht, Oudegracht, 1962).

W. G. Katz and H. P. Southerland, 'Religious Pluralism and the Supreme Court', in 'Daedalus', xcvi (1967) 180-92.

Arnold Kellett, 'Isms and Ologies' (Epworth Press, 1965).

William Kent, 'London for Heretics' (Watts, 1932).

Cardinal Franz Konig, 'The Second Vatican Council and the Secretariat for Non-Believers', in 'Concurrence', no 1 (spring 1969).

Jean Lacroix, 'The Meaning of Modern Atheism' (Gill, Dublin, 1965).

Benson Y. Landis, 'Yearbook of American Churches' (National Council of Churches, New York, 1968).

Gerhard Lenski, 'The Religious Factor', rev. ed. (Anchor Books, New York, 1963).

'Religious Pluralism in Theoretical Perspective', in 'International Yearbook for the Sociology of Religion', I (Koln-Opladen, Westdeutscher Verlag, 1965) pp. 25-42.

Marion Levy, 'Structural-Functional Analysis', in 'Encylopaedia of Social Science', iii (1968).

J. Lofland and R. Stark, 'The Concept of Seekership', in 'American Sociological Review', xxx (1963).

T. Luckmann, 'The Invisible Religion' (Macmillan, New York, 1967).

William A. Luijpen, 'Phenomenology and Atheism' (Duquesne U.P., Pittsburg, 1964).

Helen Merrell Lynd, 'England in the Eighteen-Eighties : Toward a Social Basis for Freedom' (Oxford U.P., New York, 1945).

John Edwin McGee, 'A History of the British Secular Movement' (Hadleman-Julius, Girard, Kans., 1948).

'A Crusade for Humanity: The History of Organised Positivism in England' (Watts, 1931).

Alasdair MacIntyre, 'Secularization and Moral Change' (Oxford U.P., 1967).

Horace Mann, 'Sketches of the Religious Denominations of the Present Day (and the Census)' (George Routledge, 1854).

David Martin, 'A Sociology of English Religion' (Heinemann, 1967).
'A Sociological Yearbook of Religion in Britain', vols 1 and 2 (S.C.M. Press, 1968-9).

Martin E. Marty, 'The Infidel: Freethought and American Religion' (World Publishing Company, Cleveland and New York, 1961).

Mass Observation, 'Puzzled People' (Gollanz, 1948).

C.F. G. Masterman, 'The Condition of England' (Methuen, 1909).

Stephen Mayor, 'The Churches and the Labour Movement' (Independent Press, 1967).

'Memorandum and Articles of Association of The Rationalist Press Association Limited' (May 1899).

M. W. Meyerhardt, 'The Movement for Ethical Culture at Home and Abroad', in 'American Journal of Religious Psychology and Education', iii (May 1905) 71-153.

Millett, 'A Typology of Religious Organisations Suggested by the Canadian Census', in 'Sociological Analysis' xxx 2 (summer 1969).

H. R. Murphy, 'The Ethical Revolt against Christian Orthodoxy in Early Victorian England', in 'American Historical Review', ix (July 1955).

Elizabeth K. Nottingham, 'Religion and Society' (Random House, New York, 1954).

Thomas F. O'Dea, 'The Sociology of Religion' (Prentice-Hall, Englewood Cliffs, N.J., 1966).

T. Parsons, 'Sociology and Social Psychology', in 'Religious Perspectives in College Teaching' (Ronald Press, New York, 1952).

Edward R. Pease, 'The History of the Fabian Society', 3rd ed. (Frank Cass, 1963).

S. Persons, 'Free Religion' (Beacon Press, Boston, 1963).

Albert Post, 'Popular Freethought in America, 1825-1850' (Columbia U.P., New York, 1943).

Malcolm Quin, 'Memoirs of a Positivist' (Allen & Unwin, 1924).

Howard B. Radest, 'Toward Common Ground : The Story of the Ethical Societies in the United States' (Frederick Ungar, New York, 1969).

S. K. Ratcliffe, 'The Story of South Place' (Watts, 1955).

R. J. Rees, 'Background and Belief' (S.C.M. Press, 1967).

F. Reid, 'Socialist Sunday Schools in Britain, 1892-1939', in 'International Review of Social History', xi (1966) 18-47.

Woodbridge Riley, 'Early Free-Thinking Societies in America', in 'Harvard Theological Review', xi 3 (July 1918) 247-84.

John M. Robertson, 'A Short History of Freethought, Ancient and Modern', 2 vols (Watts, 3rd ed., 1915; 1st ed., 1899; 2nded., 1906).

Roland Robertson, 'The Sociological Interpretation of Religion' (Basil Blackwell, Oxford, 1970).

B. Seebohm Rowntree and G. R. Lavers, 'English Life and Leisure : A Social Study' (Longmans, 1951).

Edward Royle, 'George Jacob Holyoake and the Secularist Movement in Britain, 1841-1861', Ph.D. thesis (Christ's College, Cambridge, 1968).

Schillebeckx,'Theological Reflections on Religio-Sociological Interpretations of Modern "Irreligion" ', in 'Social Compass', x 3 (1963) 257-84.

W. M. Simon, 'European Positivism in the Nineteenth Century: An Essay in Intellectual History' (Cornell U.P., Ithaca, N.Y.,1963).

James Ward Smith and A. Leland Jamison, 'The Shaping of American Religion' (Princeton U.P., 1961).

W. Sylvester Smith, 'The London Heretics, 1870-1914' (Constable, 1967).

P. Sorokin, 'The Western Religion and Morality of Today', in 'International Yearbook for the Sociology of Religion', ii (Cologne, 1966) 9-44.

William L. Sperry, 'Religion in America' (Boston, Beacon Press, 1963).

Frederik Spiegelberg, 'The Religion of Non-Religion' (James Ladd Delkin, Stanford, Calif., 1953).

G. Spiller, 'The Ethical Movement in Great Britain' (Farleigh Press, 1934).

R. Stark and C. Y. Glock, 'American Piety: The Nature of Religious Commitment' (Univ. of California Press, Berkeley and Los Angeles, 1968).

William W. Sweet, 'The Story of Religion in America' (Harper & Bros, New York, 1939).

G. Szczesny, 'The Future of Unbelief' (Heinemann, 1962).

G. H. Taylor, 'A Chronology of British Secularism' (National Secular Society, 1957).

T. Tribe, 'One Hundred Years of Freethought' (Elek Books, 1967).

Glenn M. Vernon, 'Sociology of Religion' (McGraw-Hill, New York, 1962). 'The Religious "Nones": A Neglected Category', in 'Journal for the Scientific Study of Religion', vii 2 (fall 1968) 219-29.

Sidney Warren, 'American Freethought, 1860-1914' (Gordian Press, New York, 1966).

Leslie D. Weatherhead, 'The Christian Agnostic' (Hodder & Stoughton, 1965).

D.E. H. Whiteley and R. Martin (eds), 'Sociology, Theology and Conflict' (Basil Blackwell, Oxford, 1969).

A.Gowans Whyte, 'The Story of the R.P.A., 1899-1949' (Watts, 1949).

E.R.Wickham, 'Church and People in an Industrial City' (Lutterworth Press, 1957).

Bryan R. Wilson, 'Religion in Secular Society' (Watts, 1966). (ed.) 'Patterns of Sectarianism' (Heinemann, 1967).

P. Worsley, 'The Trumpet Shall Sound' (MacGibbon & Kee, 1968).

J. Milton Yinger, 'Religion, Society and the Individual' (Macmillan, New York, 1957).

Index

eliminationists, 38. *See also* abolitionists
Ellingwood, Francis, 86
Emerson, R. W., 79
Encampment for Citizenship, 84
Eros, J., 114
Established Church, 82. *See also* Anglican Church, Church of England
ethic, Christian, 99
Ethical Church, 31, 79-82; cultus in, 79-81
Ethical Culture, 76, 78, 83, 97, 141;
  and morality, 74-5
ethical movement in America, 71-7, 84-5
ethical movement in England, 77-85; growth, 83
ethical societies, 43, 74, 76, 79, 82-4, 92, 113; principles of, 72-4
Ethical Union, 91-2, 94, 115;
  and charitable status, 116-17
Ethicism, 94-5, 107
evolutionary humanism, 94, 139
Existentialism, 37
experiences, irreligious, 127

Fabian Society, 70, 78
Fascism, 138
fellowship, 74
Fellowship of Religious Humanists, 86-7
Foote, G. W., lll
'Fortnightly Review', 56
Fox, W. J., 78
France, 62-3, 65, 68
'Free Enquirer', 58
free love, 98
Free Religion, 86-7
Free Religious Association, 86
free thought, 18, 86-7
Freethinkers, 41, 60, 82, 86-7, 98, 109, 112, 120
Freethinkers of America Inc., 40
free-thought in America, 58 ff.
free-thought societies, 59

About the Contributors

Stephen Bullivant is Lecturer in Theology and Ethics at St Mary's University College. He is the author of *The Salvation of Atheists and Catholic Dogmatic Theology* (Oxford University Press, 2012), and is currently writing *Faith and Unbelief* (Canterbury Press) and coediting *The Oxford Handbook of Atheism* (Oxford University Press), both due out in 2013. He is co-director of the NSRN and is a member of the editorial board of *Secularism and Nonreligion*.

Colin Campbell is Emeritus Professor of Sociology at the University of York. He is the author of half a dozen books and some one hundred articles dealing with issues in the sociology of religion, consumerism, cultural change, and sociological theory. He is probably best-known as the author of *The Romantic Ethic and the Spirit of Modern Consumerism* (Macmillan 1987, Alcuin Academic edition 2005), while his other publications on consumerism include *The Shopping Experience* (co-edited with Pasi Falk, Sage, 1997), and `The Craft Consumer: Culture, craft and consumption in a postmodern society', *Journal of Consumer Culture* 5 (1) 23-41 (2005). In the sociology of religion he is known for his contribution to work on the cult and the cultic milieu (see "The Cult, the Cultic Milieu and Secularisation" *A Sociological Yearbook of Religion in Britain 5*, 119-36, 1972), as well as the study of irreligion; while his contribution to sociological theory is evident in *The Myth of Social Action* (Cambridge University Press, 1996). His latest book, *The Easternization of the West: A Thematic Account of Cultural Change in the Modern Era*, was published by Paradigm in 2007.

Christopher R. Cotter is deputy editor and bibliography manager of *NSRN Online* and co-founder of The Religious Studies Project (http://www.religiousstudiesproject.com). He is currently editing the volume *Social Identities between the Sacred and the Secular* with Abby Day and Giselle Vincett (Ashgate, 2013).

Lois Lee is founding director of the Nonreligion and Secularity Research Network (NSRN), editor of *NSRN Online,* co-editor of *Secularism and Nonreligion* and features editor for *Studies in Ethnicity and Nationalism.* She is currently writing a book on the sociology of nonreligion and secularity, funded by the Blackham Fellowship.

183

12699475R00135

Printed in Great Britain
by Amazon.co.uk, Ltd.,
Marston Gate.